DIPLOMA
STRATEGIC MARKETING MANAGEMENT: ANALYSIS AND DECISION

First edition October 1992
Second edition September 1993
Reprinted February 1995

ISBN 0 7517 4988 5 (previous edition 0 7517 4008 X)

British Library Cataloguing-in-Publication Data

A catalogue record for this book
is available from the British Library

Published by

BPP Publishing Limited
Aldine House, Aldine Place
London W12 8AW

All our rights reserved. No part of this publication may be reproduced, stored in a retrieval system or transmitted, in any form or by any means, electronic, mechanical, photocopying, recording or otherwise, without the prior written permission of BPP Publishing Ltd.

We would like to extend our thanks to the former Senior Examiner Dr David Pearson who wrote this Workbook.

We are grateful to the Chartered Institute of Marketing for permission to use past case studies, and to Northern Consulting Associates for permission to use their case analysis of Euro Airport Ltd.

Printed in Great Britain by
Ashford Colour Press, Gosport, Hampshire

BPP Publishing Limited

1995

CONTENTS

PREFACE

The Diploma awarded by the Chartered Institute of Marketing is a management qualification which puts a major emphasis on the practical understanding of marketing activities. At the same time, the Institute's examinations recognise that the marketing professional works in a fast changing organisational, economic and social environment.

BPP Publishing has extensive experience in producing study material for a wide variety of professional examinations, and leads in many of these markets.

Strategic Marketing Management: Analysis and Decision is one of the two compulsory CIM Diploma papers. It is compulsory as the marketing professional is expected to be a *manager*. Knowledge and skills in analysis and decision, together with an appreciation of the role of marketing in the corporate structure, are essential ingredients of managerial competence in this field.

This Workbook has been written by the former Senior Examiner for candidates sitting the CIM Diploma examination in *Strategic Marketing Management: Analysis and Decision.*

This Workbook is designed to supplement the detailed case study practice offered by the Tutorial Text with two additional case studies. This Workbook is also relevant to candidates who do not need the background information in other marketing subjects provided by the Diploma.

This Workbook is divided into four parts.

(a) The CIM case study examination
(b) How to analyse the CIM case study (including the senior examiners' recommended method and a revision of some of the analytical tools which can be used)
(c) Examination technique: planning your examination
(d) Learning from experience: ensuring you pass

The last section includes detailed step by step analysis of two case studies, Brewsters Ltd and Euro Airport Ltd, so that candidates can view a variety of approaches to the material. This section is similar to the Tutorial Text although different case studies are used. The aim is to encourage candidates to take a reasoned approach to the case material which, by its very nature, reflects the uncertainties of the commercial world.

BPP's study material is noted for its thorough coverage of the syllabus and user friendly style, and is reviewed and updated each year. BPP's study material, at once clear, comprehensive and up to date, is thus the ideal investment that candidates aspiring to the Diploma can make for examination success. Good luck!

BPP Publishing
February 1995

For details of other BPP titles relevant to your studies for this examination and for a full list of books in the BPP CIM range, please turn to pages 301 and 302. Should you wish to send in your comments on this Workbook, please turn to page 303.

INTRODUCTION

1 *What is the CIM case study?*

There is no formal syllabus for the CIM's examination *Marketing Management: Analysis and Decision*. Instead the examination is based on a case study normally comprising 30 to 40 pages of narrative, charts and tables and issued to examinees by post about *four weeks in advance of the examination.*

The issue of the case study some four weeks in advance allows time for considerable analysis and discussion.

The case study is a *practical* test of the students' knowledge of marketing (gained in Certificate and Diploma, or equivalent, studies) and their ability to apply it. Normally students will also have some practical experience in marketing to bring to bear.

2 *Discussing the case study*

Students are strongly advised to conduct in-depth discussion with colleagues on the case study analysis and its issues. This is often accomplished at colleges by the forming of *syndicate groups* of four to six people and the holding of frequent *plenary sessions* where all applicants gather together. In this way, a syndicate member not only hears the view of his or her syndicate, but also those of other syndicates. In this way a much more balanced, integrated and secure approach can be developed. Students who forgo this sort of discussion are likely to fail, no matter how individually clever at analysis they might be.

3 *The examination*

There are a number of different methods of dealing with case studies and students are exposed to some of these in Part B of this Workbook, so as to promote a reasonably wide appreciation of the subject. However, some method eventually needs to be chosen, and the one recommended has been thoroughly tried and tested, and has been found to achieve a high degree of success in the CIM examinations.

One of the key success factors in case study examination (apart from being thoroughly prepared) is to be well organised in the exam room itself, freeing the mind to think more calmly and clearly about the exam questions. Students are advised to study Part C on exam techniques very thoroughly.

4 *Practice*

This manual concludes in Part D with recent case studies, examination questions and outline answers for self-assessment. It is strongly recommended that candidates conduct a practice run on at least one of these previous case studies together, with a mock exam and with answers assessed against the frameworks provided. This is the most effective way of preparing yourself for the problems you will eventually have to confront in the examination room itself.

PART A

THE CIM CASE STUDY EXAMINATION

Chapter 1

THE CIM CASE STUDY EXAMINATION

This chapter covers the following topics.

1. THE RATIONALE AND ROLE OF THE CASE STUDY EXAMINATION

1.1 The case study method of learning and teaching has played a major part in management education, training and development over the past twenty years. The Harvard Business School in the USA helped both to pioneer and to stimulate the development of the case study method on its senior management courses and quickly gained an international reputation in this field.

1.2 It has been demonstrated increasingly that:

(a) case studies make an extremely important contribution to the study, knowledge and understanding of management;

(b) case studies are being used more and more often as an examination technique by professional bodies, and in particular by the Chartered Institute of Marketing (CIM).

It is fitting that the final examination of the CIM Diploma, which once conferred, is in effect a licence to practise, should use this most searching test of management ability.

1.3 An understanding of the role of case studies is pre-requisite to being able to learn from them and how to handle them.

(a) A case study portrays, as far as possible, a real world situation and aims through its use to develop a greater ability to analyse, conclude and make decisions.

(b) Case studies are also used the encourage the *application* of theoretical concepts and techniques in a selective and evaluative way to solve practical problems.

(c) Case studies are often explored on a *group basis*, as opposed to individuals solitarily reviewing data, so as to develop broader perspectives.

1.4 In business and management education and training, the situation described by a case study is usually one faced by an organisation and would typically include some facts and figures on:

(a) the organisation's past development;
(b) its current situation;
(c) financial, marketing, and personnel aspects;
(d) competitors.

1.5 A case study can vary from a single page (often termed a mini-case or caselet) to fifty or more pages and appendices.

1.6 Cases also vary in the extent to which they are based on real life situations. Some are based entirely on a real world situation (sometimes distinguished by the term *case history*). On the other hand, a case study might be one that is fabricated by the writer so as to better test particular aspects. Often case writers deliberately distort data so as to preserve confidentiality and will intentionally introduce anomalies, jumble logical sequences and omit data so as to make the case more challenging.

1.7 *There is no one perfect solution to a case.* Solutions not only depend upon an individual's interpretation of the data (which can in turn be influenced by the nature of the analytical techniques employed) but also upon the role and relationships of the people involved in the case.

1.8 For the foregoing reasons, students can find, on their first introduction to the case method, that case studies are intimidating, irritating and frustrating. However, given the right approach and the benefits of some experience the following advantages from the use of case studies are claimed. Students can benefit in increased skills in:

(a) clear thinking through complex situations;
(b) the ability to devise credible, consistent and creative plans;
(c) the application of analytical techniques;
(d) the recognition of the relative significance of information;
(e) the determination of informational needs;
(f) oral communication in groups;
(g) the writing of clear, forceful and convincing reports;
(h) choice of career paths;
(i) recognising the importance of personal values in organisational decision taking processes and self analysis.

(Edge and Coleman *The guide to case analysis and reporting* 1986, pps 4-6)

1.9 With regard to the last item Wilson 1988 (pages 279-286) highlights individual behavioural differences pointing out that 'the more stakeholders there are, the greater is the scope for differing interpretations and assumptions'. (A *stakeholder* is a person, group or organisation with an interest in another organisation's performance.) He draws out the following four key propositions underlying the psychological typology of Jung.

(a) People have different ways of relating to other people in the world.
(b) People have different ways of gathering and using information.
(c) People have different ways of using information and making decisions.
(d) People attach different priorities to gathering and using information.

1.10 The implications of these propositions are that:

(a) *value judgements* and other affective issues are essential in defining problems;

(b) the *roles people play* need to be made explicit, as do assumptions about the people in these roles, and this is part of the learning process. In the final analysis management is about 'getting things done through people'.

Making the most of case studies

1.11 Edge and Coleman (*The guide to case analysis and reporting* 1986 pages 7-15) place the emphasis on student responsibilities in case learning. Much greater effort and cooperation is needed from students in learning from cases as opposed to lectures.

1.12 A more positive attitude can be encouraged by students working as a team on a real management situation and by role adoption.

1.13 Students need to familiarise themselves with the case in *advance* of discussion. They should both participate in, and help to manage, the discussion.

1.14 A sense of *humour* helps groups to relax, to develop a team spirit and to enjoy discussion and feedback.

1.15 When a complex and lengthy case study and analysis takes place over a period of several weeks or sessions, *regular attendance* is essential. Otherwise a student might become a burden on the group, or be seen as a malingerer.

1.16 Students must respect the contributions made by and feelings of other group members, but at the same time they should be prepared to give and take constructive criticism.

1.17 Some sympathy for the case study *leader's* role and problems in the overall management of the project will also help.

1.18 Students need to appreciate the likelihood of initial dissatisfaction with the case, the necessity for learning, and the value of keeping an open mind. At the start, confusion and frustration will be caused by the following factors.

(a) There is no one best answer.
(b) Information can be ambigious and/or irrelevant.
(c) Vital information is missing.
(d) The key issues may not be given or identified.
(e) The case study leader does not direct.
(f) The case study leader does not provide solutions.

A constructive attitude should help allay these problems.

1.19 Attention to the two matters below should help students get the most out of their case study group.

(a) The position of *chairing syndicate groups* and acting as spokesperson in plenary sessions should be rotated so that all concerned develop leadership and communication skills.

(b) The adoption of *stakeholder roles* (eg one member to act as the financial manager, another as managing director, another as spokesperson for employees' interests) by group members helps to develop greater understanding of the human relations aspects of decision making.

How to handle case studies: an overview

1.20 All writers and most case study instructors recommend a step by step approach to case study analysis. Easton (*Learning from case studies* 1982 pages 9-12) summarises these as follows:

Step 1	Understanding the situation
Step 2	Diagnosing problem areas
Step 3	Generating alternative solutions
Step 4	Predicting outcomes
Step 5	Evaluating alternatives
Step 6	Communicating the results

However the detailed methods of carrying out these steps can vary according to the nature of the case, its length and how far in advance (if at all) the case is issued.

1.21 Also, time constraints and other reasons may cause the case instructor to concentrate on particular steps. For example, the London Business School use a particular caselet purely for the purposes of generating as *many* alternative solutions as possible. This helps to encourage groups of mature business people to look beyond the first immediate solution that springs to mind.

1.22 Students being exposed to case studies as part of coursework will normally be issued with detailed guidelines on how to tackle each of the above steps or referred to recommended reading by the course instructor. For the purposes of this Workbook we are concentrating on how to handle case studies being used for examination purposes.

1.23 In the pages which follow, distinctions are drawn between:

(a) the recommended treatments for the unseen caselets (or mini-cases) which are used as part of the format for several Chartered Institute of Marketing examinations; and

(b) the major case study which is issued four weeks in advance and is the sole method of examination for the Institute's Diploma subject 'Marketing Management - Analysis and Decision'.

2. WHAT YOU CAN EXPECT IN THE EXAMINATION

2.1 It is standard practice for the CIM to supply the examination case study in the form of an A5 booklet, printed both sides of the page. There is not much room therefore for making notes in the booklet and you may prefer to expand each page on to A4 single sides for this purpose.

2.2 Typically, the CIM diploma case will be 30 to 40 pages long. It will consist of 5 to 10 pages of text followed by a number of appendices.

2.3 The information contained in the case study will most likely include some or all of the following matters.

(a) Background and historical data on the company featured.
(b) Corporate and group organisation.
(c) Marketing and sales organisation.
(d) Strengths, weaknesses, opportunities, threats (indicative only).
(e) Market size, segments, competitors, trends.
(f) Environmental factors.
(g) Marketing mix (product, price, promotion, distribution).
(h) Marketing research.
(i) Consolidated accounts (profit and loss, balance sheet).

2.4 As is usual in most management case studies, the CIM case will:

(a) include some information which is not particularly useful; and
(b) exclude some data which you might feel essential.

This is to test your powers of discrimination and also to suggest a blueprint for a marketing research plan and or improvements to the marketing information system.

2.5 You are also likely to find some anomalies and contradictions which will oblige you to make *assumptions*.

2.6 On the inside front cover of the case you will find 'Important Notes' for candidates, followed by a page 'Candidates Brief' (see Chapter 3 for details), which you must, of course read thoroughly and have in mind when interpreting the subsequent data in the case itself.

2.7 **The examiner reserves the right to issue additional information on the case with the examination paper on the day itself.**

This is to ensure thinking takes place in the examination room and to discourage excessive use of pre-prepared answers. In the most recent examinations, additional information has been provided in the examination paper and a proportion of the total marks has been allocated for its use when answering the questions set.

Questions in the examination

2.8 Typically, you may expect three or four questions of *unequal* marks requiring you to undertake some calculation of how much time to allocate to each question - see Chapter 6 on examination techniques. There is normally no choice and you are required to answer all questions.

2.9 It is normal for these three or four questions to be split between;

(a) issues of strategy formulation;
(b) more detailed tactical and operational plans.

Trends in the examination paper

2.10 The current examiner has made it clear that he wishes (on behalf of the CIM) to encourage the adoption of *longer-term strategic planning* by marketing management. It is also current policy to try to ensure that future marketing managers are *financially literate* by asking candidates to state the financial implications of their proposals.

2.11 Finally, the examiner will normally expect candidates to think through the *organisational implications* posited by the case and to be aware of the contribution that an improved marketing orientation and internal marketing can make to corporate wellbeing.

3. EXAMINATION RULES

3.1 This subject is examined as a three hour 'open book' case study examination. This means you may take as much pre-prepared material, reference books etc into the examination room as you wish, provided this does not interfere with the space and comfort of other candidates. The use of electronic calculators not requiring mains electricity is also permitted providing of course that this does not distract other candidates.

3.2 If you have any doubts on this matter it would be as well to check with the CIM. However, you would be well advised to limit your equipment to that normally required for *any* examination plus a well-indexed ring binder of pre-prepared analysis (see Chapter 6 on examination techniques). All CIM examinations are held under the jurisdiction of a professional invigilator whose decisions on any point of order must be accepted as final.

3.3 You must of course only start when the invigilator gives permission and you must stop writing immediately you are asked to do so.

3.4 All candidates will be provided with an examination slip which permits entry into the examination room. You will have been allocated an examination number which you must write on the examination script, together with the examination centre and the number of questions attempted, in the order in which they appear in the script. Your name must not appear on the script.

3.5 Additional pages must be securely fastened to the script booklet.

3.6 Answers must only be submitted on CIM script and/or paper such as graph paper supplied by the invigilator. You *cannot submit pre-prepared pages* and any material suspected of this will be treated as invalid.

4. CANDIDATES' NOTES

4.1 The Candidates' Notes are amended from time to time but stay broadly the same. The following example comes from the June 1994 case.

> **Diploma in marketing**
>
> **Marketing analysis and decision**
>
> **Important notes**
>
> The examiners will be marking your scripts on the basis of questions put to you in the examination room. Questions *may not* carry equal marks and candidates are advised to pay particular attention to the mark allocation on the examination paper. Candidates are advised to budget their time accordingly.
>
> Your role is outlined in the candidates' brief. In the position outlined you may be required to recommend clear courses of action.
>
> You *will not* be awarded marks merely for analysis. This should have been undertaken before the examination day in preparation for meeting the specific tasks which will be specified in the examination paper.
>
> Candidates are *instructed not to conduct research or analysis outside* the material provided within the case study. The introduction of extraneous material in examination answers will gain no marks and serves only to waste valuable time. Although cases are based upon real world situations, facts have been deliberately altered or omitted to preserve anonymity. No useful purpose will therefore be served by contacting companies in this industry and candidates are strictly instructed *not* to do so as it would simply cause unnecessary confusion.
>
> As in real life anomalies will be found in this case situation. Please simply state your assumptions where necessary when answering questions. The CIM is not in a position to answer queries on case data whether in writing or on the telephone. Candidates are tested on their overall grasp of the case and its key issues, not on minutiae. There are no catch questions or hidden agendas.
>
> *Additional information will be introduced in the examination paper itself which candidates must take into account when answering the questions set. Up to 15 per cent of the marks will be allocated for this purpose.*
>
> Acquaint yourself thoroughly with the case study and be prepared to follow closely the instructions given to you on the examination day. *To answer examination questions effectively, candidates must adopt report format.*
>
> The copying of pre-prepared 'group' answers written by consultants/tutors is strictly forbidden and will be penalised. The questions will demand thinking out in the examination itself and individually written answers are required.

5. CANDIDATES' BRIEF

5.1 The Candidates' Brief will of course be specific to the particular case and states your role/reporting relationships. It will normally include pointers to the areas for examination questions and is to a degree, an indication of the stance you should take on the material. The following example has been taken from the June 1992 case.

Candidates' Brief

EURO AIRPORT LIMITED (EAL)

You are Irma Bergmann the recently appointed New Business Development Manager reporting to the Commercial Director of Euro Airport Limited. This is a new position created largely by the threat of the loss of duty free sales. Also an inherent part of the justification for this appointment is however, a need for completely fresh thinking at a time of rapid change in the EC environment. EAL are wanting particularly to create a unified approach to the marketing of the airport as a whole and all applicants for vacant management positions within both the commercial and operations divisions are being judged with this requirement in mind.

You therefore have considerable scope for development of your role in the longer term. You are young, talented and ambitious.

In putting forward your proposals it is necessary to be aware that other projects will be competing for scarce resources both at company and group level.

Following your initial assessment you will be required to make clear recommendations for future action.

This case material is based upon experience with actual companies. Alterations in the information given and in the real data have not been made to preserve confidence. Candidates are strictly instructed not to contact companies in this industry.

6. CIM EXAMINER'S GUIDANCE NOTES

6.1 These are normally updated annually but remain substantially the same over a period of about three years. They contain important information on how to prepare for the examination and should be read carefully. The Guidance Notes are issued to providers of tuition for this subject for passing on to students at the tutor's discretion.

CIM examiner's guidance notes

6.2 Tutors are told the following.

(a)	Notional taught hours:	45
(b)	Method of assessment:	3 hour written examination
(c)	Number of questions:	all questions to be attempted (3 or 4)
(d)	Pass mark:	50%

Preferred sequence of studies

6.3 The culmination of the Certificate, Advanced Certificate and Diploma course is the case study. The examination has the purpose of ensuring that those who hold the Diploma qualification have not only achieved a certain level of marketing knowledge, but also have the competence to use that knowledge in addressing simulated marketing management problems.

6.4 Any aspect of the entire Certificate, Advanced Certificate and Diploma syllabuses may be applicable and if you have been exempted from parts of the course you should ensure you familiarise yourself with the detailed course requirements.

6.5 This paper should be taken at the end of your course of study.

Rationale

6.6 The guidance notes state the rationale of the case study is as follows.

> 'To extend the practice of candidates in the quantitative and qualitative analysis of marketing situations, both to develop their powers of diagnosis and to create a firm basis in decision making.'
>
> By the end of their study students will be able:
>
> (a) to identify, define and rank the problem(s) contained in marketing case studies;
>
> (b) to formulate working hypotheses regarding the solution(s) to problems identified in marketing case studies;
>
> (c) to assemble, order, analyse and interpret both qualitative and quantitative data relating to a marketing case, using appropriate analytical procedures and models;
>
> (d) to describe and substantiate all working assumptions made regarding the case problem(s) working hypotheses and data;
>
> (e) to generate and evaluate the expected outcomes of alternative solutions to case problem(s);
>
> (f) to formulate recommendations for action and feedback on case problem(s) including their financial and human resource implications;
>
> (g) to prepare and present appropriate marketing case reports.

Senior examiner's comments

6.7 The CIM Diploma is recognised increasingly widely as a licence to practise. It is in no-one's interests for it to be awarded lightly, as those who have striven hard to attain it will surely agree. The value of the Diploma depends directly upon the quality of the people holding it; in turn the respect earned from peers, superiors and clients depends on the value of the Diploma.

6.8 *Strategic Marketing Management: Analysis and Decision* is quite rightly the severest test in the CIM examinations. It is the only subject for which an exemption cannot be granted. The examination is based upon a real-life major case study and requires the application of theories, principles and techniques learned in the study of other subjects. It is not an examination to be passed by regurgitating knowledge.

6.9 Candidates must demonstrate beyond reasonable doubt that they are capable not only of in-depth analysis before the exam, but also are able to take decisions and write clear, concise and convincing marketing plans. These marketing plans need to show an understanding of the corporate and financial implications.

Question design and scope

6.10 Questions applied in case studies do not have any standardised format. They may vary in number. They may throw up a surprise situation. They will be action orientated. One inevitable and recurring theme will be the *strategic marketing* of product and services.

The examiners are aware of the time constraint of three hours and the questions are designed to enable a candidate to cover them adequately if not well, within that period. Candidates should remember that they are expected to have knowledge equivalent to the syllabuses of the other three Diploma subjects. The whole course (Certificate, Advanced Certificate and Diploma) is a legitimate source of questions.

Examination approach

6.11 Candidates are required to do what the examiners ask, to answer the question as put and in accordance with any mark allocation which is stated on the paper. This means the management of the time within the examination situation is crucial. In every case, candidates have a human role to play within the structure of either the case, the examination paper, or both, to which they are expected to be able to relate. Usually, this means that they have to respond and restructure their thinking within the examination itself; this is precisely what the examiners are seeking.

Preparation

6.12 There are two basic parts to this paper embodied in its title, Analysis and Decision. There can be no better description of these two parts than the questions put to his students by one lecturer as follows.

(a) What is wrong?
(b) What are you going to do to put it right?

Within the context of management, marketing or otherwise, the second question is the critical one, but cannot be answered without the problem identification implicit in the first.

There will be anomalies in the case, as in real life. Assumptions will therefore need to be made and clearly stated. (The CIM cannot enter into discussion on these aspects, either verbally or in writing.)

6.13 Problem identification will certainly require the application of statistical and financial analytical techniques, and of organisational and behavioural understanding and marketing knowledge. The examiners must know what these problems are, what alternative solutions to them have been considered and which alternative has been chosen by the candidate, ie:

(a) what is to be done?
(b) in what time period?
(c) by whom?
(d) with what financial and human resource implications?
(e) and with what projected outcome?

6.14 There is no such thing as a right answer to these questions. Above all, sensible recommendations are required, supported by reasoned argument. *Lists of problems and regurgitated materials from the case itself do candidates no credit.*

6.15 The evidence is overwhelming that a great many students try to seek refuge in analysis and come to their examination desks hoping that inspiration will suddenly flow to the tips of their ball-point pens! The case study is issued prior to the examination data to enable students to conducts their analysis before responding to the situation posed in the examination hall. A restatement of this analysis is insufficient to pass the examination. Decisions must be formulated and clearly articulated on the exam day.

Decisions

6.16 There is an apt Chinese proverb which says 'He who deliberates fully before taking a step will spend his entire life on one leg'. The question of taking decisions is a conceptual leap for many students. They need help. In the absence of full information, they have to make assumptions, use their judgement and be prepared to back it up on paper.

6.17 One of the difficulties, which the examiners fully understand, is the lack of knowledge about any particular industry used in the case. Marketing decisions, however, are applicable in any environment based on sound principles relevant to the situation. The examiners will not tolerate academic essays; we need to see applications and this means that candidates should adopt management report style and format to maximise their chances.

Further research

6.18 The examiners can state categorically that there is *no need* for any candidate to seek additional information outside the case study. There are three reasons for this.

(a) The examiners incorporate within the case itself enough information for the candidate to work on. It is a self-contained exercise.

(b) Some data within case studies needs to be disguised to preserve confidentiality. Trying to search out the company concerned can thus not only be a waste of time but also leads to confusion.

(c) Access to additional research data is limited, particularly for overseas students.

6.19 Nevertheless, candidates may be expected to be able to state within the examination what additional research information they would seek, for what reason, in what time period, at what approximate cost and by what method. There is every justification for encouraging student research during the course of an academic year in order to have the experience and be able to apply it to the examination case. No students will earn additional marks for external research data introduced in the examination.

7. CONCLUSION

7.1 This chapter has presented you with a sense of the context of the case study exam.

7.2 Firstly, you are given information in advance, not all of which will be relevant. You should not research outside information.

7.3 In dealing with the information, group discussion is important.

7.4 You are required to take reasoned decisions within the case's context, not to provide an ideal solution as one is not available.

7.5 The questions asked in the case can cover topics contained in the entire CIM syllabus.

PART B

HOW TO ANALYSE THE CIM CASE STUDY

Chapter 2

HOW TO ANALYSE A CIM CASE STUDY: OVERVIEW

This chapter covers the following topics.

1. Case study methodology in general
2. Mini cases
3. Longer case studies

1. CASE STUDY METHODOLOGY IN GENERAL

1.1 A number of writers have endeavoured to summarise and express the vast amount of experience gained over many years by a host of institutions using the case study approach to teaching and learning. These institutions include universities, business schools and colleges.

1.2 The following few pages are devoted to introducing you to some of the best practice and custom expressed by these writers. This will enable you to develop a broad appreciation of the ways in which most institutions approach case study teaching.

1.3 Chapter 3 will then explain the specific methods recommended by the CIM Senior Examiner for the purposes of the Diploma in Marketing case study examination. These specific methods do, of course, have their roots in the general custom and practice covered in this section.

1.4 Methods tend to vary in general according to the following factors.

(a) The length of the case.
(b) The content of the case.
(c) The culture of the teaching institution.
(d) The abilities of the students.
(e) The personality of the case tutor.
(f) The amount of time available.

2 MINI CASES

2.1 Clearly, the shorter the case study, the less is its content and the smaller is the amount of the analysis that can be conducted upon it. Another related criterion is the amount of numerical as opposed to textual data. This affects the nature of the analytical techniques that can be applied.

2.2 When writing as a Senior Examiner for the old syllabus CIM Diploma subject *Marketing Planning and Control* the senior examiner for the case study gave this advice to students faced with the typical short unseen examination case (or mini-case as it has become known).

2.3 'It needs to be stated unequivocally that the type of extremely short case (popularly called the mini-case) set in the examinations for Diploma subjects *other* than 'Analysis and Decision' cannot be treated in exactly the same way as the extremely long case set for the subject of marketing analysis and decision. If it could, there would be little point in going to all the trouble of writing an in-depth case study.

2.4 'Far too many students adopt a maxi-case approach, using a detailed marketing audit outline which is largely inappropriate to a case consisting only of two or three paragraphs. Others use the SWOT analysis and simply re-write the case under the four headings of strengths, weaknesses, opportunities and threats.

'Some students even go so far as to totally ignore the specific questions set and present a standard maxi case analysis outline including environmental reviews through to contingency plans.

2.5 'The CIM "mini-case" is not really a case at all, it is merely an outline of a given situation, a *scenario*. Its purpose is to test whether examinees can apply their knowledge of marketing theory and techniques to the company or organisation and the operating environment described in the scenario. For example, answers advocating retail audits as part of the marketing information system for a small industrial goods manufacturer, demonstrate a lack of practical awareness. Such answers confirm that the examinee has learned a given MIS outline by rote and simply regurgitated this in complete disregard of the scenario. Such an approach would be disastrous in the real world and examinees adopting this approach cannot be passed, ie gain the confidence of the Institute as professional marketing practitioners. The correct approach to the scenario is a mental review of the area covered by the question and the selection by the examinee of those particular parts of knowledge and techniques which apply to the case. This implies a rejection of those parts of the student's knowledge which clearly do not apply to the scenario.

2.6 'All scenarios are based upon real world companies and situations which are written with a full knowledge of how that organisation actually operates in its planning environments. Often, the organisation described in the scenario will not be a giant fast-moving consumer good manufacturing and marketing company, since this would facilitate mindless regurgitation of textbook outlines and be counter to the intention of this section of the examination.

2.7 'More often, the scenarios will involve innovative small or medium sized firms which comprise the vast majority of UK companies and which lack the resources often assumed by the textbook approach. These firms do, however, have to market within these constraints and are just as much concerned in marketing communications, marketing planning and control and indeed (proportionately) in international marketing, particularly the EC.

2.8 'However, as marketing applications develop and expand and as changes take root, the Institute through its examiners will wish to test students' knowledge awareness of these changes and their implication with regard to marketing practice. For example, in the public sector increasing attention is being paid to the marketing of leisure services and the concept of "asset marketing", where the "product" is to a greater extent fixed and therefore the option of product as a variable in the marketing mix is somewhat more constrained. Internal marketing has been recognised as essential to the effective operation of TQM.

2.9 'Tutors and students are referred to Examiners' Reports which repeatedly complain of inappropriateness of answer detail which demonstrates a real lack of practical marketing grasp and confirms that a learned by rote textbook regurgitation is being used. Examples would include:

(a) the recommendation of national TV advertising for a small industrial company with a local market;

(b) the overnight installation of a marketing department comprising managing director, marketing manager, advertising manager, distribution manager, sales manager, etc into what has been described as a very small company;

(c) the inclusion of packaging, branded-packs, on-pack offers etc in the marketing mix recommendations for a service.

2.10 'It has been borne in mind that the award of the Diploma is in a very real sense the granting of a licence to practice marketing and certainly an endorsement of the candidate's practical as well as theoretical grasps of marketing. In these circumstances, such treatments of the mini-case, as described above, cannot be passed and give rise to some concern that perhaps the teaching/learning approach to mini-cases has not been sufficiently differentiated from that recommended for the Marketing Analysis and Decision Paper.'

3. LONGER CASE STUDIES

3.1 With the above comments in mind, it is suggested that the following approaches should be treated as being more appropriate to the longer case study.

3.2 Cravens and Lamb (1986) recommend a six step approach to case analysis along the following lines.

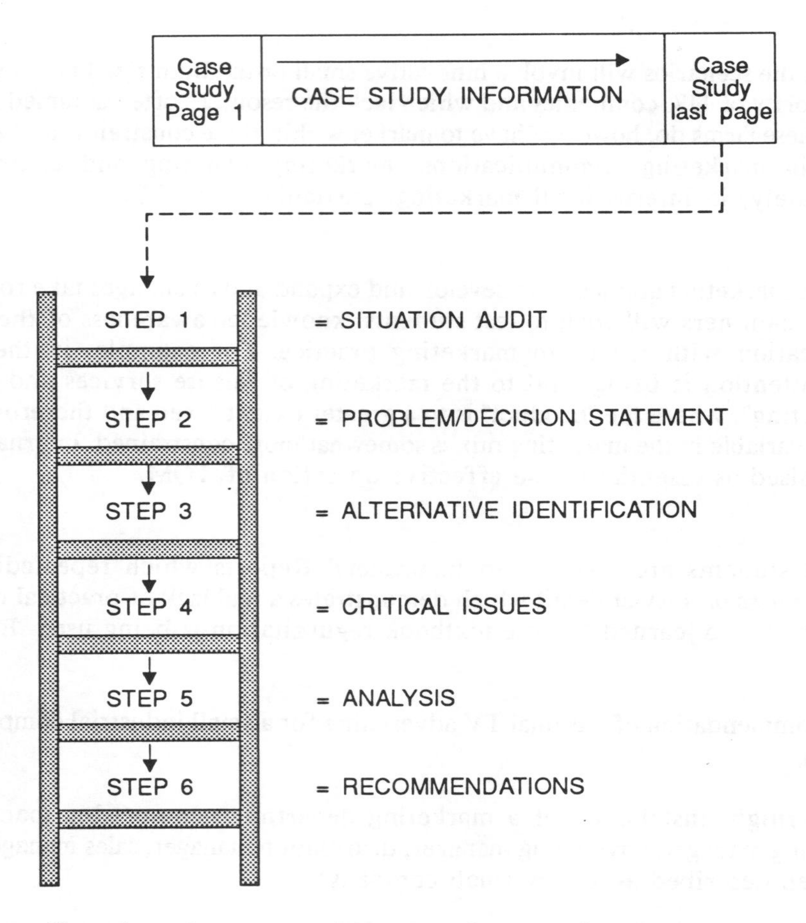

3.3 Whilst not disputing the appropriateness of any of the above steps, this model is insufficiently comprehensive for CIM major case study preparation. It suggests analysis as Step 5 whereas analysis has to take place much earlier in the process. Also CIM examination candidates would need to take step 6 (recommendations) a great deal further, for example into costings, budgets, schedules and their financial/human resource implications.

3.4 Edge and Coleman's framework for case analysis also has six steps which are, however, somewhat different in their detail from those recommended by Cravens and Lamb.

1 Comprehend case situation
↓
2 Diagnose problem areas
↓
3 State problem
↓
4 Generate alternatives
↓
5 Evaluate and select
↓
6 Defend implementation

3.5 The Edge and Coleman model adds to that of Cravens and Lamb, particularly in its first and last steps. Defending implementation is another way of saying 'justify your recommendations' which is certainly a necessity for the CIM Diploma case preparation.

3.6 Mention has already been made in Chapter 1 paragraph 1.20 of the Easton (*Learning from case studies* 1982) approach which is similar to the two outlined above but suggests a seventh step, namely that of communicating the results (of the analysis).

3.7 Easton refers to two basic methods of 'teaching' case studies in the classroom.

(a) One is the traditional Harvard method of open class discussion.

(b) The other basic method is that of asking individuals or groups (syndicates) to make formal presentations during each stage or step of the case study analysis, which then may be followed by questions and/or general discussion.

3.8 In the class discussion the case instructor may question individuals rigorously or may simply direct the groups attention to particular areas, issues or anomalies in the case. The case instructor may specify which analytical tools and techniques should be applied.

3.9 The less directive case leader will tend to chair the discussion and control the *process* rather than its *content*, guiding and advising rather than dictating solutions.

3.10 In the case of the CIM Diploma where the case study is given out at least four weeks before the examination, there is time for a structured approach aimed at developing both group and individual solutions, in the form of a complete and professional marketing plan. This is the approach which we shall be recommending in the next chapter.

4. CONCLUSION

4.1 This chapter has introduced you to the contrasts between mini-cases you will encounter elsewhere and the longer case study sat in this paper.

4.2 You have also been introduced to some of the underlying methodologies of approaching a case study.

Chapter 3

THE CASE STUDY ANALYSIS METHODS RECOMMENDED BY THE CIM SENIOR EXAMINERS

This chapter covers the following topics.

1. Introduction: a 28-step approach
2. Steps 1 to 5: confronting the case study
3. Steps 6 to 10: analysing the case study
4. Steps 11 to 16: identifying issues and developing strategies
5. Steps 17 to 23: developing your plans
6. Steps 24 to 26: control and contingencies
7. Steps 27 to 28: the examination

1. INTRODUCTION: A 28-STEP APPROACH

1.1 It has been the traditional practice for CIM Senior Examiners for the *Analysis and Decision* examination to write their own case studies dedicated to the particular standards and teaching/learning objectives set by the CIM and its academic Boards. These case studies are individually tailored to the testing of particular areas of marketing management abilities.

1.2 Over the years a considerable expertise has been built up through extensive dialogue with Course Tutors; by teaching and directing actual case study courses; through student appraisals and not least by the need for case study writers to submit marking schemes, examiner's reports and specimen answers.

1.3 This expertise is synthesised in the following recommendations.

Objectives

1.4 (a) A thorough understanding of the situation and of the key issues should be gained through a rigorous analysis of the information provided in the specific examination case being tackled.

(b) A complete and credible marketing plan should be produced which is appropriate to the specific case study, and which addresses the key issues and is underpinned by the prior analysis.

Rationale

1.5 Whilst it would be unlikely for the examiners to ask for the presentation of this *complete* marketing plan in the examination paper (owing to time constraints), the questions are inevitably going to invoke *parts* of this plan.

1.6 Rather than gamble on which parts of the plan are likely to be tested in the exam *and therefore run the risk of failure*, it is better to be prepared for *all* eventualities. Whilst other subjects can be revised relatively easily in the event of failure, each case study is unique. To resit the case examination essentially means *starting again from scratch.*

Basic approach

1.7 A *group* approach to analysis and decision is recommended. It is extremely unlikely that a person working alone (however clever) will be able to develop the wider perspectives necessary to a thorough understanding of the case. Additionally, the challenges provided by the group to an individual's recommendations constitute an excellent forum for developing appropriate justification. This process also helps to moderate excesses and provide a balanced, reasoned report.

1.8 The *ideal* approach is that whereby a study group is formed consisting of a group of say 24 people who then work in four syndicates each of six people in a programmed way through each of the steps recommended below.

1.9 At the end of each syndicate session, the syndicates should report formally back to the plenary group of 24, through a rotating syndicate spokesperson. Each syndicate's presentation should be open to questions, challenges and constructive criticism from the other syndicates and be followed by general discussion. All sessions should ideally be programmed and guided by an objective case instructor of the less directive nature (see Chapter 2, paragraphs 3.7 to 3.9).

1.10 Continuity, commitment, discipline and organisation within the syndicates is essential to producing the quality of marketing planning required.

1.11 Failing this ideal, candidates working alone are, *as a minimum* urged to discuss aspects of the case with as many colleagues as they can muster and to continually challenge their own assumptions, conclusions and solutions. Analyses of the case are available at modest prices from a number of sources normally advertised in *Marketing Success* published by the CIM. These analyses do at least provide other perspectives, usually generated by a small group of marketing consultants.

Summary of the 28 steps recommended when tackling the CIM case

Step 1	Read the case.
Step 2	After an interval, re-read the case.
Step 3	Reflect on the instructions and candidates' brief.
Step 4	Think yourself into the role and the situation
Step 5	Re-read the case, write a précis. Discuss with colleagues.
Step 6	Conduct a marketing audit. Discuss with colleagues.
Step 7	Do a SWOT analysis. Discuss with colleagues.
Step 8	Conduct analyses/cross analyses of appendices. Discuss with colleagues.
Step 9	Reconsider your précis, marketing audit and SWOT analysis.
Step 10	Conduct a situational analysis. Discuss with colleagues.
Step 11	Decide key issues. Discuss with colleagues.
Step 12	Develop a mission statement. Discuss with colleagues.
Step 13	Decide broad aims. Discuss with colleagues.
Step 14	Identify and analyse major problems. Develop and analyse alternative solutions.Discuss with colleagues.
Step 15	Develop quantified and timescaled objectives. Discuss with colleagues.
Step 16	Consider alternative strategies and select those most appropriate. Discuss with colleagues.
Step 17	Draw up detailed tactical plans covering the marketing mix. Discuss with colleagues.
Step 18	Draw up a marketing research plan and MKIS. Discuss with colleagues.
Step 19	Consider organisational issues and make recommendation for changes towards complete marketing orientation as felt necessary. Discuss with colleagues.
Step 20	Consider the organisation's culture and make recommendations for internal marketing programmes as felt necessary. Discuss with colleagues.
Step 21	Consider the financial and human resource implications of your plans/ recommendations. Discuss with colleagues.
Step 22	Assess costs and draw up indicative budgets. Discuss with colleagues.
Step 23	Draw up schedules showing the timing/sequence of your plans/recommendations. Discuss with colleagues.
Step 24	Specify review procedures and control mechanisms. Discuss with colleagues.
Step 25	Outline contingency plans. Discuss with colleagues.
Step 26	Review your complete marketing plan.
Step 27	Draw up your examination plan.
Step 28	Practise writing in true report style.

1.12 This, then, is the 28 step approach to a thorough preparation for the CIM examination. It can be seen that this specific approach is necessarily more comprehensive than the more general approaches recommended by other authors. It encompasses many different steps of *analysis* and *decision* which are the basic ingredients of this subject and of marketing management in general. Nevertheless the above steps are only in summary form and need expansion into more practical detail in the remainder of this chapter

2. STEPS 1 TO 5: CONFRONTING THE CASE STUDY

Step 1. Read the case

2.1 The first thing to remember is not to panic when the actual case study falls through your letterbox. This is not good marketing management practice. Keep calm, remember you have at least four weeks (normally) to prepare and that thanks to this workbook, you have an excellent game plan. Resist the temptation to drop everything, miss your breakfast, frantically pore over the case and immediately start analysing all the tables.

2.2 Choose a time when your brain is receptive. Set aside no more than *one hour* for this purpose. Find somewhere quiet where you will not be disturbed.

2.3 Read the case through very quickly *twice* then put it away, ideally until the next day, when you've slept upon it and your sub-conscious mind will have sifted it through for you and made more sense of it.

> Resist the temptation to read the case slowly and thoroughly because if you do, you are highly likely to become obsessed with the detail and never see the wood for the trees.

2.4 Speed reading tests show that quicker reading not only saves time but also actually *improves* retention of the content (up to a point of marginal returns). Reading very quickly twice, rather than very slowly once, is therefore more effective. Go on, try it. Force yourself.

Step 2. After an interval, re-read the case

2.5 This time read the case through *once* very quickly - as you did yesterday, then once again more slowly. Allow yourself a maximum of *two hours*.

Step 3. Reflect on the instructions and candidates' brief

2.6 All CIM case studies contain a page of instructions under the heading of *Important notes* and a further page headed *Candidates' brief* prior to the text of the actual case itself. Both pages give important clues, need to be read carefully and given close consideration.

2.7 The *Important notes* will tell you that no useful purpose will be served by conducting research or analysis outside the material in the case. So do not waste your valuable time by doing this. They also tell you that you will not be awarded marks for mere analysis. Analysis is expected to have been undertaken between receiving the case and the four week period before the examination. It is to be used in the examination solely for the purpose of underpinning your decisions. The notes will emphasise that you must adopt report format, hence the need for practice as recommended in Step 28 of our approach. Finally the notes will warn you that pre-prepared 'group' or syndicated answers written out blindly without reference to the actual questions set, will be failed. You really do have to think in the examination itself, *select* data from your analysis, manipulate it and add to it, in order to pass.

The page headed *Candidates' brief* is equally important since it will not only tell you which role to adopt but remind you of the need to justify the financial and human resources demanded by your proposals, against competing projects. The candidates' brief will often also indicate at least one of the key issues which act as pointers towards possible examination questions.

Step 4. Think yourself into the role and situation

2.8 You will note later in the Examiner's Reports that candidates lose marks for failing to adopt the role designated in the Candidates' Brief, for example, writing 'What Irma should do...' when they are supposed to be Irma.

2.9 Sometimes candidates are placed in the role of a *consultant*. In this case, it would be unsuitable to adopt the *tell* style and more appropriate to position yourself in an advisory capacity. The more you can adopt your role and think yourself into the situation described in the case, the better will be your grasp, and the more realistic will be your recommendations.

2.10 *Without* re-reading the case, start thinking about it and make strong efforts to adopt the company/organisation as your own. What are the major problems? What business are you in? What is the present position? Where would you like to take the company over the next few years?

2.11 *Avoid detail*. You are in the position of an artist trying to decide the nature of your next painting. You decide upon a rural scene, approximate size and *broad* content, sky, water, trees, a hill. This is sufficient for a visualisation, a rough sketch. The details of cloud types, tree varieties, number of leaves etc can come later. *This overview is most important*. The ability to see the most *important* things in the case situation is crucial. You need to see the ball clearly *now* in order to keep your eye firmly upon it in subsequent and more detailed stages.

2.12 You will find the précis called for in the next step is a useful technique towards confirming your overall initial grip on the situation.

Step 5. Re-read the case, write a précis. Discuss with colleagues

2.13 The pre-précis reading of the case should be a quick one, merely serving as a reminder to you of its contents and to confirm initial impressions of the more important facts.

2.14 You are now asked to précis the 30-40 pages of the case in not more than two A4 sides. This is a really good way of forcing yourself to decide what is truly basic to the case and what is relatively less important.

2.15 One case study tutor has remarked that some of his course members when put to the task of doing a précis, produce one considerably longer than the original text. Let us therefore remind ourselves of what a précis is.

'A *concise* summary of the essential *facts* or statements of a book article or other text'. (Dictionary)

2.16 It is important to avoid putting your own opinions, assumptions or interpretations into your précis. Stick to the facts. Many people find it difficult to avoid suggesting solutions to problems in their précis, a sign that they will find it difficult to stick to the question in their examination. This is not the purpose of the précis.

2.17 How to do the précis? Well, one way is to do it in easy stages. Go through each page and pencil lightly at the side I. for important, V.I. for very important. Try not to treat each page the same. Some pages may have no important information on them and others a great deal.

2.18 You may find you have pencilled about a third. If so you can boil it down still further until you really have condensed it down to two pages or can do so when using your *own* words, rather than those given in the text. Now you can either maintain the order in which the case is printed or you can re-order. You might want to add structure, such as which parts of your précis come under the headings of objectives (or problems or opportunities or indeed the marketing mix), if you think this will help to give you a better grip on the essential facts.

2.19 Now, and only now, *discuss* your précis and what you feel to be most relevant important issues, with your colleagues. Remember there is no one wholly correct answer. It is quite normal to find that someone with an *accounting background* will think the *financial data* to be more important than someone from the social sciences. You should find that while there are a number of different perspectives, all should share some common ground and that your own knowledge of the case study has been significantly improved.

3. STEPS 6 TO 10: ANALYSING THE CASE STUDY

Step 6. Conduct a marketing audit. Discuss with colleagues

3.1 What is a marketing audit? Here is Kotler's definition.

'A marketing audit is a comprehensive, systematic, independent and periodic examination of a company's - or business unit's - marketing environment, objectives, strategies and activities, with a view to determining problem areas and opportunities and recommending a plan of action to improve the company's performance'.

3.2 It is, therefore, a pre-requisite to the setting of objectives. If you think about it, the clearer the view of where we are now and how we arrived at this position, the more likely we are to set realistic objectives. The further our actual position is from that imagined, the more unrealistic will be the targets set.

3.3 The marketing audit should therefore be rigorous. It is well worth a considerable investment in time and resources. Wherever possible, comparisons should be drawn with competitors. For example, in discussing advertising you might ask the following questions.

(a) How much did we spend on advertising last year?
(b) How much did our competitors spend?
(c) How effective is our advertising compared with competitors?
(d) How do our advertisements compare in terms of media used, size of advertisements, the use of colour, copy platforms etc?

3.4 The full marketing audit has two parts, the *internal* (or micro) audit and the *external* (or macro) audit, a summary of which follows.

(a) *Marketing environmental audit*. Political, legal, economic, sociological and technological factors. Markets, competitors, distributors, suppliers, publics.

(b) *Marketing strategy audit*. Mission, objectives, strategies.

(c) *Marketing organisation audit*. Formal structure, functional efficiency, interface efficiency.

(d) *Marketing systems audit*. MIS, planning systems, control systems. Marketing research inputs.

(e) *Marketing productivity audit*. Profitability analysis, cost-effectiveness, analysis.

(f) *Marketing function audits*. Products/services, price, distribution, selling, advertising, sales promotion and public relations. If services, add people, process and physical evidence (see paragraphs 5.6, 5.7, 5.8).

3.5 In the context of the CIM case study we have to adapt models, frameworks, tools and techniques to suit our own purposes. It would, for example, be folly not to examine the financial position of the company in the case bearing in mind we are likely to be required to give the financial implications of our proposals. With this in mind it is suggested that you add audits of other functions as follows.

(a) *Financial audit*. Revenue/profit trends, financial ratio trends, financial accounts.
(b) *Production audit*. Production facilities, constraints, developments.
(c) *Personnel audit*. Organisation, training, human resources.

3.6 When auditing the case study, it would also be sensible to use a *marketing planning framework* bearing in mind what we are trying to accomplish is a comprehensive marketing plan. We could ask questions such as 'What do we know about the corporate mission? Do we have one? Is it good, bad or indifferent?' etc. A simple schematic approach for this is suggested below.

3.7 It is recognised that a full marketing audit using the checklist in Chapter 4 (section 3 of that chapter), is difficult to apply on the relatively scant information given in the typical case study. However, you could use this checklist to identify *the information you have not got* but would ideally require and which therefore might constitute part of the information specification for your marketing research plan or marketing information system.

3.8 After completing this audit and discussing it with your colleagues, your understanding of the case should have again improved. However, a great more analysis is needed before we can start our decision making process.

AUDITING THE MARKETING PLAN - SCHEMATIC APPROACH

Planning	*Auditing*
Corporate mission	Correct? Understood?
Corporate objectives	Feasible? Being achieved?
Corporate strategies	Appropriate? Have environmental factors changes? What are competitors doing?
Marketing objectives	Feasible? Being achieved?
Marketing strategies	Appropriate? Working? Competitors? (Direct, indirect)
Marketing mix plans	Harmonised? Tailored for each segment? Positioning OK? Check price, place, product/ service and promotion. Internal audits, customer audits
Marketing research plan	Is the right data provided at the right time in the right format?
Budgets/performance measures	Appropriate? Being achieved?
Organisation, integration, co-ordination	Working harmoniously? Is the organisation effective?
Overall	How do we compare with last year and the years before? How do we compare with competitors?

Step 7. Do a SWOT analysis. Discuss with colleagues

3.9 The following sheet (purposely designed for use on CIM case studies) illustrates the approach used to identify from the comprehensive marketing audit those areas of Strengths and Weaknesses, Opportunities and Threats. You should have come across SWOT in your *Strategic Marketing Management: Planning and Control* Study Text.

3.10 It is a popular analytical tool because it is quick and easy to use and it can form the blueprint for the marketing plan. Companies can attempt to exploit strengths and correct weaknesses so as to form the basis of a short-term tactical plan. Strengths and weaknesses emanate from within the company and are, therefore, classed as internal, controllable variables.

3.11 Opportunities and threats come from outside the company. These variables, being external, are to a greater extent uncontrollable (eg we cannot directly control competitors). Operating in ways to seize and develop opportunities, and so stave off or negate threats, can form the basis of longer term strategic plans.

3.12 The SWOT analysis has its limitations.

(a) It is essentially subjective.

(b) One person can see an attribute as a *strength*, whilst another might see it as a *weakness*.

(c) Under particular circumstances, a strength can become a weakness and vice versa.

(d) People have difficulty in deciding whether something is a strength or an opportunity and whether something is a weakness or a threat.

(e) It can produce almost endless lists with variations on themes and so can result in too much detail to be effective.

3.13 Ways in which the SWOT analysis can be made more effective are as follows.

(a) Keep strictly to the *internal* versus *external* criteria when deciding between strengths and opportunities, weaknesses and threats.

(b) Categorise all items by function, for example a particular strength as being a marketing strength, or a financial strength and so forth.

(c) Rank each strength in relative importance on a scale of *major* to *minor*.

(d) Draw up a list to show in descending order of ranks which items are most important.

(e) Take it as read that there are always opportunities to correct weaknesses and exploit strengths.

(f) Use the broad frameworks of other techniques to develop the SWOT analysis. Here are two examples.

(i) *Ansoff:* we have a broad opportunity to develop new products/services for existing markets (which new products and for which existing markets?).

(ii) SLEPT (Social, legal, economic, political and technological) factors representing opportunities or threats - which particular legal factors? - do these emanate from the national legislation, or Europe or other international sources?

(g) Do not equivocate. *Decide*, for the purposes of what follows, *how* an item should be categorised.

(h) Keep the SWOT analysis under continuous review.

(i) Use the *ref.* column to indicate the page number in the text of the case (p1) and/or appendix number (A10) from which you have extracted each item. This not only underpins your analysis more objectively, but saves time during the discussion periods, and other occasions when disputes may arise.

SWOT ANALYSIS SHEET

STRENGTHS	Ref	Function	WEAKNESSES	Ref	Function
1			1		
2			2		
3			3		
4			4		
5			5		
6			6		
7			7		
8			8		
9			9		
10			10		
11			11		
12			12		
13			13		
14			14		
15			15		
16			16		
17			17		
18			18		
19			19		
20			20		

OPPORTUNITIES	Ref	Function	THREATS	Ref	Function
1			1		
2			2		
3			3		
4			4		
5			5		
6			6		
7			7		
8			8		
9			9		
10			10		
11			11		
12			12		
13			13		
14			14		
15			15		
16			16		
17			17		
18			18		
19			19		
20			20		

Step 8. Conduct analyses/cross analyses of appendices. Discuss with colleagues

3.14 CIM case study appendices normally considerably enrich the information afforded by the text. However, many of the appendices may be in the form of tables and the data contained therein may need analysis and interpretation in order to extract information for decision-taking purposes. Remember, information which cannot be used for taking decisions is by definition useless as far as we are concerned.

3.15 Many people (usually the more numerate ones) get carried away by figures and will argue endlessly whether the extra cost of switching from hard toilet paper to soft is £2.27 per week or £2.35 per week, depending on whether or not we can negotiate a retrospective volume discount. Quite honestly, such debates waste the valuable time of a group and so the format suggested on the following page is designed deliberately to simplify the data. What do the figures mean? Without meaning, figures are useless. We must also recognise that some tables may be deliberate red herrings and add very little to our understanding. Be aware that figures can be interpreted differently. For example, a series (representing annual turnover net of inflation as an index, 1988 = 100) reading 100, 99.8, 99.5, 99.4 may be interpreted by the more statistically minded person as a declining trend. However, looked at from a marketing management viewpoint the series could, on the contrary, be said to represent a highly stable market.

3.16 Does the appendix corroborate data in the text, In other words, does it:

(a) strengthen; or
(b) contradict

something in the text? If so, which is right?

You are, in the latter case, entitled to make your own assumptions but if the data in the text emanated from a newly appointed cleaner whilst that in the appendix came from a statistically sound survey, it would be more sensible to opt for the appendix. Data in one appendix can of course corroborate or contradict data in another appendix. What is the source of the date? How old is it? How reliable is it? Is the data quantitative or qualitative? What value can we place upon it? - are all worthwhile questions to ask.

3.17 Finally on this subject of appendix analysis, look for *synergy* by cross analysis. You can often gain valuable extra information by doing so. For example if Appendix 2 reveals that half our customers are female and Appendix 12 that female customers currently spend twice as much on our goods or services as males, then we can deduce that female customers are responsible for about two thirds of our turnover of £300,000 or approximately £200,000.

CASE APPENDICES - ANALYSIS/CROSS ANALYSIS

Appendix number	*What is it essentially saying?*	*How does it help us?*	*Which other appendices or text can it be related to?*	*If so what other extra information and insights does this reveal?*

Step 9. Re-consider your précis, marketing audit and SWOT analysis

3.18 Now is the time to recap on your work so far. It may well be that new knowledge acquired from your appendix analysis would warrant some modifications to your previous outputs. In some instances it may have given you fresh insights and in others, confirmed your views.

Step 10. Conduct a situational analysis. Discuss with colleagues

3.19 The situational analysis is both time consuming and rewarding. After a great deal of effort, you want to end up with a statement between half and one page long which puts the case study situation in a nutshell.

3.20 Imagine you are a retail stores' group manager. You visit one of your hypermarkets and ask the manager 'What's the situation?' He or she might well reply - 'Well we've had a good month but that's down to the new city festival. Overall, we're down this year to date against last year, mainly on the premium brands. I'm worried about the high rate of pilferage and suspect the back stores have got a racket working. On the staff side, we're struggling a bit and I've worked it out that we've been two down on establishment on average this year. All in all, I reckon that we'll pan out about 98% of budgeted revenue this year but there'll be some compensation from costs of only 96%. We should just about hit targeted profit'.

3.21 You can see that the store manager knows the situation very well and has been able to sum it up in just a few sentences. However, to get there will have taken many hours of analysis and enquiry.

3.22 The *situational analysis* seeks to bring out the relevant *relationships* between the often overlapping and contradictory aspects of the SWOT. An example would be the importance of purchasing to marketing and corporate success.

3.23 The situational analysis puts a time dimension by looking at likely future market trends and by looking for a prognosis (where is the company headed - glorious success, grim survival or somewhere in the middle ground). Establish factual information and value judgements.

3.24 A situational analysis should cover at least the following issues, concentrating on the areas identified as important.

External	*Internal*
Economic environment	Sales
Market environment	Market share (if relevant)
Competitive environment	Profit margins
Technological environment	Product range and development
	Price
	Distribution
	Promotion

3.25 You should use analytical methods and models, wherever possible (eg product life cycle, diffusion of innovation, buyer behaviour models, product portfolio, customer portfolio, profit impact of marketing strategies), to establish understanding of the case material and gain fresh insights on the relationship between different pieces of information.

3.26 You should have a thorough understanding of:

(a) buyer behaviour;
(b) competition and competitive strategies;
(c) distinctive competence.

3.27 This is the time to apply all your knowledge and use your full set of analytical tools, models and techniques, some of which are given for your convenience in the next chapter. The more perspectives you can bring to bear on the case then the greater will be your understanding and the higher your payoff in terms of examination marks. Take for example, buying behaviour models. You cannot know your markets without knowing your customers and understanding their buying behaviour. In the case study Euro Airport Ltd you would have learned a great deal by constructing a flow chart, depicting the stages which a typical passenger goes through from leaving work or home to arriving at the destination in a foreign country. At many of these stages lie opportunities for gaining, or losing, sales.

3.28 The less analytical reader will by now be impatient to start making some real decisions, so let us do just that.

4 STEPS 11 TO 16: IDENTIFYING ISSUES AND DEVELOPING STRATEGIES

Step 11. Decide the key issues. Discuss with colleagues

4.1 The current senior examiner is on record as having said that any good case study should yield, *upon proper and thorough analysis*, its key issues and that any good examiner should set exam questions around these key issues in order to maintain good faith. So this is it. This is absolutely crucial to your exam success. Have you done your analysis thoroughly? If not, you have only yourself to blame if you haven't identified the right key issues and therefore the likely exam question areas.

4.2 In a retail situation you might have identified purchasing as a critical success factor, following analysis and discussion. A key issue might then be the method(s) of organising purchasing within the corporate and marketing plan.

4.3 In Part D of this text you will be able to practise and test your ability to identify key issues in two actual exam case studies. Having identified the key issues we can now proceed to address these in our marketing plan.

Step 12. Develop a mission statement. Discuss with colleagues

4.4 The mission statement is an important part of strategy. It has an important role in providing a *consensus* between different viewpoints and a *focus* for business activity.

4.5 The mission statement is likely to have a degree of generality so that it can integrate various stakeholders' interests over a long period of time. Stakeholders could be defined as 'any group or individual who can affect or is affected by the achievement of an organisation's purpose'. Stakeholders could be grouped as follows.

Market place stakeholders	*External stakeholders*	*Internal stakeholders*
Customers Competitors Suppliers	Government Political groups Financial community Trade associations Activist groups	Owners Decision makers Unions and employees

4.6 Generality can be part of a *focus* by the use of open objectives. This type of objective is appropriate for areas that are difficult to quantify or express in measurable terms, eg 'to be a leader in technology'. Open objectives in your mission statement can avoid over centralisation, opposition, rigidity to change and alerting competitors.

4.7 The mission is shaped by five key elements.

(a) The organisation's history.
(b) The current preferences of owners and managers (stakeholders).

(c) Environmental considerations.
(d) Resources.
(e) The organisation's distinctive competences.

4.8 Examples of some mission statements are given below.

(a) *What business are we in?*

Firm	*Product view*	*Market view*
Revlon	We make cosmetics	We sell hope
Xerox	We make copying equipment	We help improve office productivity

(b) *Mission statement*

(i) RCA. 'To be technological leader again in its core business of electronics and communications.'

(ii) Apple. 'Apple (computers) is not in the game or toy business but in the computer business. What Apple does best is to take a high cost idea and turn it into a low cost, high quality solution.'

(iii) 'To make a lot of money' is not a mission statement but Toyota's 'Global 10' mission 'to have 10 per cent of the world auto market by 1990' does give form to business activity.

Step 13. Decide broad aims. Discuss with colleagues

4.9 Most people find it difficult to proceed directly from a mission statement into quantified and timescaled objectives. They are also perhaps overly concerned with the problems the company in the case study is facing.

4.10 For these reasons the step of deciding broad aims is often found to be very useful. You do not immediately have to decide by how much and when. For example, in the Brewsters case your broad aim might be to maintain sales, despite having to sell off a large proportion of your pubs, or to reduce your dependence on the UK market. In the Euro Airport case, it might be to replace the loss of duty-free sales.

4.11 Your broad aims must be consistent with your mission statement. (In fact, consistency throughout the different parts of your marketing plan is something you must aim for and continually check from now on.)

4.12 Generally speaking broad aims must be capable of *later* refinement into quantified and timescaled objectives, such as to increase sales (net of inflation) from the current £36m in 1992 to £63m by 1997.

4.13 However, this can be difficult in the case of a broad aim being for example 'to become more marketing orientated'. Nevertheless you could convert this into a marketing objective of 'to be fully marketing orientated by the end of 1997' and go on to suggest strategies and tactics by which this could be achieved. You could also say in what respects the company is not yet fully marketing orientated and the measures you would take at the end of 1997 to check whether your objective has been achieved.

4.14 The advantage of deciding broad aims *before* doing problem analysis is that you have the vision of your mission statement behind you, and are not held back by problems which upon subsequent analysis may turn out to be relatively minor.

Step 14. Identify and analyse major problems. Develop and analyse alternative solutions. Discuss with colleagues

4.15 Identify *all* the problems first and then decide which of these are relatively minor and which are major. Generally speaking your tactical plan will address the more minor, short term problems, whilst your strategic plan will focus upon the more major, long-term problems.

4.16 Having identified the major problems you must not immediately jump to ill-thought out solutions. The more responsible and managerial approach is to generate alternative solutions and then to evaluate each solution by examining its advantages and disadvantages, in order to arrive at the best selection.

4.17 A format for doing this is given on the next page and it is suggested you set yourself the task of analysing the six most important problems in this way, as a minimum. You should, of course, discuss your results with colleagues and be prepared to change your stance, given sufficient logical argument.

4.18 One way in which to decide which are the most major problems is to ask yourself 'Which of these problems most stands in the way of the achievement of my broad aims?'

Step 15. Develop quantified and timescaled objectives. Discuss with colleagues

4.19 Although modern marketing management must allow for some objectives which at first sight may be judged as qualitative, they should, if worked at, be capable of measurement over time. The hard business approach is that unless an objective can be measured over time, there is no accountability and no management objective, only a delusion.

4.20 The case study is difficult enough without making a rod for your own back unnecessarily. So choose your objectives carefully and do not parade too many in your answer. Remember that for each objective you need at least one strategy and for each strategy you need a set of tactics, a budget and a schedule. It is better to stick to key or main objectives and (only if you must) then use the subterfuge of sub-objectives to avoid over-complicating your plan.

PROBLEM NO.	ALTERNATIVE SOLUTIONS	MAIN ADVANTAGES	MAIN DISADVANTAGES
1.0	1.1	1.1.1	1.1.1
		1.1.2	1.1.2
		1.1.3	1.1.3
	1.2	1.2.1	1.2.1
		1.2.2	1.2.2
		1.2.3	1.2.3
	1.3	1.3.1	1.3.1
		1.3.2	1.3.2
		1.3.3	1.3.3
	1.4	1.4.1	1.4.1
		1.4.2	1.4.2
		1.4.3	1.4.3
	1.5	1.5.1	1.5.1
		1.5.2	1.5.2
		1.5.3	1.5.3

PROBLEM NO.	ALTERNATIVE SOLUTIONS	MAIN ADVANTAGES	MAIN DISADVANTAGES
2.0	2.1	2.1.1	2.1.1
		2.1.2	2.1.2
		2.1.3	2.1.3
	2.2	2.2.1	2.2.1
		2.2.2	2.2.2
		2.2.3	2.2.3
	2.3	2.3.1	2.3.1
		2.3.2	2.3.2
		2.3.3	2.3.3
	2.4	2.4.1	2.4.1
		2.4.2	2.4.2
		2.4.3	2.4.3
	2.5	2.5.1	2.5.1
		2.5.2	2.5.2
		2.5.3	2.5.3

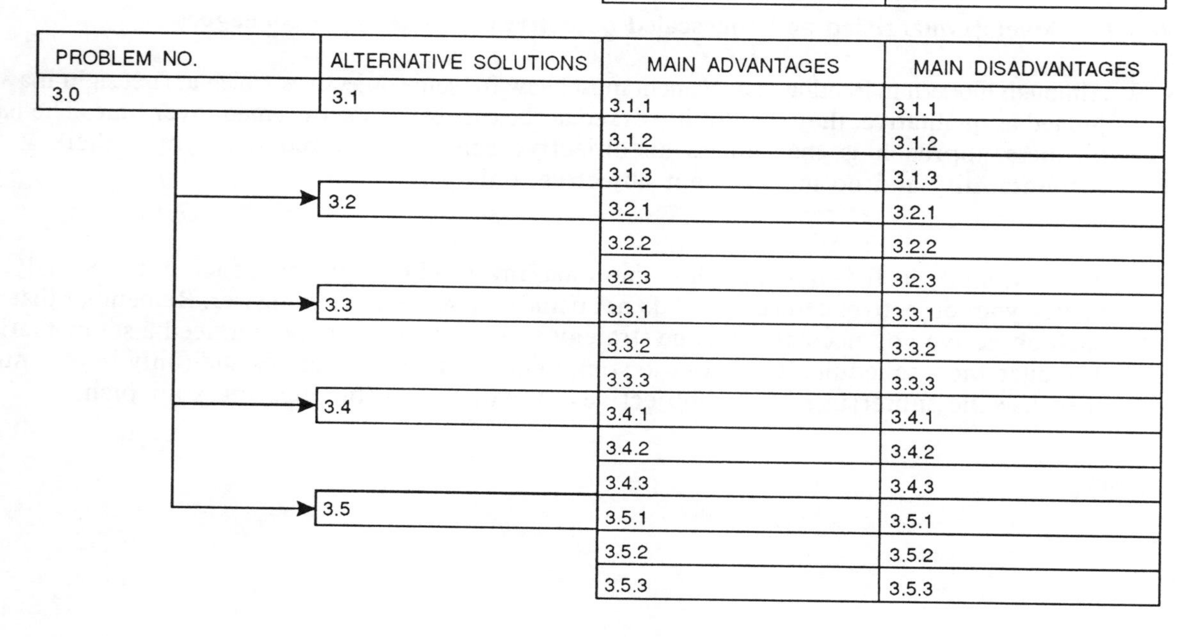

PROBLEM NO.	ALTERNATIVE SOLUTIONS	MAIN ADVANTAGES	MAIN DISADVANTAGES
3.0	3.1	3.1.1	3.1.1
		3.1.2	3.1.2
		3.1.3	3.1.3
	3.2	3.2.1	3.2.1
		3.2.2	3.2.2
		3.2.3	3.2.3
	3.3	3.3.1	3.3.1
		3.3.2	3.3.2
		3.3.3	3.3.3
	3.4	3.4.1	3.4.1
		3.4.2	3.4.2
		3.4.3	3.4.3
	3.5	3.5.1	3.5.1
		3.5.2	3.5.2
		3.5.3	3.5.3

4.21 Many people get confused between corporate objectives and marketing objectives, also between objectives and strategies, which is not surprising since most authors seem themselves confused or are at least incapable of writing clear differentiations.

4.22 It may help you to assume that corporate objectives are usually concerned with profitability, growth and risk reduction and to realise that all the functions are deployed *strategically* towards achieving these objectives.

4.23 For example, the marketing function can grow sales profitably, the production function can reduce costs, the finance function can manage funds more efficiently and the personnel function can recruit better people at less cost. In other words, all functions work together to achieve the corporate objective of profitable growth. Looked at from the viewpoint of corporate management the functions are means to ends and are therefore strategies. However, at functional level, the corporate strategies become objectives eg a marketing objective of increasing sales from X to Y by N date, whilst maintaining costs. The means by which the marketing function achieves a sales growth objective may be by introducing new products and/or entering new markets ie *strategy* (Ansoff), or indeed via the marketing mix (advertising, pricing etc) which are tactics to the marketing manager. Both strategies and tactics are means to ends, the difference is merely one of detail and the level at which you are looking from.

CORPORATE OBJECTIVES (SETTING)

Profitability -	ROCE increase
Growth -	Turnover, size, prestige
Risk reduction -	Increase product base, customer base, market base

FUNCTIONAL OBJECTIVES ARE CORPORATE STRATEGIES

How is the marketing function deployed to meet corporate objectives? (Ask the same of production, finance and personnel functions.)

Say the *marketing objective* is to increase market share from X% to Y% by end of 19X9.

How is this done?

Devise a strategy

- new products
- new customers

These become the objectives for the following.

- New product development manager, to introduce 'N' *new products* by ....
- Sales manager, to obtain 'N' *new customers* by ....

TACTICS ARE DETAILS

Advertising objective	=	To increase awareness from X to Y by ....
Strategy	=	Press
Tactics	=	Mirror, Times, ½ page black and white once monthly

Step 16. Consider alternative strategies and select those most appropriate. Discuss with colleagues

4.24 Please bear in mind the work 'select' and do not try to pursue every available strategy. Good marketing management is about strategic *choice*. Your starting point should be *Ansoff* (see a reminder in Chapter 4). Leaving aside diversification for the moment, since this would normally involve corporate management, you need to ask yourself the following questions.

(a) Is the current market saturated, or is there room for greater market penetration?
(b) What opportunities are there for product development?
(c) What are the possibilities for market development?

4.25 The basic Ansoff analysis should of course be expanded to define which new products and which new markets should be developed and then into more detail such as:

(a) product modification;
(b) re-packaging;
(c) market segments;
(d) niche markets;
(e) positioning.

Your strategic choices should also be advised by competitor analysis. Again a reminder of the major techniques used in competitor analysis will be found in Chapter 4.

5. STEPS 17 TO 23: DEVELOPING YOUR PLANS

Step 17. Draw up detailed tactical plans covering the marketing mix. Discuss with colleagues

5.1 Although some of the broader marketing mix decisions such as pull or push promotional policy, skimming or penetration pricing, overseas market entry etc, are quite rightly seen as strategic decisions by some authors, for the sake of simplicity we are treating the marketing mix plans here as tactical. Certainly in the case study answers we will need to go into the tactical detail, since the senior examiner is on record as saying that his examination papers will contain a mix of strategic and tactical questions.

5.2 If you wish, you can in your marketing mix plans distinguish by headings between promotional strategy and promotional tactics, pricing strategy and pricing tactics and so on, but as was said earlier the distinction depends to some extent upon the level from which you are looking and you are likely to be placed in a *more* senior role than that of a manager of an element of a marketing mix (such as advertising manager, or sales promotion manager).

5.3 To help you in drawing up your detailed marketing mix plans, you will find a reminder of the normal types of decisions and considerations you need to identify, under each of the 4 P's, on the following page.

5.4 Promotion is then expanded into its sub-mix on the next page and following that, for good measure, is a general purpose screening model. This has been included because screening quite often crops up in exam questions and many students seem to lack knowledge of this important process. Screening of new product/service ideas or concepts can be seen as both part of the new product development plan and part of the marketing research.

PRODUCT SUBMIX

Product policies:
- product life cycle
- portfolio analysis
- product mix

Product strategy and tactics:
- branding
- new product development
- screening
- licensing
- organisational aspects

PRICING SUBMIX

Pricing policies:
- role of pricing
- approaches to pricing policies
- pricing and the PLC
- legal considerations

Pricing objectives

Pricing methods and tactics:
- experience and costs
- offensive pricing

MARKETING ELEMENTS - SUBMIX PLANNING

DISTRIBUTION SUBMIX

Distribution strategies and tactics:
- channels
- stock levels
- ordering systems
- speed of response
- dealer relationships
- depots/warehouses
- transportation

PROMOTIONAL SUBMIX

Promotional strategies and tactics:
- advertising
- sales promotion
- public relations
- personal selling

NB: detailed breakdowns of each of the above headings are suggested on the next page.

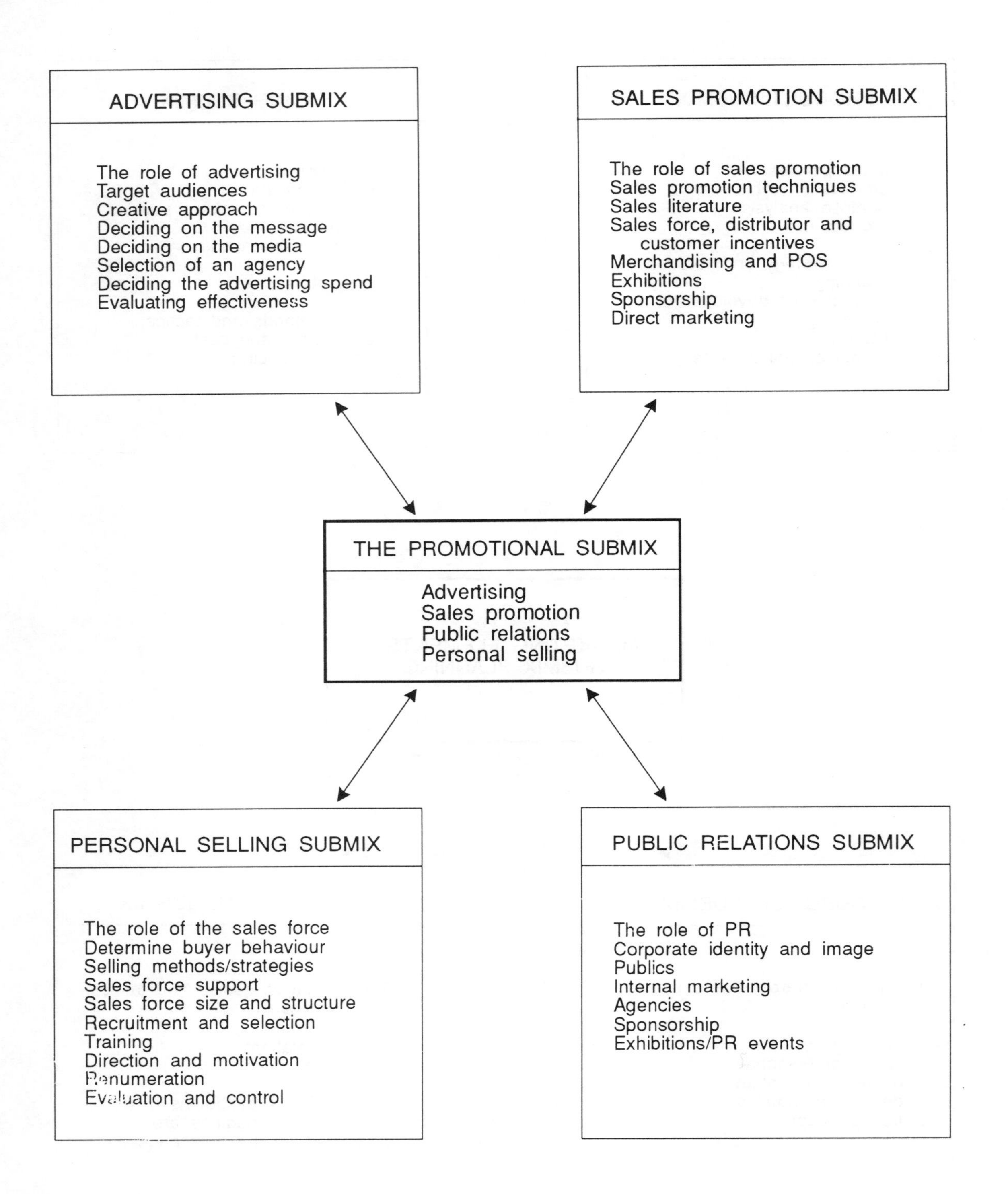
ADVERTISING SUBMIX
The role of advertising
Target audiences
Creative approach
Deciding on the message
Deciding on the media
Selection of an agency
Deciding the advertising spend
Evaluating effectiveness
SALES PROMOTION SUBMIX
The role of sales promotion
Sales promotion techniques
Sales literature
Sales force, distributor and customer incentives
Merchandising and POS
Exhibitions
Sponsorship
Direct marketing
THE PROMOTIONAL SUBMIX
Advertising
Sales promotion
Public relations
Personal selling
PERSONAL SELLING SUBMIX
The role of the sales force
Determine buyer behaviour
Selling methods/strategies
Sales force support
Sales force size and structure
Recruitment and selection
Training
Direction and motivation
Renumeration
Evaluation and control
PUBLIC RELATIONS SUBMIX
The role of PR
Corporate identity and image
Publics
Internal marketing
Agencies
Sponsorship
Exhibitions/PR events

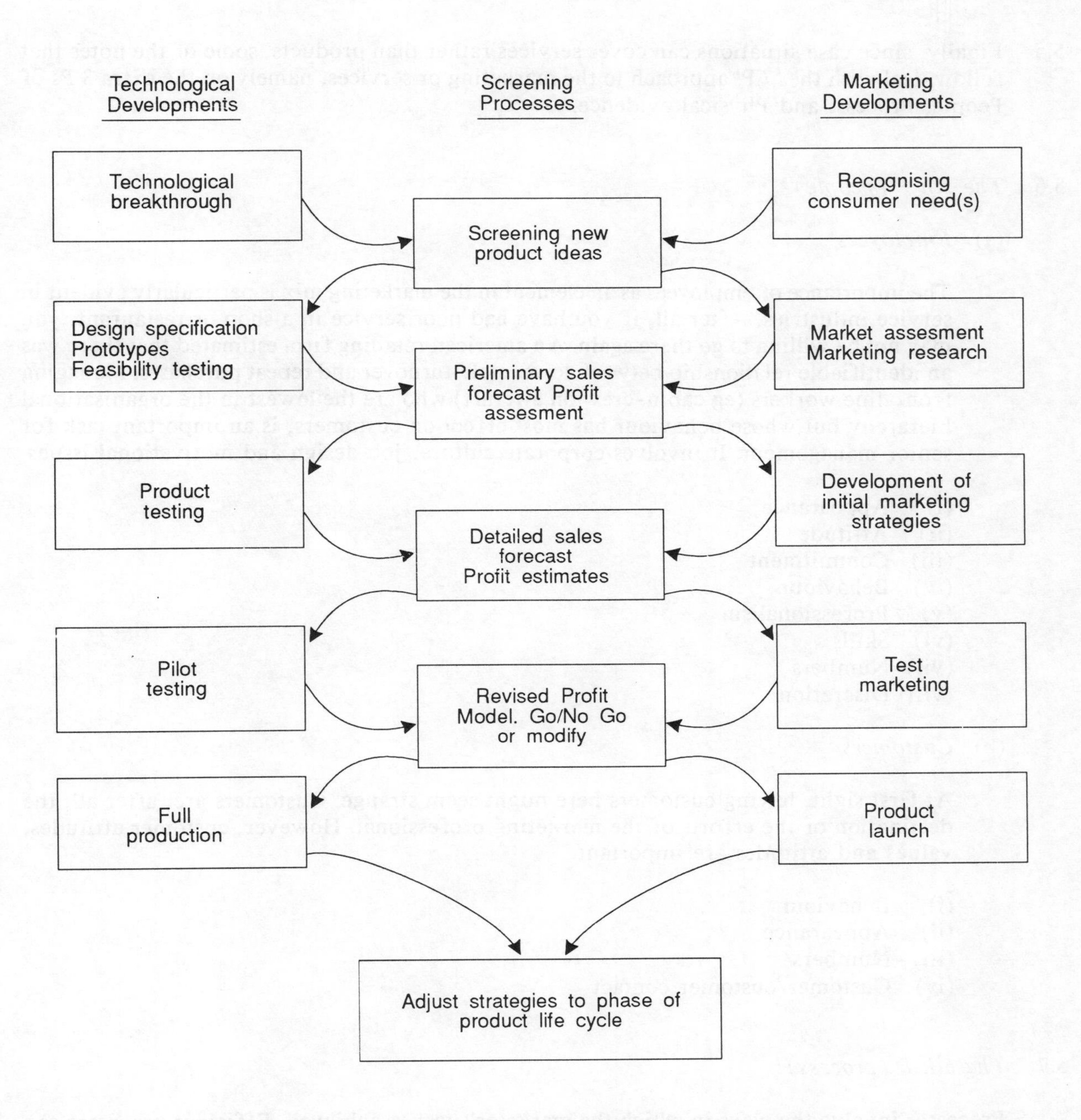

General purpose screening model for new product ideas

5.5 Finally, since case situations can cover services rather than products, some of the notes that follow deal with the '7 P' approach to the marketing or services, namely on the extra 3 Ps of People, Process, and Physical evidence.

5.6 *The 5th P (people)*

(a) *Employees*

The importance of employees as an element in the marketing mix is particularly evident in service industries. After all, if you have had poor service in a shop or restaurant, you may not be willing to go there again. An american retailing firm estimated that there was an identifiable relationship between lower staff turnover and repeat purchases. Managing front-line workers (eg cabin-crew on aircraft) who are the lowest in the organisational hierarchy but whose behaviour has most effect on customers, is an important task for senior management. It involves corporate culture, job design and motivational issues.

(i) Appearance
(ii) Attitude
(iii) Commitment
(iv) Behaviour
(v) Professionalism
(vi) Skills
(vii) Numbers
(viii) Discretion

(b) *Customers*

At first sight, having customers here might seem strange. Customers are, after all, the destination of the efforts of the marketing professional. However, customer attitudes, values and attitudes are important.

(i) Behaviour
(ii) Appearance
(iii) Numbers
(iv) Customer/customer contact

5.7 *The 6th P (process)*

Processes involve the ways in which the marketer's task is achieved. Efficient processes can become a marketing advantage in their own right. For example, if an airline develops a sophisticated ticketing system, it can encourage customers to take connecting flights offered by allied airlines. Efficient processing of purchase orders received from customers can decrease the time it takes to satisfy them. Efficient procedures in the long term save money.

(a) Procedures
(b) Policies
(c) Mechanisation
(d) Queuing
(e) Information
(f) Capacity levels
(g) Speed/timing
(h) Accessibility

5.8 *The 7th P (physical evidence)*

Again, this is particularly important in service industries, for example where the ambience of a restaurant is important. Logos and uniforms help create a sense of corporate identity.

(a) *Environment*

(i) Furnishings
(ii) Colours
(iii) Layout
(iv) Noise levels
(v) Smells
(vi) Ambience

(b) *Facilities*

(i) Vans/vehicles/aeroplanes
(ii) Equipment/tools
(iii) Uniforms
(iv) Paperwork

(c) *Tangible evidence*

(i) Labels
(ii) Tickets
(iii) Logos
(iv) Packaging

Step 18. Draw up a marketing research plan and MkIS. Discuss with colleagues

5.9 Marketing research is usually dealt with separately by most authors since it does not easily fit into the standard planning outline of objectives, strategy and tactics.

5.10 Marketing research is, however, key to all the planning stages. It is needed for the adequate audit of the marketing environment prior to the formation of objectives. Internal data is used together with competitor information and market information when deciding objectives. Marketing research is also necessary to decide strategy (eg which new products and/or which new markets?). Finally, marketing research should be employed to decide the best marketing *mix* for given market segments and to check on the progress of the plan in achieving the objectives.

5.11 Because of its pervasive importance to marketing planning, marketing research (research into all aspects of marketing) often forms the basis of at least one of the examination questions. This can be in the form of an information specification eg 'what information is needed in order to determine the best means of entry into mainland Europe?' or an outline marketing research plan itself. Occasionally you will be asked to differentiate between information needed for a particular project or sub-plan and that which should be ongoing and part of the company's MkIS (marketing information system).

5.12 You also need to distinguish between:

(a) the detailed information sought ie the information specification, its type (product, market etc); and

(b) the method used (postal questionnaire, personal interview etc).

5.13 To help you with drawing up this sub-plan within your total marketing plan, a typical format is given below.

OUTLINE OF A MARKETING RESEARCH PLAN

(a) Research objectives.

(b) The information specification.

(c) Research methods - survey design - desk research, field research (postal, telephone, personal visit, observations).

(d) Questionnaire design - drafting, pilot testing.

(e) Respondent selection - sample size, sample frame, characteristics.

(f) Timing considerations - survey, report, decisions.

(g) Briefings - in-house and/or agencies.

(h) Analysis - method, staff.

(i) Report - format, writer, readers.

(j) Budget - costs of each plan element.

(k) Contingency - for overspend, delays, faults etc.

Step 19. Consider organisational issues and make recommendations for changes towards complete marketing orientation as felt necessary. Discuss with colleagues

5.14 You need to remember that the CIM case study is a test of all your marketing knowledge gained in previous studies. When auditing the organisation described in the case study you need to ask yourself questions such as the following.

(a) To what extent has this organisation adopted the marketing concept?

(b) Do all functions in the company (not just marketing) accept the idea of customer sovereignty?

(c) To what extent does the company work together to satisfy customer needs?

(d) Is the marketing function on an equal footing alongside the other functions in the organisation or is it organisationally subservient?

(e) Is adequate marketing research being conducted to keep the organisation fully in touch with changing customer needs?

(f) Is the organisation structure flexible enough to respond to changing customer needs?

(g) To what extent does the marketing organisation reflect the importance of critical success factors in the particular market (such as in retail marketing - packaging, merchandising, point-of-sale)?

(h) Would the organisation benefit from a matrix approach?

(i) To what extent might brand managers, product managers or market managers be appropriate?

(j) Is the salesforce organisation properly aligned to customer buying behaviour, market segmentation etc?

5.15 By the use of these and other questions you might be able to identify ways in which the company could make organisational changes to gain greater competitive advantage and reap dividends in terms of increased sales and repeat business.

Extra information on these aspects has been provided in Chapter 22 at the end of this workbook.

Step 20. Consider the organisation's culture and make recommendations for internal marketing programmes as felt necessary. Discuss with colleagues

5.16 This step is closely related to the previous one and both steps have been tested in recent examinations, so it would pay you to read up on marketing orientation, internal marketing (under TQM) customer care and relationship marketing. More books and articles are being published on these aspects, which are seen as intrinsic to modern marketing. Remember the CIM has to conserve its image as being at the forefront of the cutting edge of marketing and all senior examiners reserve the right to test you on your knowledge of recent events in marketing development.

5.17 Any organisation can make cosmetic alterations, for example changing the title of the sales manager to sales and marketing manager but these do not themselves result in full marketing orientation. A change of culture will require total commitment from the top and often take several years of careful internal marketing planning and training. British Rail have brought about many improvements to their marketing mix but despite internal marketing, staff attitudes to customers still leave a lot to be desired.

Extra information on these aspects has been provided in Chapter 22 at the end of this workbook.

Step 21. Consider the financial and human resource implications of your plans/recommendations. Discuss with colleagues

5.18 The CIM has in the past been criticised by industry for turning out marketers who are financially illiterate. For far too long it had been accepted that marketers, being creative, were therefore necessarily innumerate. In order to work effectively within the corporate team marketing managers and directors need to understand the basics of return on investment, cashflow and risk. They also require to be able to interpret a balance sheet and profit and loss account, at least as well as production and personnel managers.

5.19 The definition of marketing by the CIM ends with the work 'profitably'. No longer can marketers go on spending money in the hope of increasing market share without recognising the importance of a return on investment and that other projects within the company might return more profit at a lower risk and within a shorter period.

5.20 The CIM have made it clear that future members will need to provide evidence of financial literacy and that financial acumen will be tested in the case study.

5.21 As a minimum you will be expected to show the anticipated results of your proposals in terms of revenues, costs and gross margins. Hopefully you would also be able to demonstrate an understanding of how your plans might increase tensions on cashflow, affect rates of stockturn, require capital injections etc. A checklist of financial implications is given below for your convenience.

FINANCIAL IMPLICATIONS CHECKLIST

Capital investment	Stock
Risk	Liquidity
Revenue	Depreciation
Profit, profitability, break-even	Forecasting
Working capital	Budgets
Cash flow	Financial planning/organisation
ROI/ROCE	Financial control
Creditors/debtors	Costs-staffing etc

5.22 Equally you need to be able to show an appreciation of the *human resource* implications of your plans. Every proposed action will require time by people, time that may not be available. Proposed actions may demand from people skills or knowledge which they do not have.

5.23 Recruitment and training not only cost money but also take time and may not have the desired result. For every basic salary there are considerable related employment costs.

5.24 Changes in personnel have knock-on effects and may adversely affect team spirit and company *culture*. When proposing action you should at least indicate who is involved in taking it and who will monitor or control results.

Step 22. Assess costs and draw up indicative budgets. Discuss with colleagues

5.25 Within the four weeks time available to study the case, it should be relatively easy for marketers to acquire rough costs for advertising, market research, salaries, training etc.

5.26 You are not expected to be accurate beyond a 'ball park' figure. For example, it does not matter too much whether you indicate a cost of £1,000 or £1,500 per group discussion in a marketing research plan (they vary anyway) as long as you don't show £100 or £10,000.

5.27 The examiner does, however, expect you to have some knowledge of how to construct a marketing budget. Candidates who quote a total promotional budget of £100,000 appear to have plucked this out of the air. If this was supposed to cover everything from a series of exhibitions to an extensive TV advertising campaign they would reveal their ignorance. Far better to show the examiner that you know how this figure is built up viz:

	£'000	£'000	£'000
Literature	6		
Reps display materials	22		
Exhibitions	60		
Trade advertising	12		
		100	
Contingency reserve at 10%		10	
			110

5.28 Or if this were an advertising budget

	£'000		
Local radio	10		
TV	-		
Press*	82		
Cinema			
Poster	8		
		100	
Contingency reserve at 10%		10	
			110

* Monthly ½ page black and white advertisements in the Daily Dozen (£42,000), and quarterly full page adverts in the Monthly Review (£40,000).

5.29 To help you we have included the *typical contents of marketing budgets* below.

(a) *The selling expenses budget*

(i) Salaries and commission
(ii) Materials - literature - samples
(iii) Travelling - car cost, petrol, insurance etc. Entertaining
(iv) Staff recruitment, selection and training
(v) Telephones, postage, fax
(vi) After-sales service
(vii) Royalties
(viii) Office rent and rates, lighting, heating etc
(ix) Office equipment
(x) Credit costs, bad debts etc

(b) *Advertising budget*

(i) Trade journals - space
(ii) Prestige media - space
(iii) PR space (cost of releases, entertainment etc)

(iv) Blocks and artwork
(v) Advertising agents commission or
(vi) Staff salaries, office costs etc
(vii) Posters
(viii) Cinema
(ix) TV
(x) Signs

(c) *The sales promotion budget*

(i) Exhibitions - space, equipment, staff, transport, hotels, bar etc
(ii) Literature - leaflets, catalogues
(iii) Samples/working models
(iv) Point of sale display, window or showroom displays
(v) Special offers - salesforce, dealer and consumer incentives
(vi) Direct mail shots - enclosure, postage, design costs

(d) *Research and development budget*

(i) Market research - design and development and analysis costs
(ii) Packaging and product research - departmental costs, materials, equipment
(iii) Pure research - department costs, materials and equipment
(iv) Sales analysis and research
(v) Economic surveys
(vi) Product testing
(vii) Patents

(e) *The distribution budget*

(i) Warehouse/depots - rent, rates, lighting, heating
(ii) Transport - capital costs
(iii) Fuel - running costs
(iv) Warehouse/depot and transport staff wages
(v) Packing (as opposed to packaging)

Step 23. Draw up schedules showing the timing/sequence of your plans/recommendations. Discuss with colleagues

5.30 Far too many candidates lose valuable marks by failing to schedule their proposals. Others simply put timings such as X = 6 months, Y = 3 months, Z = 1 year, without indicating their sequence.

5.31 The easiest and quickest way to indicate schedules in the examination is by means of a Gantt chart similar to that shown below, which enables you to show activities, which are relatively short-term along with others which are ongoing.

A modified Gantt chart for scheduling activities

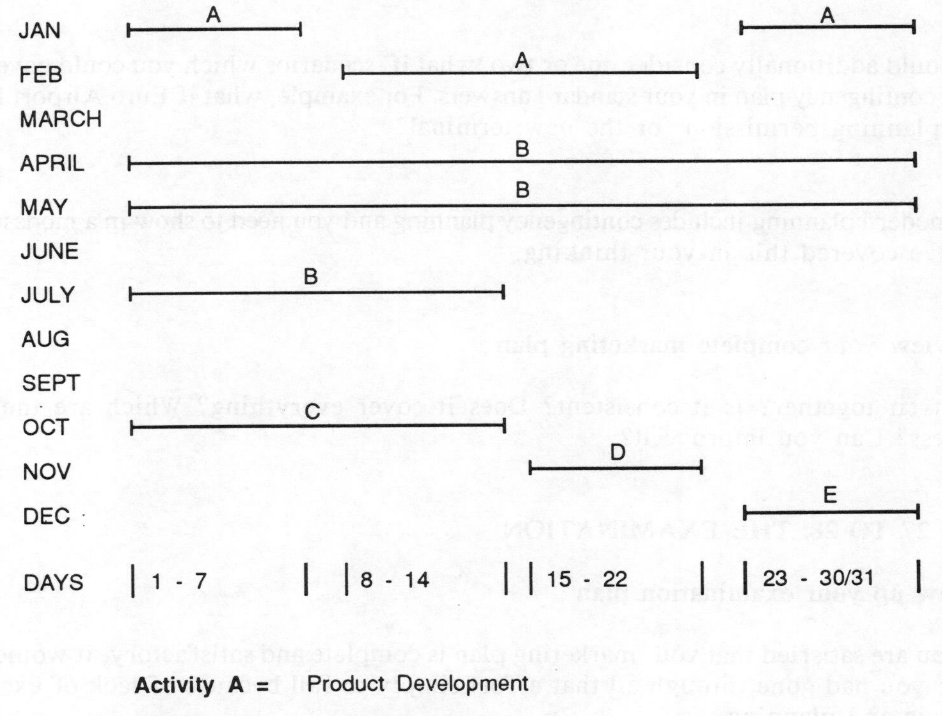

Activity A = Product Development

Activity B = Launch Planning

Activity C = Pre-launch promotion

Activity D = Exhibitions and in-factory demonstrations

Activity E = Post-launch promotion

6. STEPS 24 TO 26: CONTROL AND CONTINGENCIES

Step 24. Specify review procedures and control mechanisms. Discuss with colleagues

6.1 Students' performance is generally weak in this area. If you excel here, this *might* identify you as a distinction grade graduate.

6.2 It is not enough to simply list items such a budgets, meetings, ratio analysis. You need to indicate clearly which budgets are used, which parts of the management accounting system are involved; which people should attend the meetings, when and for what purpose; and which particular ratios are important and so on.

6.3 Read up on this in your BPP CIM Study Text on *Strategic Marketing Management: Planning and Control*.

Step 25. Outline contingency plans. Discuss with colleagues

6.4 The CIM examiner reserves the right to introduce extra material into the actual examination paper. Since this right has been exercised in recent examinations, it is as well to think through this contingency.

6.5 What sorts of extra information might you, if you were the examiner yourself, introduce? Bear in mind this would have to be modest, fair and not over-demanding.

6.6 You should additionally consider one or two 'what if' scenarios which you could cover with an outline contingency plan in your standard answers. For example, what if Euro Airport Ltd failed to get planning permission for the new terminal?

6.7 Good modern planning includes contingency planning and you need to show in a modest way that you have covered this in your thinking.

Step 26. Review your complete marketing plan

6.8 Does it fit together? Is it consistent? Does it cover everything? Which are the areas of weakness? Can you improve it?

7. STEPS 27 TO 28: THE EXAMINATION

Step 27. Draw up your examination plan

7.1 Now you are satisfied that your marketing plan is complete and satisfactory, it would be a sad folly if you had gone through all that effort simply to fail because of lack of examination technique and planning.

7.2 Examination planning should cover everything you need to do between now and when you finally put your pen down as the invigilator calls time in the examination hall. Many hardworking and clever people fail through lack of examination technique. This aspect is so important that it has been given a chapter to itself (Chapter 6). Please be sure to study it carefully and take the necessary action.

Step 28. Practise writing in the report style

7.3 Most of us have been conditioned at school, college and/or university to write essays for both assignments and examinations. However, essays are not the stuff of business communications. Business needs succinct, clear reports which take the minimum of time to assimilate, rather than elegant but wordy prose. Many candidates are unclear about what true business report style is, simply because they have not received any tuition during studies or training in this aspect.

7.4 Marketing managers need to be able to produce good business reports for their colleagues and seniors. You must demonstrate this ability in order to gain the CIM Diploma. Furthermore, you will find it is almost impossible to cover all the points you need to make when answering the case study questions, within the time available, when writing in essay style. So get some practice in. You will find further details on report style in Chapter 6.

8 CONCLUSION

8.1 You have now reviewed the CIM examiner's recommended method.

8.2 It covers everything from your mental state as you read the study from the first time to writing reports at the end.

8.3 Help yourself succeed, and follow the method.

Chapter 4

ANALYTICAL TECHNIQUES: OTHER MAJOR TOOLS

This chapter covers the following topics.

1. Introduction
2. A concise framework for the marketing plan
3. Marketing audit checklists
4. A simple consumer buying behaviour model
5. Industrial buying behaviour: the DMU
6. Bases for market segmentation
7. The product life cycle (PLC)
8. The Ansoff matrix
9. The Boston matrix
10. Diffusion of innovation
11. The PIMS database
12. Competitor and customer analysis
13. Communication models: AIDA

1. INTRODUCTION

1.1 The case study is intended to bring together and to test all your previous studies and knowledge of marketing. It would be impossible to cover all that here in one manual. Hopefully you will be familiar with all the major techniques and models through previous studies for your other Certificate and Diploma subjects. If not, it is recommended that you study the BPP CIM Study Texts for other subjects, in particular *Marketing Planning and Control.*

1.2 A great many techniques and formats have been included in the previous section. All we wish to do here is to *remind* you of some of the other more usual tools you should consider when conducting your situational analysis and which might be applicable to your actual exam case study.

1.3 This section exists to jog your memory. If you want a full explanation of the techniques covered, look elsewhere.

2. A CONCISE FRAMEWORK FOR THE MARKETING PLAN

A CONCISE FRAMEWORK FOR A MARKETING PLAN

1. ANALYSIS OF CURRENT SITUATION (Using Marketing Research)

1.1 THE MARKET

Mkt size (units)
Mkt share (units)
Mkt size (cash)
Mkt share (cash)
Mkt trends/forecasts
Co. strengths/weaknesses and key features of marketing mixes
Brand strengths/weaknesses and key features of marketing mixes
Compertitor strengths/weaknesses and key faetures of marketing mixes
Customer profiles, buying behaviours
Company sales forecasts

83	84	85	86	87	88	89	90	91	92	92

1.2 DISTRIBUTION

Available channels
Sales by outlet
Competitors distribution methods

1.3 ENVIRONMENTAL FACTORS

2. BUSINESS MISSION/OBJECTIVES

What business are we in?
What business would we like to be in 5-10 years hence. Corporate objectives - profitability, growth risk reduction. Marketing objectives - market share, sales.

3. STRATEGIES - ANSOFF

	Existing Products	New Products
Existing Markets	Market Penetration	Product Development
New Markets	Market Development	Diversification

SEGMENTATION

- Bases for
- Characteristics and measurement
- Segmentation strategy

4. TACTICS/OPERATION PLAN - MKG MIX PROPOSALS

4.1 PRODUCT DECISIONS

- Objectives
- Branding
- Packaging
- Pre/After Sales Service

4.2 PRICING DECISIONS

- Objectives
- Strategy - Penetration v. Skimming
- Discounts

4.3 DISTRIBUTION DECISIONS

- Objectives
- Channels
- Intensive/selective/exclusive distribution

4.4 PROMOTION DECISIONS

- Objectives - roles
- Salesforce size/organ/motivation
- Sales promotion/PR, merchandising
- Advertising expenditure
- Media - target audiences
- Copy/creative platforms
- Agencies

5. BUDGETS

Sales Forecasts, Sales budgets
Periods - 1-5 years
Costs - selling marketing - advertising etc

3. MARKETING AUDIT CHECKLISTS

3.1 A marketing audit analyses all of a company's marketing activities. here are two checklists with some of the issues which will arise in such an audit.

Internal checklist

3.2 (a) *Current position*

(i) *Sales*

(1) Total sales in value and in units.
(2) Total gross profit, expenses and net profit.
(3) Percentage of sales for sales expenses, advertising etc.
(4) Percentage of sales in each segment.
(5) Value and volume sales by area, month, model size etc.
(6) Sales per thousand consumers, per factory, in segments.
(7) Market share in total market and in segments.

(ii) *Customers*

(1) Number of actual and potential buyers by area.

(2) Characteristics of consumer buyers, eg income, occupation, education, sex, size of family etc.

(3) Characteristics of industrial buyers, eg primary, secondary, tertiary, manufacturing; type of industry; size etc.

(4) Characteristics of users, if different from buyers.

(5) Location of buyers, users.

(6) When purchases made: time of day, week, month, year; frequency of purchase; size of average purchase or typical purchase.

(7) How purchases are made: specification or competition; by sample, inspection, impulse, rotation, system; cash or credit.

(8) Attitudes, motivation to purchase; influences on buying decision; decision making unit in organisation.

(9) Product uses - primary and secondary.

(b) *Products*

(i) *Current product information*

(1) Quality: materials, workmanship, design, method of manufacture, manufacturing cycle, inputs-outputs.

(2) Technical characteristics, attributes that may be considered as selling points, buying points.

(3) Models, sized, styles, ranges, colours etc.

(4) Essential or non-essential, convenience or speciality.

(5) Similarities with other company products.

(6) Relation of product features to user's needs, wants, desires.

(7) Development of branding and brand image.

(8) Degree of product differentiation, actual and possible.

(9) Packaging used, functional, promotional.

(10) Materials, sizes, shapes, construction, closure.

(ii) *Competitors' products*

(1) Competitive and competing products.
(2) Main competitors and leading brands.
(3) Comparison of design and performance differences with leading competitors.
(4) Comparison of offering of competitors, images, value etc.

(iii) *Future trends*

(1) Likely future product developments in company.
(2) Likely future, or possible future, developments in industry.
(3) Further product line or mix contraction, modification or expansion.

(c) *Distribution*

(i) *Current distribution position.*

(1) Current company distribution structure.

(2) Channels and methods used in channels.

(3) Total number of outlets (consumer or industrial) by type.

(4) Total number of wholesalers or industrial middlemen, broken down into areas and by types.

(5) Percentage of outlets of each type handling product broken down into areas.

(6) Attitudes of outlets by area, type, size.

(7) Degree of cooperation, current and possible.

(8) Multi-brand policy, possible or current.

(9) Strengths and weaknesses in distribution system, functionally and geographically.

(10) Number and type of warehouses; location.

(11) Transportation and communications.

(12) Stock control; delivery periods; control of information.

(ii) *Competitors' distribution*

(1) Competitive distribution structure; strengths and weaknesses.
(2) Market coverage and penetration.
(3) Transportation methods used by competitors.
(4) Delivery of competitors.
(5) Specific competitive selling conditions.

(iii) *Future development*

(1) Further likely and possible developments in industry as a whole or from one or more competitors.

(2) Probably changes in distribution system of company.

(3) Possibilities of any future fundamental changes in outlets.

(d) *Promotion and personal selling*

(i) *The sales force*

(1) Size and composition of sales force.

(2) Calls per day, week, month, year by salesman.

(3) Conversion rate of orders to calls.

(4) Selling cost per value and volume of sales achieved.

(5) Selling cost per customer.

(6) Internal and external sales promotion.

(7) Recruiting, selection, training, control procedures.

(8) Methods of motivation of salesmen.

(9) Remuneration schemes.

(10) Advertising appropriation and media schedule, copy theme.

(11) Cost of trade, technical, professional, consumer media.

(12) Cost of advertising per unit, per value of unit, per customer.

(13) Advertising expenditure per thousand readers, viewers of main and all media used.

(14) Methods and costs of merchandising.

(15) Public and press relations; exhibitions.

(ii) *Competitors' sales activities*

(1) Competitive selling activities and methods of selling and advertising; strengths and weaknesses.

(2) Review of competitors' promotion, sales contests, etc.

(3) Competitor's advertising themes, media used.

(iii) *The future*

(1) Future developments likely in selling, promotional and advertising activities.

(e) *Pricing*

(i) *Current pricing*

(1) Pricing strategy and general methods of price structuring in company.

(2) High or low policies, reasons why.

(3) Prevailing pricing policies in industry.

(4) Current wholesaler, retailer margins in consumer markets or middlemen margins in industrial markets.

(5) Discounts, functional, quantity, cash, reward, incentive.

(6) Pricing objectives, profit objectives, financial implications such as breakeven figures, cash budgeting.

(ii) *Competitors' pricing*

(1) Prices and price structures of competitors.
(2) Value analysis of own and competitors' products.
(3) Discounts, credit offered by competitors.

(iii) *Future developments*

(1) Future developments in costs likely to affect price structures.

(2) Possibilities of more/less costly raw materials or labour that would affect prices.

(3) Possible competitive price attacks.

(f) *Service*

(i) *Current service*

(1) Extent of pre-sales or customer service and after-sales or product service required by products.

(2) Survey of customer needs.

(3) Installation, education in use, inspection, maintenance, repair, accessories provision.

(4) Guarantees, warranty period.

(5) Methods, procedures for carrying out service. Returned goods, complaints.

(ii) *Competitors' services*

(1) Services supplied by competitive manufacturers and service organisations.
(2) Types of guarantee, warranty, credit provided.

(iii) *Future service policies*

(1) Future possible developments that might require a revised service policy.

(g) *Organisational points* (eg design of marketing organisation, sales, production or marketing orientation)

External checklist

3.3 (a) *Environmental audit: national and international*

(i) Social and cultural factors likely to impact upon the market, in the short and long term.

(ii) Legal factors and codes of practice likely to affect the market in the short and long term.

(iii) Economic factors likely to affect market demand in the short and long term.

(iv) Political changes and military action likely to impact upon national and international markets.

(v) Technological changes anticipated and likely to create new opportunities and threats.

(b) *Marketing objectives and strategies*

(i) *Current plans*

(1) Short term plans and objectives for current year, in light of current political and economic situation.

(2) Construction of standards for measurement of progress towards achieving of objectives; management ratios that can be translated into control procedures.

(3) Breakdown of turnover into periods, areas, segments, outlets, salesmen etc.

(4) Which personnel required to undertaken what responsibilities, actions etc when.

(ii) *Competitors' plans*

(1) Review of competitors strengths and weaknesses, likely competitive reactions and possible company responses that could be made.

(iii) *Future developments*

(1) Long term plans, objectives and strategies related to products, price, places of distribution, promotion, personnel selling and service.

4. A SIMPLE CONSUMER BUYING BEHAVIOUR MODEL

4.1 Buyer behaviour is a topic connecting the consumer's needs, wishes and desires - normally studied by the psychologist - with the economic and commercial objectives of a firm.

4.2 The model below indicates the main issues in buyer behaviour. One of the consequences of a purchase might be to encourage an additional purchase (especially true in service industries). Post-purchase feelings are therefore important.

STEPS IN THE BUYING PROCESS

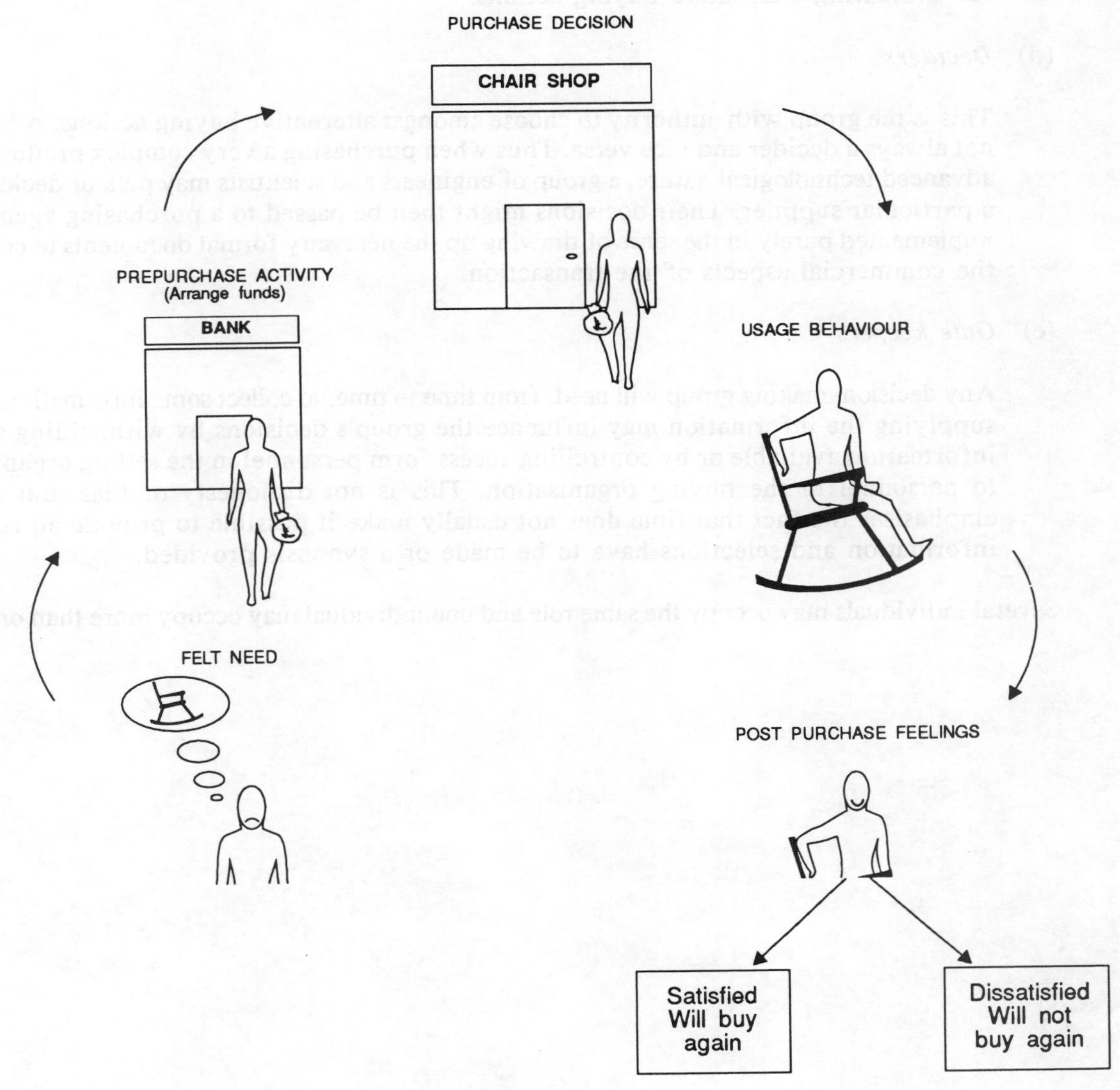

5. INDUSTRIAL BUYING BEHAVIOUR: THE DMU

5.1 The decision making unit involves five roles.

(a) *Users*

This group includes all those in the organisation who use or are going to use the product being purchased. It will include people at all levels in the organisation - thus the decision to purchase a particular type of powered hand-tool may well be influenced by the shopfloor workers who tried out the samples.

(b) *Buyers*

In most organisations, there is a *purchasing or buying department*. Certain members of this department will have formal responsibility and authority for signing contracts for purchases on behalf of the organisation. These are, in this context, the purchasing agents together with any other persons with such authority.

(c) *Influencers*

This is usually a large ill-defined group as it includes all those who influence the decision process directly or indirectly by providing information and setting the criteria for evaluating alternative buying actions.

(d) *Deciders*

This is the group with authority to choose amongst alternative buying actions. A buyer is not always a decider and vice versa. Thus when purchasing a very complex product of an advanced technological nature, a group of engineers and scientists may pick or decide upon a particular supplier. Their decisions might then be passed to a purchasing agent to be implemented purely in the sense of drawing up the necessary formal documents to complete the commercial aspects of the transaction.

(e) *Gate keepers*

Any decision-making group will need, from time to time, to collect some information. Those supplying the information may influence the group's decisions by withholding certain information available or by controlling access form personnel in the selling organisation to personnel in the buying organisation. This is not dishonesty or bias, but simply emphasises the fact that time does not usually make it possible to provide all relevant information and selections have to be made or a synopsis provided.

Several individuals may occupy the same role and one individual may occupy more than one role.

6. BASES FOR MARKET SEGMENTATION

6.1 Segmentation classifies the market so that there are fewer people in a market segment, than the whole market. They have more in common with each other than with others in the wider market.

6.2 *Segmentation variables useful in deciding why people buy*

(a) *Psychographic*

(i) Life styles
(ii) Attitudes
(iii) Self concept
(iv) Culture

(b) *Benefits sought*

(i) Economy
(ii) Convenience
(iii) Prestige
(iv) Service

6.3 *Segmentation variables useful in targeting marketing effort*

(a) *Demographic*

(i) Age, sex, education, religion
(ii) Social class, occupation
(iii) Residence, life cycle (eg with children)

(b) *Geographic*

(i) Urban, suburban, rural
(ii) Climate

6.4 Other types of segmentation include usage behaviour.

6.5 Some segmentation variables for industrial markets include the following.

(a) Industrial demographics: industry, company size, geographical location.

(b) Usage: light, medium or heavy.

(c) Purchasing criteria: companies seeking lower prices or higher quality, better service etc.

(d) Conditions of purchase: stringent or light?

(e) Company personality: risk taking, loyal, bureaucratic, power seeking etc.

(f) Ordering characteristics: frequency, size of order, urgency of order etc.

7. THE PRODUCT LIFE CYCLE (PLC)

7.1 This concept suggests that most products are services will, over time, exhibit stages of growth, maturity, and decline as follows.

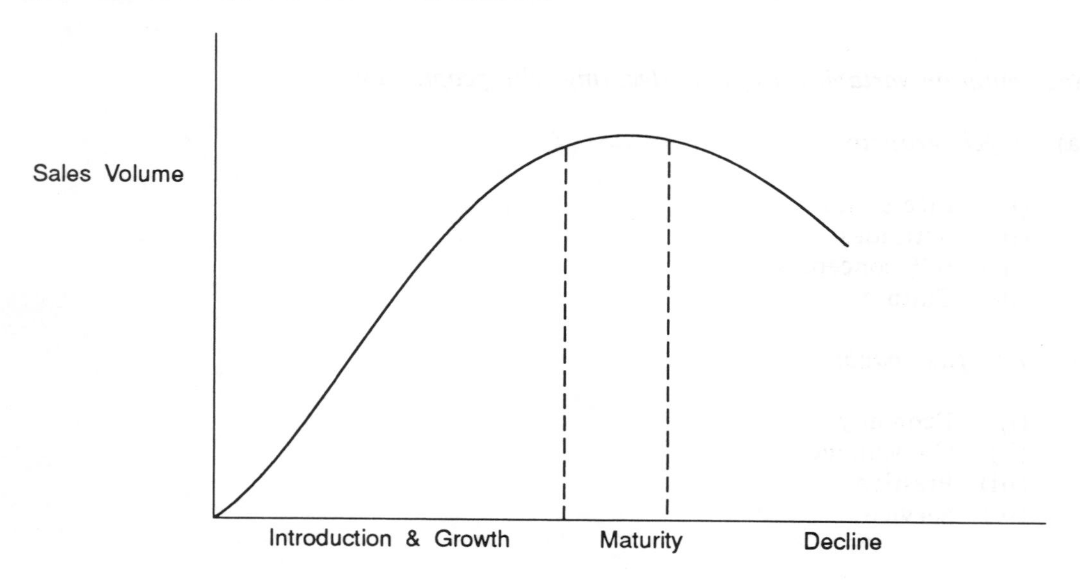

Simplified Version of the Product Life Cycle

7.2 The concept is useful inasmuch as it draws attention to the need for marketing action to lengthen a product's life, regenerate or replace it. Whilst some critics argue that the PLC has been responsible for far too many premature product withdrawals and others argue that coal, bread etc have been in demand for thousands of years, there is little doubt that a great many individual products do exhibit PLC tendencies unless modified. Thus, smokeless fuels replaced standard coal in the home and now most homes have central heating. Likewise, less bread is eaten in terms of ounces per capita and new varieties (eg slimming breads), have now appeared to challenge the standard British loaf. Hovis is now packaged and available in a sliced variety, more in tune with modern needs.

7.3 In practice, some products and services can be re-cycled, as in the case of sixties' music and mini skirts. However, it would be difficult to accept the possibility of a future boom in horse-drawn carriages in place of the motor car as a viable means of modern transportation!

7.4 **The utility of the PLC in indicating the need for action is perhaps best demonstrated in the following diagram where it can be seen that unless something is done urgently, the likelihood is that total turnover and profit will radically decline. This is because Product A is in decline whilst Products B and C have reached maturity and are about to enter into decline.**

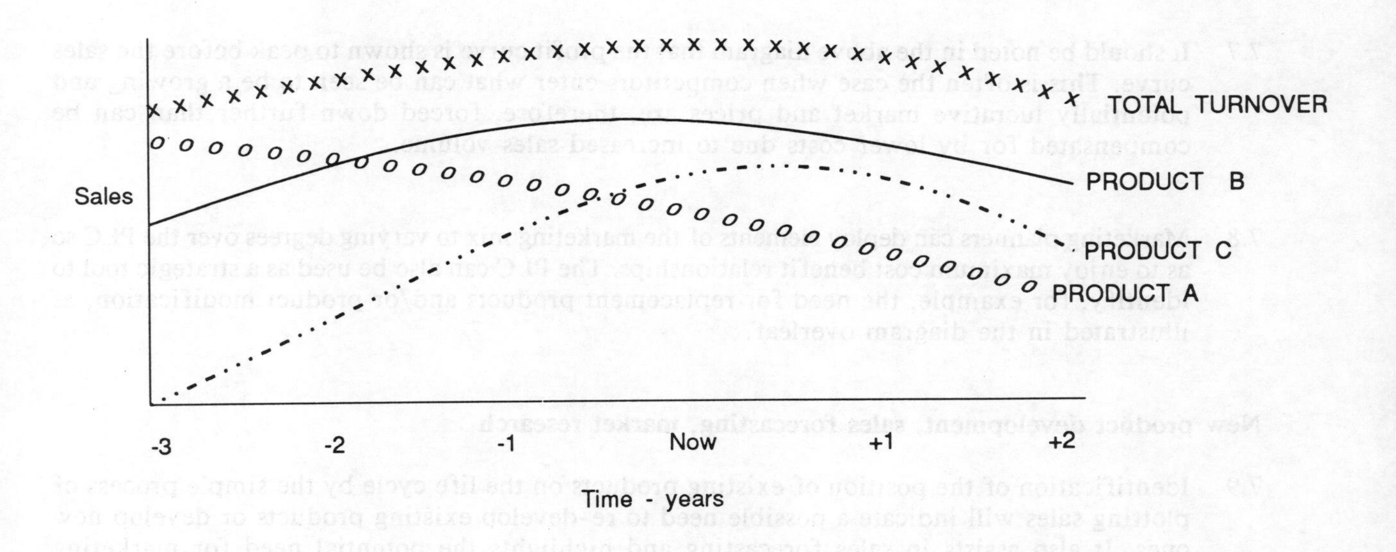

7.5 **We can now move to a more sophisticated treatment of the PLC, one that adds the pre-launch and the deletion stages to the picture and paints in the aspects of cashflow and profitability.**

Diagram

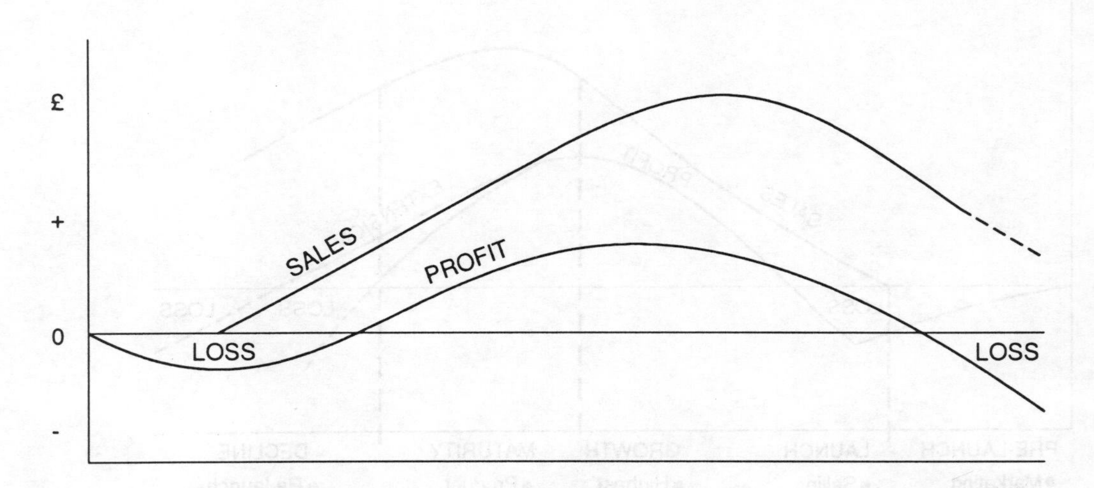

7.6 At the pre-birth stage, costs are involved in conducting research and product development so that a negative cash flow occurs. This situation tends to worsen on launch, in that heavy promotion and distribution are added whilst relatively few sales are made. However, during the growth stage, marketing planners expect to generate positive cash flow and go into profit, a position which should last until a point in the decline stage where sales drop below break-even and deletion becomes desirable unless regeneration is possible.

7.7 It should be noted in the above diagram that the profit curve is shown to peak before the sales curve. This is often the case when competitors enter what can be seen to be a growing and potentially lucrative market and prices are, therefore, forced down further than can be compensated for by lower costs due to increased sales volume.

7.8 Marketing planners can deploy elements of the marketing mix to varying degrees over the PLC so as to enjoy maximum cost benefit relationships. The PLC can also be used as a strategic tool to identify, for example, the need for replacement products and/or product modification, as illustrated in the diagram overleaf.

New product development, sales forecasting, market research

7.9 Identification of the position of existing products on the life cycle by the simple process of plotting sales will indicate a possible need to re-develop existing products or develop new ones. It also assists in sales forecasting and highlights the potential need for marketing research, particularly at the decay stage of an existing product and/or the generation stage of a new product.

Marketing mix relative to product life cycle

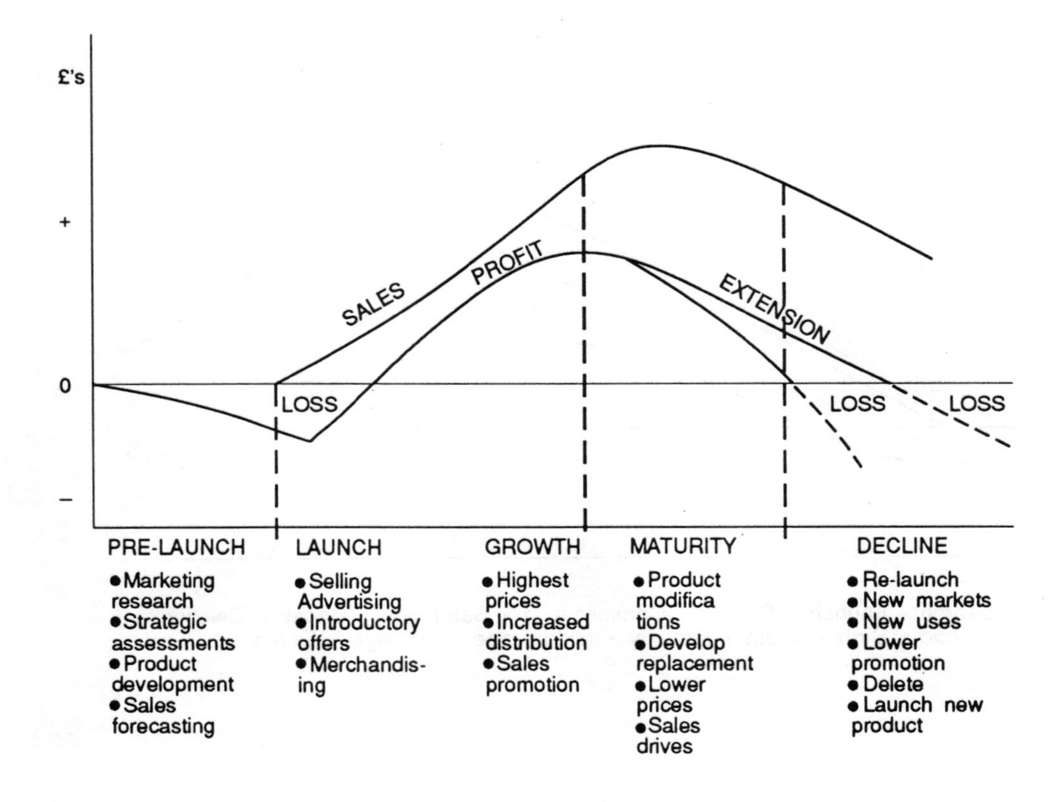

Advertising, sales promotion, selling

7.10 The communications job will be particularly demanding at the sell-in stage of new products and will continue at somewhat lower levels during the stages of growth and maturity. Lower prices, special offers, development of the existing product, improvement of the service elements etc are resorted to in an attempt to counter decline which, if continued, will lead to efforts to find new outlets, new uses and new markets. If decline continues, promotional support is often removed in order to postpone the point at which the product's sales fall to break-even and efforts to develop a new replacement product are increased.

Distribution and pricing

7.11 The planning of increases in the number of outlets in harmony with production (and transport) capacity is particularly important during the growth stage. New outlets, particularly in less sophisticated markets abroad, may be sought during the decline stage. Price levels may be high during the period of high demand in order to recover development costs but may be forced down before sales peak, with the onset of competition

Arresting decline. Where new products to replace those in decline are not available in time, marketing planners can attempt to arrest decline by finding new users, perhaps in developing markets overseas. New uses may be developed for existing products or they can be modified in some way or perhaps re-packaged. Thus, the Ford Escort's PLC has been extended by a continuous process of product modification. The addition of diesal engined versions may lead to new users, ie those interested more in economy than acceleration. The development of estate or hatchback versions may lead to new uses, eg as a freight carrier.

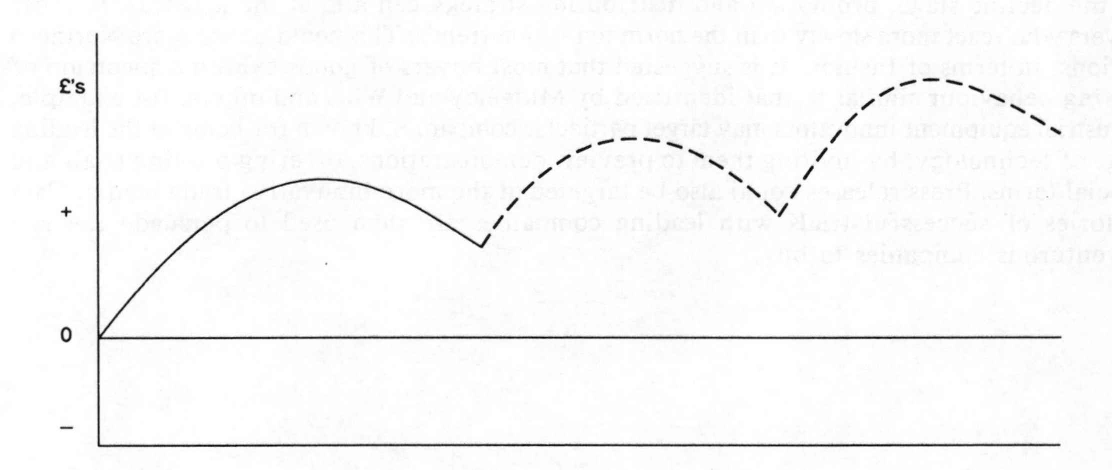

7.12 A further strategic aspect of the PLC is that of considering the relative buying behaviour patterns. Studies by Midgeley and Wills, 1974 indicated that relationships between types of buyers and PLC exists in fashion markets, which can be exploited in terms of more accurate targeting of the marketing mix over time. Thus, at the launch stage, buyers are likely to be the more adventurous, innovative, leader types. Promotional messages, media chosen, pricing and distribution outlets can be targeted accordingly.

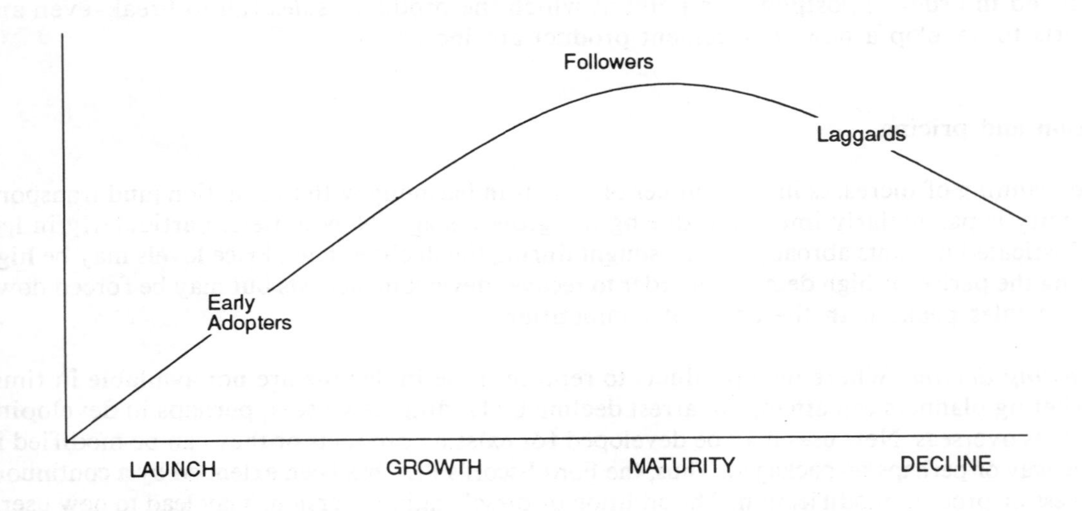

7.13 At the growth stage, the marketing strategy can move towards mass media and mass distribution outlets with alterations in messages appealing to the followers of the trend setters and opinion leaders (early adopters).

7.14 At the decline stage, promotion and distribution strategy can aim at the laggards, ie those buyers who react more slowly than the norm to fashion trends. This could be the more Northern regions, in terms of fashion. It is suggested that most buyers of goods exhibit a spectrum of buying behaviour similar to that identified by Midgeley and Wills and others, for example, industrial equipment innovators may target particular companies, known for being at the leading edge of technology, by inviting them to preview demonstrations, offering proving trials and special terms. Press releases could also be targeted at the more innovative trade media. Case histories of successful trials with leading companies are then used to persuade the less adventurous companies to buy.

8. THE ANSOFF MATRIX

8.1 The Ansoff matrix is used to analyse the appropriate product - market strategies, by the type of product and market.

ANSOFF

Product / *Market*	*Existing*	*New*
Existing	Market penetration	Product development
New	Market development	Diversification

8.2 Here are some examples of the type of strategies that might be used.

	Existing products	*New product*
Existing markets	*Market penetration strategy* 1 More purchasing and usage from existing customers. 2 Gain customers from competitors. 3 Convert non-users into users (where both are in same market segment).	*Product development strategy* 1 Product modification via new features. 2 Different quality levels. 3 'New' product.
New markets	*Market development strategy* 1 New market segments 2 New distribution channels 3 New geographical areas. EG exports.	*Diversification strategy*

9. THE BOSTON MATRIX

9.1 You may find the Boston Consulting Group's analysis of products into stars, cash cows, dogs and question marks quite a useful one. Bear in mind, though that this is simply a *model* and a tool, involving subjective judgements and prone to change over time.

BOSTON CONSULTANCY GROUP GROWTH - SHARE MATRIX

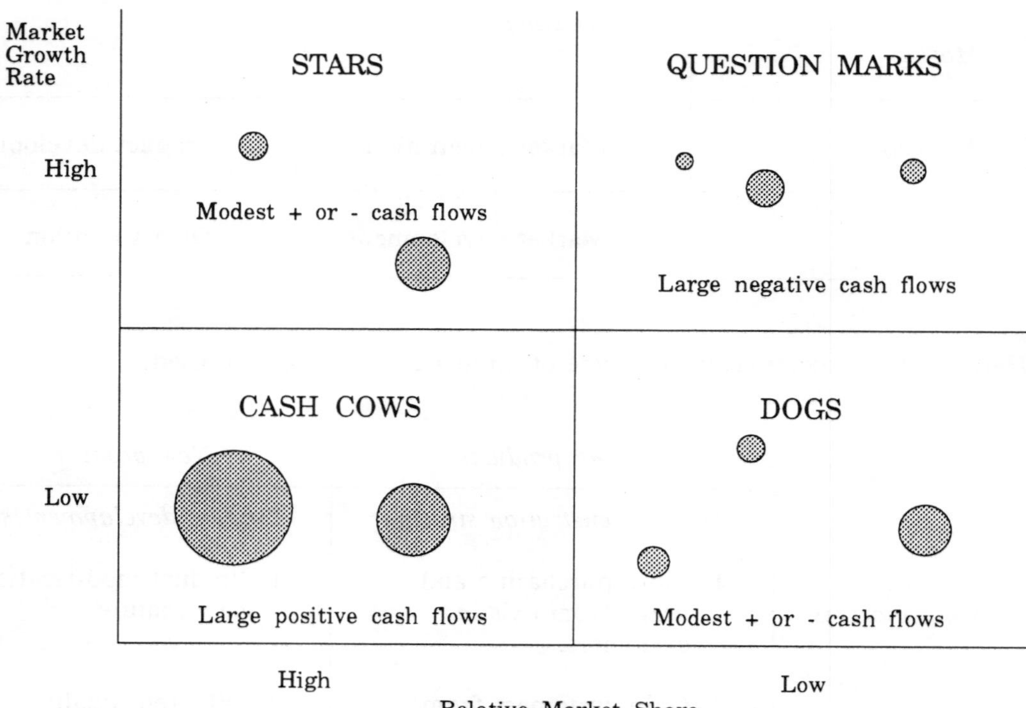

10. DIFFUSION OF INNOVATION

10.1 This is another buyer behaviour model. Take the example of the compact disk player. When first introduced, it was a speciality item. Now, certainly for classical music, it has become standard.

DIFFUSION OF INNOVATION CURVE: STATISTICAL PATTERNS IN BUYER BEHAVIOUR

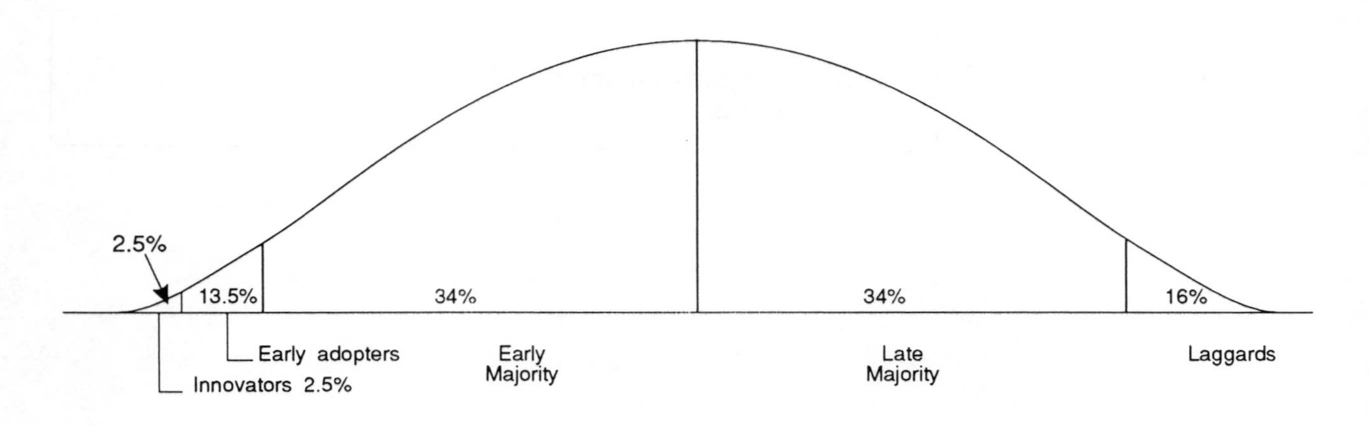

11. THE PIMS DATABASE

PIMS (Profit Impact of Market Strategy)

11.1 In the words of Tom Peters in his book *A Passion for Excellence* PIMS 'has at its command the most extensive, strategic information data base in the world'. This is currently in excess of 28,700 businesses which have been extensively analysed to identify the most significant determinants of profit.

11.2 From a marketing management viewpoint it is possible to identify two factors which consistently have been the important determinants of profit.

(a) The competitive position of the company - with relatively high market share and relatively high product quality being the most important factors.

(b) The attractiveness of the served market - here market growth rate and the customers' characteristics are extremely important factors.

PIMS is available through the Strategic Planning Institute, a non-profit membership organisation based in London.

12. COMPETITOR AND CUSTOMER ANALYSIS

12.1 A great deal can be accomplished in understanding competitors and customers by relatively simple numerical analysis, and financial and market review.

12.2 *Competitors*

(a) How many?
(b) Sizes?
(c) Growing or declining?
(d) Market shares and/or rank orders
(e) Likely objectives and strategies
(f) Changes in management personnel
(g) Past reactions to:

(i) price changes
(ii) promotional campaigns
(iii) new product launches
(iv) distribution drives

(h) Analysis of marketing mix strengths and weaknesses
(i) Leaders or followers?
(j) National or international
(k) Analysis of published accounts

12.3 *Customers*

(a) Numbers and trends
(b) Types - demographics, lifestyles
(c) Sizes

(d) Average order size and trends
(e) Average frequency or orders and trends
(f) Buying behaviour
(g) Attitudes
(h) Database compilation and analysis
(i) Acorn classifications

13. COMMUNICATION MODELS: AIDA

13.1 *The AIDA communications model (as applied to a training agency advertisement)*

(a) Attract	**A**ttention - picture of trainers, trainees, training in action
(b) Create and hold	**I**nterest - words explaining the benefits of group activities
(c) Stimulate	**D**esire - special training courses/packages available
(d) Motivate/generate	**A**ction - contact group training at the address mentioned.

14. CONCLUSION

14.1 No one of these techniques can provide all the answers. Not all of them are appropriate to every situation. However they are invaluable to help you analyse the case study, and to make sense of the mass of data presented to you.

Chapter 5

ADOPTING THE ROLE AND CREATING THE PLAN

This chapter covers the following topics.

1. Syndicates
2. Personalities and teamwork

1. SYNDICATES

1.1 This relatively short section is really aimed at getting the best out of syndicate work. Syndicates are an ideal way of enlarging individual perspectives, moderating excesses and producing results in more detail and of a higher quality than could normally be achieved by any individual working alone.

1.2 These benefits depend on the collective ability of the members of the syndicate to work as a team, to agree on a division of labour for the more menial and time consuming tasks, and, above all, to be organised and disciplined.

1.3 First of all, an individual syndicate member can adopt the role of *devil's advocate*, deliberately taking an opposing view to test the syndicate's logic. The role of devil's advocate can be adopted by each individual in turn, as can the adoption of the role specified in the candidates' brief. Other syndicate members can in discussion, adopt the role of the person reported to, the managing director, the financial director and so forth.

1.4 For maximum effectiveness a syndicate should elect a chairperson, for each session, and a spokesperson. Again these two roles should be passed round in turn.

1.5 The *chairperson's* job is:

(a) to ensure the task is completed on time;
(b) to maintain order; and
(c) to arbitrate in the case of a dispute.

It is not to steamroller his or her views on the syndicate.

1.6 Likewise, the *spokesperson's* job is to relay the syndicate's views objectively to the plenary assembly, not his or her own personal views.

1.7 There are occasions when the syndicate should work together (eg on the *mission statement*). At other times, individuals should work entirely on their own (eg *on the précis*) and times when the syndicate, say of eight persons for example might be advised to split into four pairs to work on the SWOT analysis, for example.

1.8 In the latter instance one pair could work on strengths, another on weaknesses, a third on opportunities and the fourth on threats. Very little is lost as a result, and a great deal is gained in the amount of items gathered. The team would, of course, come together to amalgamate their work at the end of the session.

1.9 Many syndicates leave the write-up for the presentation of their work to the very last minute and therefore often do not do themselves justice as a result. *It is strongly recommended that writing up is done as you go along* and this is particularly important when producing overhead projection transparencies.

1.10 Syndicates can also benefit by organising 'swap shops', between syndicate groups, to exchange work. This helps to avoid excessive note-taking during plenary sessions when all come together and encourages maximum debate.

1.11 Extra work outside course hours can also be conducted voluntarily within the syndicates. Alternatively, special assignments suggested by the case study tutor, can be accepted as extra workload.

1.12 Work allocated to syndicates can play to each syndicate's strengths, as can work shared among syndicate members. If a given syndicate contains a large number of people in marketing communications, it might be allocated the task of producing a promotional plan. If within a syndicate there is a person from an accounting background he or she might be asked to analyse the appendix containing the accounts.

1.13 This is not to absolve *individuals* from creating their own personal plans, but merely to make best use of limited syndicate and plenary group time. Individuals can and should sit in critical judgement of other people's contributions, accepting the best, rejecting the poorer and adding their own contributions.

2. PERSONALITIES AND TEAMWORK

2.1 Syndicate members will get the best out of their team if they pull together, retain a sense of humour and recognise the value of interplay between personalities. Individuals should endeavour to categorise themselves eg as being too dominant or too quiet and attempt to overcome these faults in their own and the group's interests.

2.2 The following categorisation is offered for self-analysis and with the tiniest pinch of salt.

(a) The *Jumper*. Usually better qualified than the average, this person knows the best solutions instantly and feels that, the development of alternative solutions and the weighing up of each solution's advantages/disadvantages before making a choice, is a menial task suited to his or her less well qualified colleagues but unnecessary for someone of his or her acumen. 'It's obvious' is the catchphrase, delivered with thinly disguised scorn for those people who cannot see the argument (including the tutor). This person is impatient, quick-thinking and finishes the job in half the time, making other team members feel that it is they who are doing something wrong.

(b) The *Sitter*. This person finds it difficult to come to a decision and sits on the fence equivocating brilliantly on both sides. He or she seems to forget that the subject examined is 'Analysis and *Decision*'.

(c) The *Xerox*. With no strong personal views and no real inclination to hard work, this person copies other people's ideas - unfortunately often those of the Jumper. The Xerox is caught out by the exam questions which puts a slightly different slant on the matter and blindly copies out the pre-prepared answer notwithstanding.

(d) A *tree* never sees the wood. This person tends to receive the case and plunge into analysis of all tables to the nth degree with calculator smoking. This person works hard and is extremely difficult to beat in discussion since he or she can bring more and more data to bear on the question, endlessly splitting hairs, crossing t's and dotting i's. This person can pass with honours if only he or she would sit back and objectively review what it is they are really trying to achieve.

(e) A *blinker* sees things only from his or her narrow experience. This person tends to have one textbook approach for all situations, and adamantly sticks to this in face of all opposition or evidence to the contrary. This person worships Kotler, or Baker, or Smallbone, or Levitt, and apart from this one, all other authors are idiots not worth reading. Favourite catchphrases are 'I once knew a company which ...' and 'the company I once worked for [usually the Post Office as a Christmas temp] do it this way'. A favourite examination technique is to write out whatever pre-prepared views he or she has on the world, irrespective of the actual exam question or for that matter the case study.

3. CONCLUSION

3.1 This chapter has endeavoured to give you some advice as to how to relate to your colleagues in the syndicates, and you can get the most out of group work.

PART C

EXAMINATION TECHNIQUES: PLANNING YOUR EXAMINATION

Chapter 6

EXAMINATION TECHNIQUES: PLANNING YOUR EXAMINATION

This chapter covers the following topics.

1. Preparing for the examination day
2. Report format
3. Examination day
4. What not to do

1. PREPARING FOR THE EXAMINATION DAY

1.1 As a professional marketing manager you should possess two attributes, namely to be able:

(a) to visualise the future; and
(b) to organise for it.

Please apply these two attributes to preparing for your examination.

1.2 If you are typical of most candidates, you will have amassed a great deal of paperwork comprising your analysis and your complete marketing plan.

1.3 What you do now is to reduce it to manageable proportions. None of us likes to throw away the results of our hard work, but you can at least produce neat, concise summary sheets of each section. Relegate the remainder to the status of back-up detail, to be consulted and used only if needed. All your work should be placed in an A4 ring binder and *indexed* for quick and easy access. The best way to index it is to use the framework for your marketing plan since this is the most logical and practical access system for your exam and you are already familiar with it.

1.4 An outline for your index is suggested overleaf but however you organise your ring binder, be familiar with it. Know exactly where everything is and how to locate it quickly.

EXAMINATION RING BINDER INDEX: SUGGESTED FORMAT

(a) Analysis

- (i) Précis
- (ii) Marketing audit
- (iii) SWOT analysis
- (iv) Appendix analysis
- (v) Situational analysis
- (vi) Problem analysis
- (vii) Key issues

(b) Mission statement/broad aims

(c) Objectives

(d) Strategies

(e) Tactics/marketing mix

- (i) Product/service plan, packaging
- (ii) Pricing
- (iii) Promotion
  - (1) Advertising
  - (2) Sales promotion
  - (3) Selling
  - (4) PR
- (iv) Place - Distribution
- (v) People
- (vi) Process
- (vii) Physical evidence

(f) Organisation/internal marketing

(g) Budgets/financial and human resources

(h) Scheduling

(i) Control

(j) Contingencies

(k) Ready reckoner (see below Page 82)

1.5 You will need at least 42 hours to apply the 28 step approach recommended in this text to the actual examination case. You have about four weeks to do this; let us say this works out at 12 hours a week. You must find the time and plan it out properly.

1.6 Take a copy of the case study - ideally you should enlarge this from A5 size pages to A4 to allow you space to make notes.

1.7 The principles of marketing planning and control should also be applied to your examination scripts. In the Chartered Institute of Marketing's (CIM) major case study examination there are usually three or four questions each scoring a different percentage of marks eg 20%, 30%, 50%, or 15%, 15%, 30%, 40%. Your time needs to be apportioned accordingly.

1.8 A spacial control as well as a temporal control is recommended. How long does it take you to write an *A4 page*, legibly is essay style and report style? Make allowances for fatigue setting in part way through a three hour paper. For example, you may find you can write a legible A4 page in essay style, in ten minutes, when you are fresh but this increases to twelve minutes when fatigued. The figures for report style become five minutes and six minutes respectively.

1.9 You can now calculate the number of pages you should target for any given question (after deducting thinking and planning time) and pencil in a 'spatial control' on your script paper. A three part report for 30% of the marks might be allocated a total time of 50 minutes, of which 15 minutes is allocated to thinking and planning, and five minutes for checking what you have written. This leaves 30 minutes for report style writing when fresh, which equals six pages or two pages for each section of your report.

1.10 This sort of planning can of course be conducted before you enter the examination hall to avoid unnecessary waste of precious examination time.

1.11 In the examination room itself, use the following 'ready reckoner' to quickly allocate time proportionately to question marks. Have a copy of this ready reckoner handy in your ring binder and indexed.

1.12 This table shows how many minutes to allocate to each question in a three hour exam, based on the number of marks per question.

Marks	*Minutes*
5	9
10	18
15	27
20	36
25	45
30	54
35	63
40	72
45	81
50	90
55	99
60	108
65	117
70	126
75	135
80	144
85	153
90	162
95	171
100	180

1.13 Think through and prepare your ancilliary equipment for the examination.

(a) Your exam entry documentation

(b) Pens and pencils, pencil sharpener

(c) Calculator. Your calculator needs to be silent and should not require mains electricity. You are not likely to need it if you have thoroughly prepared you analysis, but take one in case.

(d) Rubber/White 'Tippex' fluid

(e) Stencils for drawing organisation charts, boxes, or anything that may help you to save time as well as being neat. If you pre-prepare charts do them in black ink on a white background and on an A4 sheet. If you slide these behind your CIM exam script paper you will find they show through sufficiently well for you to copy neatly in double quick time.

(f) Blanks of charts - organisation, Gantt schedules, graphs, pie charts etc in black ink on white paper

(g) Ruler

(h) The case study itself

(i) Indexed ring binder

(j) Sweets?

(k) Watch/clock

(l) Marketing text book. Although you will not have time in the exam to keep looking things up, it is as well to take a text book with you as an insurance policy. You could take this Workbook, or alternatively, the BPP Tutorial Text, which contains inputs from the other diploma subjects relevant to the case study.

1.14 Check where the examination centre is and estimate how long it will take you to get there. Allow for contingencies like traffic and parking delays. *You will not be allowed into the exam hall more than 15 minutes after the start.*

1.15 Plan to get there early so that you do not put undue pressure on yourself.

1.16 Plan to get to bed early the night before the examination day and to dress comfortably for the weather.

1.17 Remember that space (ie the desktop and around the desk) will probably be extremely limited.

Consultant's analysis

1.18 You should consider purchasing one of the consultant's analyses advertised in *Marketing Success* (such as that offered by Northern Consultancy Associates). Extracts from an analysis for the Euro Airport Ltd, case study set in June 1992 can be found elsewhere in this text and costs around £12.

1.19 You would normally receive this analysis about two weeks before the examination. Whilst it should not of course *substitute* for your own analysis, it can rather act as a check on what you have done and hopefully add additional perspectives, which can be particularly useful if you have not been working with a syndicate group.

1.20 Copies of all consultants' analyses are lodged by the CIM and cannot be copied out in the exam without risk of failure, not that there are exam questions based solely on analysis. The one produced by Northern Consultancy Associates is the work of a team of experienced marketing lecturers but you must realise that whilst it is a professional piece of work it will have been produced within a very short lead time and it is *not* intended to be perfect.

2. REPORT FORMAT

2.1 Report style is *always* mandatory for the major case study, and is often mandatory or recommended for the mini-case studies as far as the CIM is concerned. You are being examined in Marketing Management and busy managers do not thank you for wasting their time by using too many words to get to the point in essay format, when report format will convey information not only more quickly but more clearly.

The use of charts of diagrams is also recommended wherever possible.

2.2 Many of the questions related to planning will require costing and activity scheduling in the answers to score good marks.

2.3 Many candidates are unclear about report style and use a quasi-report style which is really an essay split into sectors under headings rather than true report style. Here are a couple of examples. The question addressed by each relates to the criteria on whether to launch product A.

Quasi-report style: WRONG

> 'The first criterion is whether this will be profitable over the estimated life cycle of product A. Another criterion which is related to the first criterion is that of estimated volume sales at the proposed price. A third criterion which needs to be considered when deciding whether or not to launch Product A is....'

Report style: RIGHT

> (a) Decision criteria in rank order
>
> (i) Profit (ROI) over product life cycle
> (ii) Sales volume at proposed price
> (iii) ...

Question structure

2.4 Try to structure your answers in the same way in which the question is structured so that there is no doubt as to which parts of your report relate to which parts of the question. An example of how to do this against the CIM June 1985 paper follows.

Example

2.5 As Roger Mead, your first task is to organise your team to complete a fact finding mission derived from your client's brief. You have learned since your appointment and original briefing of the following changes.

1. A policy decision has been taken to discontinue the hire of touring caravans. Existing used caravan stock is to be moved to permanent sites in France and Belgium or sold.

2. The new Baxter Kestrel is an 18 feet 4 berth luxury caravan to be sold at £6,750 including VAT, which is to replace the Baxter Hawk which will be withdrawn in December 1985.

3. Don Adams has been taken seriously ill and is not expected to rejoin the company.

4. The decision on time sharing phase II at Parque Montana has been confirmed by the board of the Spanish company.

You are required to report on the following.

(a) The implications, in brief, of the new information at your disposal for A & R Baxter Ltd business operations. (20 marks)

(b) Detail the additional information requirements you would require Brenda Gardner and Nigel Harding to obtain to assist in the achievement of the consultancy assignment. (20 marks)

(c) The methods you would employee to market the time sharing of Parque Montana Phase II and the financial potential to be realised. (40 marks)

(d) Make justified recommendations on the future siting and official opening of three additional travel shops and one flight only retail outlet over the next two years. (20 marks)

2.6 A specimen layout of report is given below

A & R BAXTER LTD

FROM: Roger Mead, Senior Consultant
Mead & Franklin Associates

SUBJECT: A & R Baxter Ltd

DATE: June 1985

CONTENTS

(a) *Implications of new information*

(i) Touring caravans
(ii) Product development
(iii) Don Adams' illness
(iv) Time sharing Parque Montana II

(b) *Information requirements*

(i) Company information
(ii) Financial information
(iii) Legal information
(iv) Marketing information

(c) *Marketing time shares for Parque Montana Phase II and the related financial potential*

(d) *Recommendations for new outlets*

(i) Resumé of current position
(ii) Options
(iii) Siting of travel shops over next two years
(iv) Three sites only
(v) Official opening

Succinct writing

2.7 Practise writing succinctly. Critically review your own wording. In fact 'staccato' style is often more appropriate than long sentences.

Example

2.8 Consider the following *actual extract* from an exam script for the June 1992 exam paper.

> '(a) Proposals for change in the organisational structure.
>
> (i) *Creation of 'strategic business units' centred around each terminal*
>
> This would allow each terminal to be represented at board level with each managers having his own operational and commercial staff beneath him. This will involve a huge restructuring of the organisation and individual job roles/responsibilities, however this move is necessary in order that commercial and operations staff work alongside each other and cooperate to solve problems in the most effective way, to the benefit of EAL in serving the needs of its customers. All commercial versus operations conflicts would be solved lower down the hierarchy which will in turn be flattened out as a result of restructuring. Each terminal general manager must have beneath him his appropriate support staff for his commercial and operations roles eg catering manager, retail operations manager, quality control engineers.'

Total words = c 140
Total time = 8 minutes

2.9 Keeping the same heading we might change the section to read as follows.

> Each terminal to become an *SBU* under a general manager with his own support staff (catering, retail operations, quality control etc).
>
> BENEFITS
>
> Although requiring much restructuring and reformulation of job descriptions:
>
> (i) commercial and operations staff would work together in meeting the needs of the customer;
>
> (ii) all commercial v operations conflicts would be solved lower down the flatter hierarchy;
>
> (iii) each terminal would be represented at board level.

Total words = c 70
Total time = 4 minutes

2.10 Quite apart from the re-wording halving the original word length, it is easier to understand and mark. If this saving was replicated throughout the paper there would be at least an *extra hour* to make extra points and gain extra marks.

2.11 You really do owe it to yourself to work at this if you are the sort of person who writes 'quasi-essays' instead of reports. Not only will you be much more likely to pass the examination but you will also become a more effective communicator for your company.

3. EXAMINATION DAY

3.1 Hopefully, you will have gone to bed the previous evening, risen early, gone through your normal ablutions and breakfast routine and are now feeling organised.

3.2 Check through your exam kit once more and pack it in your brief case if you have not already done so.

3.3 Allow yourself the luxury of a short walk round the block to clear your head and make you feel good.

3.4 Psychology is important. *Tell yourself* that you are *well prepared*, you are *intelligent*, you have a track record of *success*. Look forward to performing well.

3.5 Try not to feel nervous (although some nerves are normal and can enhance performance). Remember that the examiners want you to pass - all you have to do is to give them sufficient excuse.

3.6 In your mind's eye, imagine yourself in the exam room. Imagine yourself sitting there calm and organised organised whilst others are fussing about, all 'uptight'. Don't feel intimidated if you see other examinees entering the hall with the equivalent of the Encyclopedia Brittanica as their case ring binder. Instead, anticipate a glow of satisfaction and superiority once the exam has started and you can see and hear the endless shuffling of mountains of paper.

3.7 Always make it a point of honour *not* to be the first to start writing. Do all your thinking up front. Plan your answers. Make sure you have read the questions properly and understood them and any instructions.

3.8 Plan your time and stick to it. Allow adequate time for checking. If you have really thought through and planned your answers thoroughly, all the hard work is done. You know you will pass. All you need to do now is to put the flesh on the bones.

4. WHAT NOT TO DO

4.1 Please do *not:*

(a) write out the questions;

(b) write a lead sheet for each section of the report (just do one at the beginning);

(c) repeat information from the case (your reader will know this);

(d) write lengthy introductions, current situations, executive summaries, background information or other time wasting waffle - get straight down to business;

(e) answer only part of the question (a good technique is to pencil in the key words in the question at the start of each answer and stick rigidly to these);

(f) write endless assumptions;

(g) submit uncalled for SWOT analyses.

4.2 Hopefully you will find the following guide to examination failure both instructive and amusing.

HOW NOT TO PASS EXAMS
SOME KEY RULES

(a) Play it by ear	'Candidates don't plan to fail, they fail to plan'
(b) Don't revise	Do not have a revision plan either
(c) Aim to just pass	That way you won't waste effort
(d) Have no exam technique	Exams are bad enough without having to think about techniques
(e) Do not anticipate questions	You may get it wrong
(f) Do not read previous papers or exam reports and avoid any student aids like the plague	*You're* no wimp
(g) Just do the first five questions	They're all as bad anyway
(h) Write want you want to say. Don't worry about the question	It's more interesting
(i) Ignore instructions	They only put you off
(j) Do not check the time	Whilst you're doing this you could write a few more words
(k) Never check your answers	There'll only be a few minor errors
(l) Always start with an introduction and finish with a summary	That way you can forget about the middle
(m) When in doubt - waffle	It will probably con the marker into thinking you know what you're talking about.
(n) Write illegibly, especially the words that really matter	The examiner will always give you the benefit of the doubt
(o) Do not structure your answers when it is a multi-part question	Let them guess which part belongs to which - it's what they are paid for isn't it?

(p)	If it is a two-part paper do the last bit first	It shows initiative - makes you stand out from the crowd
(q)	Arrive late and leave early	What's a few minutes between friends
(r)	Be disorganised	You can always ask the invigilator if you can borrow his/her pen, and for the odd toilet break or two
(s)	Have just a little drink before the exam	It helps you to relax doesn't it?
(t)	Don't bother to put the question numbers down	Well it should be obvious shouldn't it and you never know your luck!
(u)	Tell the examiner what a hard life you've had and don't forget the good wishes for Christmas, Easter, the hols etc.	Should earn you a few 'Brownie points'. Well they're only human aren't they?

If all else fails - ignore the above - do not take any action, do not change your ways one iota.

5. CONCLUSION

5.1 You have by now learned the Senior Examiner's recommended method to approach this paper, and you have revised some analytical techniques.

5.2 You have also been instructed in exam technique. And, should you *intend* to fail, perhaps for the pleasure of retaking the case study, we have even told you how to manage that as well.

5.3 Now it is time for you to practise some real cases.

PART D

LEARNING FROM EXPERIENCE: ENSURING YOU PASS

Chapter 7

INTRODUCTION TO PAST CASES

This chapter covers the following topic.

1. Practice on previous cases

1 PRACTICE ON PREVIOUS CASES

1.1 There is no better way to prepare for your examination than to practice on actual previous case studies used for CIM exams. This means systematically analysing the case study using the methodology described in Chapter 3 and then tackling the actual exam questions set using the techniques given in Chapter 4. You will then see for yourself how the methodology and techniques work to ensure you pass. This will build up your confidence and of course your expertise. It will help you to avoid making costly errors in the examination paper and to make best possible use of the limited time available.

1.2 To make it easier for you we shall, after each stage of your analysis, give you examples of other students' analyses. There are not necessarily the best examples or in any way perfect analyses but rather the sort of acceptable standard you would normally get from a syndicate working under pressure. Remember there is no one correct answer. Different people interpret the same data in different ways. The purpose of the analysis is to widen your perspectives so as to better understand the case situation and to identify its key issues.

1.3 The senior examiner in his Examiner's Report states 'A good case study should, given competent and thorough analysis, yield its key issues. These key issues should normally be the basis on which the examination questions are set, so as to preserve the integrity of the case'.

1.4 The first case study you are recommended to practise on is Brewsters Ltd as set for the CIM December 1991 examination and based upon a large national brewer faced with a declining home market and a legal requirement to dispose of a large proportion of its tied outlets.

1.5 The first step is of course to read the case study which is presented on the following pages exactly how you would have received it through your letter box about four weeks before the exam.

2. CONCLUSION

2.1 You should now turn to Chapter 3, paragraphs 2.1 to 2.19 of this Workbook for *full* details of how to conduct Steps 1 to 5 of the analysis namely:

(a) read the case;
(b) after an interval re-read the case;
(c) reflect on the instructions and candidates' brief;
(d) think yourself into the role and the situation;
(e) re-read the case and write a précis.

(NB. Most students need between three and six hours to complete these steps.)

Chapter 8

BREWSTERS LTD: CASE STUDY DOCUMENTATION

This chapter includes the case study information sent to candidates.

1. Candidates' brief
2. Brewsters Ltd: text
3. Brewsters Ltd: appendices

(*Note.* The CIM case does not number the paragraphs as we have done here. This has been done to help you find your way around, especially when cross referencing.)

1. CANDIDATES' BRIEF

1.1 In your capacity as David Downing the Marketing Director of Brewsters Ltd for the past six years, you have a clear brief to develop longer term marketing strategy in a wider European context.

1.2 A number of external uncontrollable factors as described in the case are affecting the brewing industry sufficiently for you to need to re-think your strategic marketing plans.

1.3 In putting forward your proposals it is necessary to be aware that other projects will be competing for scarce resources both at company and group level.

1.4 Following your initial assessment you will be required to make clear recommendations for future action.

1.5 This case material is based upon experience with actual companies. Alterations in the information given and in the real data have been made to preserve confidence. Candidates are strictly instructed not to contact companies in this industry.

2. BREWSTERS LTD: TEXT

2.1 Brewsters Ltd represents the beer brewing interests of a large group (Leighlow Leisure plc). The Leighlow Group describes itself as a UK company with businesses involved in the production and distribution of drinks; the ownership and franchising of pubs, hotels and restaurants; the manufacture, distribution and servicing of amusement machines; and the operation of a diverse range of leisure facilities.

2.2 Its mission is one of creating value for shareholders, customers, and employees by supplying products and services of high quality in all its businesses. It also conducts its operations with a high regard for the interests of the general public and the environment.

2.3 Like most large brewers, Brewsters Ltd owns the freehold of several thousand pubs and hotels but is being obliged by the Monopolies and Mergers Commission (MMC) to dispose of a proportion of these.

2.4 About a third of all UK pubs are known as 'tied' houses because they are managed by brewery staff or independently tenanted but obliged to sell the brewer's brands (See Appendix 1 in paragraph 3.1 of this Chapter). However, in 1988 the Office of Fair Trading in the UK asked the MMC to investigate the brewing industry on the grounds that consumer choice was being unfairly restricted by this system and prices were unnecessarily high. At that time tenanted pubs made up about 33,000 of the 82,000 pubs and bars in the UK. Tenants pay a rent to the brewer on a leasehold arrangement and take a margin on all goods and services old including drinks, food and takings from pool tables, fruit machines, juke boxes etc. Whilst rents were charged below commercial rates tenants were reasonably happy with this arrangement, but in recent years brewers were also charging tenants up to 40% more for a barrel of beer than some licensees in the 'free' trade (those owning their own pubs and bars and therefore not tied to a brewery), taking advantage of the captive market.

2.5 The 1973 Fair Trading Act defines monopoly in two ways. A 'scale monopoly' is where a company takes 25% or more of any market. However, the largest brewer claimed only 21%. What the MMC examined therefore was the possibility of a 'complex monopoly' which exists where companies which together command 25% or more or a market act in a way which prevents, restricts or destroys competition.

2.6 In 1989 the MMC declared its findings that a complex monopoly existed and made the following recommendations.

(a) No brewer to own more than 2,000 on-licenced premises including pubs and restaurants.

(b) Tied tenants to be allowed to sell 'guest' draught beers and beers brewed by companies other than the pub's owners.

(c) Tied tenants also to be free to buy low alcohol beers, wines, spirits, cider and soft drinks from the most competitive suppliers.

(d) No new loan ties, which oblige owners of so-called 'free houses' to sell only one brewer's products. (It was common for brewers to offer low interest loans, provided owners agreed to stock their drinks).

(e) Protection and security of tenure for tied tenants under the Landlord and Tenant Act.

(f) Brewers to publish and adhere to wholesale price lists.

2.7 The above recommendations are to be put into effect by March 1992 and will have considerable implications for the strategic marketing plans of all brewers.

2.8 The introduction of guest beers would, for example, allow strong regional beer branch brewers to manoeuvre themselves on to the bars of the major national brewers' pubs. It is felt that some brewers might decide to opt out of brewing in favour of transforming their pubs into retail outlets offering a wide variety of choice (where high proportions of their profits are derived from retailing). The City press also considers that other brewers might dispose of their pubs altogether to concentrate on brewing and that foreign brewers might seize the opportunity to buy into the UK market. Yet further possibilities are that pubs will be bought by their licencees (tenants) or perhaps by groups of licencees in management buyouts. Some licencees might buy several pubs. Regional brewers whose estates are currently below the 2,000 limit might also be tempted into buying.

2.9 Legal changes are only one of a number of environmental factors affecting the brewing industry over the last decade.

2.10 Reports indicate that social change is radically altering British drinking habits.

2.11 The 1980s greatly increased the internationalisation of world consumer markets (lager brands being a notable example). UK consumers have become more discerning and more cosmopolitan in their outlook. As a result, former core products in the drinks market such as stout and whisky have given ground to more 'exciting' items (often imported) such as light spirits, wines, mineral waters, lagers and fruit juices.

2.12 Other trends are as follows.

(a) A move away from alcoholic towards soft drinks.

(b) A tendency towards 'healthy' drinks.

(c) A preference for lighter, less alcoholic drinks rather than the heavier, stronger types.

(d) Increased market share of the off licence (shops and supermarkets) over the on-trade (pubs and bars) resulting from more drinking at home.

(e) Drinks once seen as the preserve of particular sections of society are now being consumed by all members of society.

(f) Demographic changes including a smaller proportion of young people and people generally living longer are also having effects on brewers' markets.

2.13 These factors combined with the advent of 1992 (the freeing of marketing within the European Community) and the current UK economic climate are causing Brewsters Ltd's Marketing Director David Downing much concern. He is already foreseeing the need for a professional salesforce (perhaps with special account executives) as a result of greatly increased competition in the future. Up to the present, Brewsters Ltd has been in the happy position of being able to tell its tied trade what they should stock and so has not felt the need for a truly professional sales force as such. The salesforce's role has been more to maintain and develop existing business rather than seek new outlets. External trade has tended to be negotiated by the Brand or Product Group Managers (through Sales Administration Managers) whether for the home market or abroad. Exports are effected either direct or through distributors according to the nature of the product (draught beer in barrels or bottled/canned), the size and nature of the outlets (pubs/bars or retail shops) and the logistics involved. An export division is operated by the Group to handle the physical distribution aspects of all its companies.

2.14 The product portfolio is particularly in need of constant review in light of all the changes referred to above.

2.15 Quality circles were recently extended to include white collar office staff (as opposed to blue collar brewery production workers, as formerly) as part of a total quality management programme.

2.16 Following brainstorming sessions by these quality circles, some novel ideas have emerged from the office staff which are worthy of further consideration despite the somewhat piecemeal and amateurish nature of the outline marketing plans submitted (Appendices 2, 3 and 4, paragraphs 3.2, 3.3 and 3.4 of this Chapter).

2.17 David Downing, inspired by the notion of developing 'Continental' brands from scratch, rather than endeavouring to internationalise UK brands, has received authority from the Managing Director to form a project team derived from all functions to investigate the viability of this notion using the three brainstormed ideas as prospective new products for Europe 1992.

2.18 The question of branding raises a number of issues such as whether to produce beer under private or own label as well as under the brewer's brands. In the latter case a brewer may use its corporate name as a manufacturer's brand but then use sub-brands to attack particular market segments.

2.19 When attaching overseas markets, brewers have to decide whether to use standard formulations for their beer brands or to adapt these to suit individual market tastes. Unlike the US, where beer is the same in most states, European beers in particular areas can be quite different. In Europe lager beers predominate.

2.20 Some companies prefer to position brands within niche markets such as those for really strong beers or those with a low alcohol content.

2.21 The final outcome of the debate on the extent to which European homogeneity takes preference over national distinctions may in time come to mirror the present UK situation where there are both national brands (mainly lagers) and also regional brands catering usually for a particular market segment.

2.22 Other complications in Europe occur with regard to packaging and 'green issues'. Whilst cans predominate in the UK take home market, returnable bottles form the main medium in mainland Europe, strengthening the position of local brewers due to the need to have cost effective re-cycling networks.

2.23 Advertising restrictions vary. France has banned the advertising of alcohol on television whilst the Spanish have doubled their TV rates for alcohol advertisements. The position in the UK with regard to advertising is largely governed by a code of practice as indicated in Appendix 5 (paragraph 3.5 of this Chapter).

2.24 For the British brewer the key to the market is felt to be the distribution system. The major options for foreign brewers seeking to enter a beer market would be as follows.

(a) Direct export using local wholesalers.

(b) Joint ventures with local companies, possibly involving cross shareholding or the setting up of a new company. A variation on this theme is an alliance.

(c) Licensing where the product is attractive but the brewer lacks the means to distribute it.

(d) Acquisition (although this can be difficult given the way some continental companies are structured).

2.25 Included in the area of product strategy are the concepts of company, brand and product brand life cycles in addition to that of the product life cycle. Some brands appear to have a built-in obsolescence and so the strategy needs to take this possibility into account. 'Cash cows, rising stars, questions marks and dogs', can be identified, but at a brand level rather than a product level.

2.26 Nevertheless, despite these considerable problems David Downing is convinced that opportunities for developing strong European brands exist for Brewsters Ltd and he is determined to investigate these fully.

3. BREWSTERS LTD: APPENDICES

No.	*Subject matter*
1	Brewers' ownership of tied houses; pub and restaurant ownership in the UK
2	Quality circle department A: Charmonix du Monde
3	Quality circle department B: Vronsky or Minsk
4	Quality circle department D: Effré
5	Code of advertising practice: alcoholic drinks
6	Brewsters Ltd: ratio analysis
7	Sales analysis
8	Market data
9	Extract from recent article on the price of beer
10	Marketing and sales organisation charts

3.1 Appendix 1

(a) Brewers' ownership of tied houses in the UK

Brewer	*% of Beer market*	*Tied pubs independently tenanted*	*Managed by brewery staff*
1	21	4,642	2,545
2	13	4,600	2,300
3	13	3,655	1,509
4	13	5,000	1,500
5	10	1,400	850
6	9	4,600	400

Source - Trade (1988)

(b) Pub and restaurant ownership in the UK

Brewer	*Number*	*Number to be divested*
1	7,300	5,300
2	6,600	4,600
3	6,100	4,100
4	6,500	4,500
5	2,300	300
6	5,100	3,100
Total	33,900	21,900

Source: MMC (1989)

3.2 Appendix 2

Quality circle department A

Product concept: 'Charmonix Du Monde'

A low alcohol sparkling wine mixed with a fruit juice in a range of flavours including peach, pineapple, kiwi and blackcurrant. Presentation would be in distinctive glass bottles with a cocktail image and of individual long drink size. Major market segment seen as wealthier 25 to 40 year olds aspiring to sophistication. Positioning - the fashionable drink of the '90s.

Justification

(a) The general move away from alcohol drinks towards soft drinks.
(b) Increased preference for 'healthy' drinks.
(c) Trend towards light, less alcoholic drinks (as opposed to strong and heavy).
(d) Increasing success of off-licence retailing as more people drink at home.
(e) Greater consumption of mineral water and fruit juices.
(f) Global warming resulting in greater demand for refreshing drinks.
(g) Opportunities for a European brand aimed at 'sophisticates'.

3.3 Appendix 3

Quality circle department B

Product concept: 'Vronsky' or 'Minsk'

A strong high quality, refreshing lager drink with an appealing flavour capable of becoming an acquired taste. Distinctively packaged in a black 300 ml bottle with a red star shaped label (most of the competitive brands are 275 ml) to reinforce the image of robustness, vigour and solidity and enhance on-shelf impact.

Positioning is seen as a mix of both humour and seriousness demanding a response from the consumer. Copy platforms based on statements such as 'This is the beer that came in from the cold' and 'What kept the Russians warm during the cold war?' The name Vronsky or Minsk depends on the outcome of further market research.

Justification

(a) The market size was five million barrels for draught and premium lager in 1990.

(b) The bottled lager market is of the order of 360 million units per annum.

(c) Our target market size for the Russian theme premium lager would be 20 million units of 300 ml glass bottles.

(d) Environmental consideration indicate that a preference for a glass bottle exists. An EC beverage directive giving global recycling/refilling targets within five years seems likely. Germany and Denmark have already implemented legislation to promote recycling. 35% of consumers consider drink cans an environmental issue.

(e) The premium lager market segment has grown by 72% since 1985 and is characterised by many brand names occupying relatively small market shares.

(f) We need something distinctive with an international appeal in order to counteract current trends and competition.

(g) The concept would proact with current political climates whilst at the same time remain flexible in its interpretation, over time.

3.4 Appendix 4

Quality circle department C

Product concept: - 'Effré'

Effré was chosen as a more inviting alternative to other well known carbonated mineral waters, which nevertheless would benefit from a favourable attitude towards a French name for a water product. It is felt Effré reflects an image of quality, sophistication and naturalness. The bottle will be made of glass in a long circular shape with a gold metal sealed screw-type replaceable cap and frosted to give it the 'cool' appearance. The formulation would be carbonated water (drawn from local sources) available with a hint of flavour, packaged in both a small size - 375 ml (for pub consumption) and a litre (for hotels and restaurants). In both cases this capacity is deliberately slightly larger than competitors to give Effré a value edge without degrading the image. Effré would be launched initially unflavoured, with flavoured versions rolling out and riding on the back of the initial publicity.

Justification

(a) The idea of developing an alcoholic drink was rejected on the basis of a static beer market scenario, combined with the perceived public interest moving away from alcoholic drinks due to increasing severity of the drink-drive laws throughout Europe.

(b) A non alcoholic drink would be good for Brewsters Ltd's image.

(c) Brewsters Ltd is sited in an area renowned for its water springs.

(d) Within the soft drinks market, sales of bottled water grew by 70% in 1988/89.

(e) Hotter summers.

(f) Increased concern over water quality in the UK and Europe.

(g) Consumers are more discerning and cosmopolitan with increased interest in 'healthy' drinks.

3.5 Appendix 5

Code of advertising practice: alcoholic drinks

1 Introduction

1.1 Moderate drinking is widely enjoyed and helps to make social occasions cheerful and pleasant.

1.2 The alcoholic drinks industry, with others, is aware that a small, but significant minority cause harm to themselves and others through misuse of alcohol. They share the concern about this social problem, the causes of which are complex and varied. There is no evidence connecting such misuse with the advertising of alcoholic drinks.

1.3 The industry is concerned that its advertisements should not exploit the immature, the young, the socially insecure, or those with physical, mental or social incapacity. The industry accepts that its advertising should be socially responsible and should not encourage excessive consumption.

1.4 The industry believes that it is proper for advertisements for alcoholic drinks:

(a) to indicate that they given pleasure to many, are of high quality and are widely enjoyed in all classes of society;

(b) to seek to persuade people to change brands and/or types of drinks;

(c) to provide information on products;

(d) to employ such accepted techniques of advertising practice as are employed by other product groups and not inconsistent with detailed rules.

2. Implementation and interpretation

2.1 The industry has therefore proposed the following rules for inclusion in the British Code of Advertising Practice. The CAP Committee has accepted this proposal and the Advertising Standards Authority has agreed to supervise the implementation of the rule.

2.2 The rules are to be interpreted in the light of the considerations set out in paragraphs 1.1 to 1.4 above. So far as the scope and general interpretation of the rules are concerned, the provisions of the British Code of Advertising Practice apply, as they do to those aspects of advertisements for drink, not covered by the rules.

2.3 'Drink', for the purposed of this Appendix, is to be understood as referring to alcoholic beverages and their consumption.

Continued

3. **Rules**

3.1 *Young people*
Advertisements should not be directed at young people or in any way encourage them to start drinking. Anyone shown drinking must appear to be over 21. Children should not be depicted in advertisements except where it would be useful for them to appear (eg in family schemes or in background crowds) but they should never be drinking alcoholic beverages, nor should it be implied that they are.

3.2 *Challenge*
Advertisements should not be based on a dare, nor impute any failing to those who do not accept the challenge of a particular drink.

3.3 *Health*
Advertisements should not emphasise the stimulant, sedative or tranquillising effects of any drink, or imply that it can improve physical performance. However, references to the refreshing attributes of a drink are permissible.

3.4 *Strength*
Advertisements should not given the general impression of being inducements to prefer a drink because of its higher alcohol content or intoxicating effect. Factual information for the guidance of drinkers about such alcoholic strength may, however, be included.

3.5 *Social success*
Advertisements may emphasise the pleasures of companionship and social communication associated with the consumption of alcoholic drinks, but it should never be implied that drinking is necessary to social or business success or distinction, nor that those who do not drink are less likely to be acceptable or successful than those who do.

Advertisements should neither claim nor suggest that drinking makes the drinker more attractive to the opposite sex.

3.6 *Drinking and machinery*
Advertisements should not associate drink with driving or dangerous machinery. Specific warnings of the dangers of drinking in these circumstances may, however, be used.

3.7 *Excessive drinking*
Advertisements should not encourage or appear to condone over-indulgence. Repeated buying of large rounds should not be implied.

3.6 Appendix 6

Brewsters Ltd ratio analysis

	1987	1988	1989	1990	1991
(a) *Profitability*					
Return on capital %	12.9	13.8	14.8	15.2	15.7
Return on assets %	9.9	10.9	11.3	11.7	11.9
Profit margin %	11.4	12.0	13.1	13.9	14.8
(b) *Efficiency ratios*					
Asset utilisation	87.5	90.9	86.2	88.1	87.9
Sales/fixed assets	1.2	1.3	1.2	1.2	1.2
Turnover/stocks ratio	11.7	12.2	13.2	13.8	14.2
Credit period extended (days)	29.0	27.0	23.0	25.0	28.0
Liquidity ratio	0.8	0.9	0.8	0.8	0.8
Creditor/debtor ratio	0.8	0.7	0.7	0.7	0.8
Quick ratio	0.5	0.5	0.5	0.6	0.6
(c) *Financing ratios*					
Equity gearing ratio	0.7	0.6	0.6	0.7	0.7
Borrowing ratio	7.7	9.1	12.9	13.8	13.9
(d) *Employee ratios*	£	£	£	£	£
Average remuneration	5,839	5,940	6,479	7,062	7,782
Sales per employee	40,498	44,011	44,776	45,701	52,556
Profit per employee	4,600	5,292	5,869	6,227	6,630
Capital employed per employee	35,569	38,459	39,606	40,552	41,099

3.7 Appendix 7

Sales analysis

(a) *Index*	1987	1988	1989	1990	1991
Group turnover	100	118	137	149	165
Brewsters Ltd turnover	100	120	140	145	160

(b) *Segmental sales analysis (percentages)*

	1990	*1991*
Brewing	29	30
Pub retailing	21	22
Hotels and restaurants	15	11
Leisure	20	18
Soft drinks	9	9
Other	6	10

	Internal sales %	
	1990	*1991*
Brewing	38	39
Pub retailing	-	-
Hotels and restaurants	-	-
Leisure	2	3
Soft drinks	8	15

	External sales %	
	1990	*1991*
Brewing	62	61
Pub retailing	100	100
Hotels and restaurants	100	100
Leisure	98	97
Soft drinks	92	85

(c) *Group turnover %*

	1990	*1991*
UK	86	91
Rest of Europe	5	5
USA	8	3
Rest of world	1	1
	100	100

3.8 Appendix 8

Market data (sources: industry and internal estimates)

(a) *% of consumer expenditure at constant 1980 prices*

	1980	*1986*	*1992(est)*
(i) *Alcoholic drinks*			
Beer	45.7	38.1	33.0
Spirits	23.3	20.4	18.0
Wines, cider and perry	16.4	21.0	26.0
	85.4	79.5	77.0
(ii) *Soft drinks*			
Carbonates	10.4	15.1	15.0
Concentrates	2.0	1.8	2.0
Fruit juices and mineral water	2.4	4.6	6.0
	14.8	21.5	23.0

(b) *International comparisons 1984 (Consumption per head per year)*

(i) *Beer*

	Pints
West Germany	255
East Germany	250
Czechoslovakia	247
Denmark	236
Belgium	220
UK	194

(ii) *Wine*

	Litres
Portugal	84
France	82
Italy	80
Argentina	66
Switzerland	50
UK	11

(iii) *40% spirits*

	Litres
Hungary	13
East Germany	12
Poland	11
Czechoslovakia	8
USSR	8
UK	4

(iv) *Carbonates*

	Litres
West Germany	66
Belgium	62
Netherlands	58
Spain	55
UK	46
Italy	30
France	20

(v) *Bottled water*

	1984	*1992(est)*
	Litres	*Litres*
France	72	74
Belgium	54	55
Italy	54	55
Germany	53	58
Spain	20	26
Netherlands	9	10
UK	2	8

(c) *Combined market shares of four largest brewers in each country (1988)*

Country	*% share*
Japan	99
Australia	98
Canada	95
Netherlands	95
France	92
Denmark	90
UK	60

(Source: Financial Times)

Notes

Overseas trade in beer is not heavy. Most countries have their own native industry. Only Holland is significant in Europe with a third of its output exported. British allies tend to be sought as specialist beers in a number of countries but little British lager is exported. Many British lagers are, in any case, imitations of foreign beers. Imports of beer to the UK in 1988 were 7% of total consumption whilst exports were 2%.

(d) *UK exports of beer by country of destination (1988)*

	%
USA	36
Eire	23
Belgium	13
Italy	6
Others	22
Total	100 %

(e) *Average number of brands per pub/bar (1989)*

Country	*Draught*	*Packaged*	*Total*
UK	6.5	9.8	16.3
West Germany	2.2	1.7	3.9
France	1.9	4.7	6.6
Denmark	0.6	8.5	9.1
Ireland	8.5	9.2	17.7

(f) *World drinking trends (litres of pure alcohol consumed per head per year)*

	Country	*1987*	*1988*	*1989*	*1992(Est)*
1	France	13.0	13.4	13.4	13.5
2	Luxembourg	12.1	12.0	12.5	12.8
3	Spain	12.7	11.9	12.0	12.5
4	East Germany	10.8	11.0	11.1	12.0
5	Switzerland	11.0	11.0	10.9	11.0
6	Hungary	10.7	10.5	10.7	11.0
7	West Germany	10.6	10.4	10.4	10.0
8	Portugal	10.9	9.9	10.4	10.6
9	Austria	10.1	10.1	10.3	10.3
10	Belgium	10.7	10.0	9.9	10.0
11	Denmark	9.6	9.7	9.6	9.6
12	Italy	11.0	9.9	9.5	10.0
13	Bulgaria	8.9	9.1	9.3	9.8
14	Czechoslovakia	8.6	8.5	8.7	9.2
15	Australia	8.5	8.3	8.5	8.7
16	Netherlands	8.3	7.9	8.3	8.3
17	Romania	7.8	7.7	7.9	8.0
18	New Zealand	8.4	7.7	7.8	7.8
19	Canada	7.8	7.3	NA	7.5
20	Finland	7.1	7.6	7.6	7.6
21	United Kingdom	7.5	7.6	7.6	7.5
22	USA	7.6	7.5	7.5	7.5
23	Argentina	8.9	8.0	7.1	7.2
24	Cyprus	6.3	6.7	7.0	7.0
25	Poland	7.2	7.1	7.0	7.3

(g) *Advertising beer in the UK in 1989*

Lagers received twice as much expenditure as other beers and 40% of the expenditure on others was on low/non alcohol types. Total advertising expenditure was estimated at £102m, 90% of which was on TV.

Lager Brand	*£m on advertising (Est)*
Carlsberg	8.5
Carling Black Label	6.3
Heineken	3.7
Castelmaine XXXX	3.4
Fosters	4.2
Pils	3.1
Labatts	2.9
Miller Lite	2.3
Tennants Extra	4.6
Lowenbrau	1.9

In the UK about 73% of beer consumed is in draught form, and 27% is packaged. Low or non-alcohol beer has about 1.5% of the total market split 0.4% draught, 1.1% packaged. Lager accounts for 51% of consumption of all beers.

3.9 Appendix 9

Extract from newspaper article June 1991

Brewing giants pumped up the price of a pint by 10p yesterday. And it puts the final froth on a mind-blowing 1,150 per cent increase in ale costs over the last 20 years.

Now a survey has revealed that, even when inflation is taken into account, beer has rocketed way ahead of other items. In 1971, the year we went decimal, you could sup your favourite tipple for 12p a pint - now the average price is a whopping £1.50. In contrast to beer, bread has gone up just 500 per cent and butter 217 per cent.

The rise will affect big-selling brands like Fosters, Carlsberg, Budweiser, John Smiths, Manns and Samuel Websters. Other big breweries are expected to follow.

In the South, lager is likely to soar to £1.60 a pint and bitter to £1.48 while in the North and the midlands the cost will be around £1.35 and £1.20.

The cheapest pint in Britain is from Manchester brewer Joseph Holt. Their mild sells for a mere 79p a pint and bitter for 84p.

Courage last night defended their increase. 'Our prices are still competitive when compared to other breweries' a spokesman said. But furious Labour Consumer Affairs spokesman Nigel Griffiths is demanding an urgent government inquiry. He said 'I'll be referring this to the Director General of the Office of Fair Trading for him to investigate.'

Profit

Last night beer drinkers slammed the rise. The Campaign for Real Ale's Iain Loe said 'Brewers should stop being so greedy. I don't know how they can justify it.'

Taxes swallow almost one third of the cash which drinkers spend on their pint. But our breakdown of exactly where the money goes shows the brewer stands to make a tidy profit.

Landlords fear the latest round of price rises could force them to call time on their hard-pressed businesses. Tenants of brewery-owned pubs have already been hit by crushing rent increases and the economic slump. A spokesman for their union, the National Licensed Victuallers' Association, stated: 'This couldn't be more unwelcome. The budget added up to 10p on a pint and now this. The price just keeps going up and up. It's crippling us.'

'It won't be long before you see the £2.00 pint.'

The £1.50 Pint: This is now cash breaks down

VAT	22p
Excise duty	23p
Raw materials	3p
Production and distribution	21p
Advertising	3p
Pub costs (landlord's salary, heating, maintenance etc)	57p
Profit	21p

Where the money goes

3.10 **Appendix 10**

(a) *Marketing organisation*

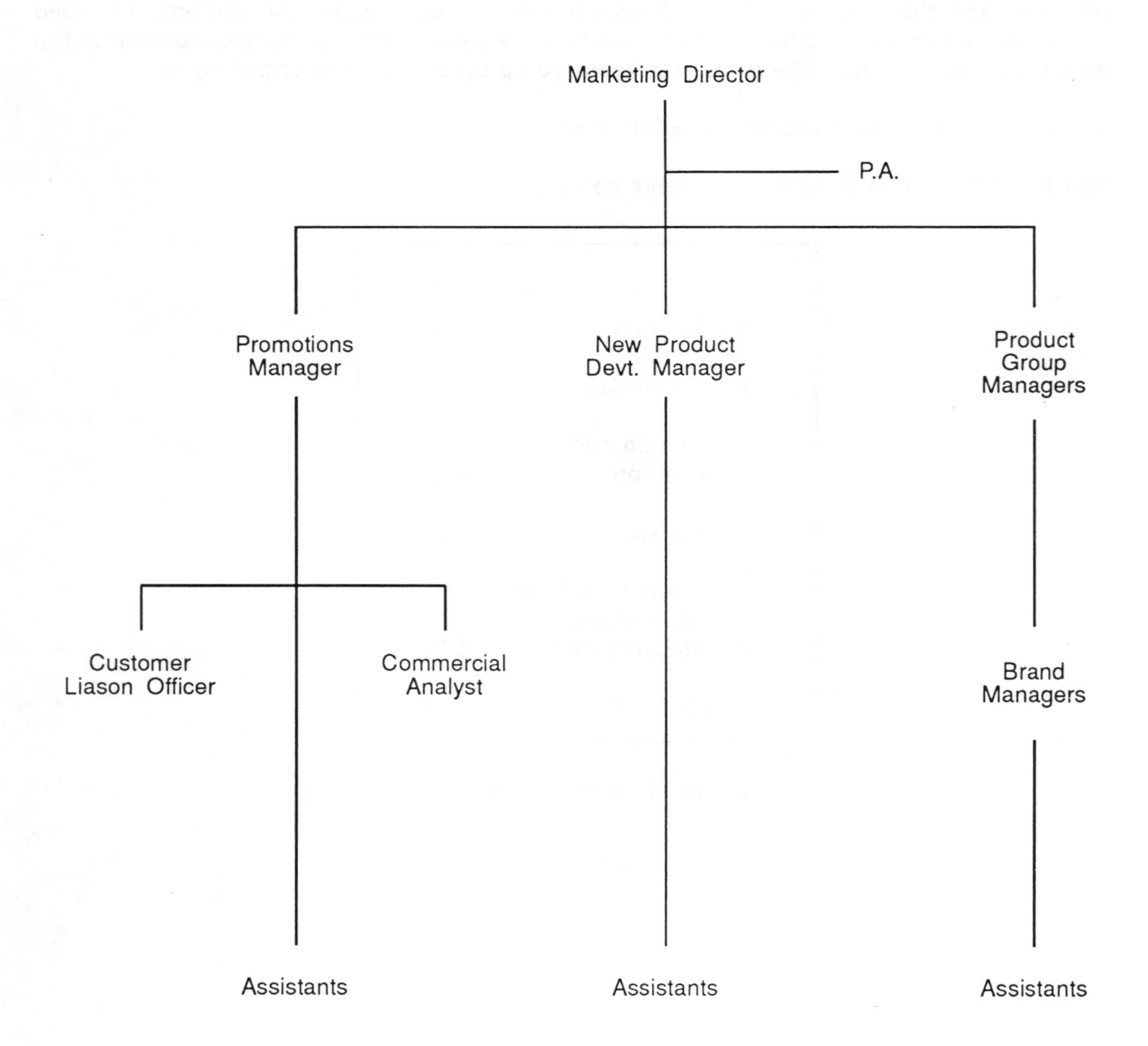

(b) *Sales organisation*

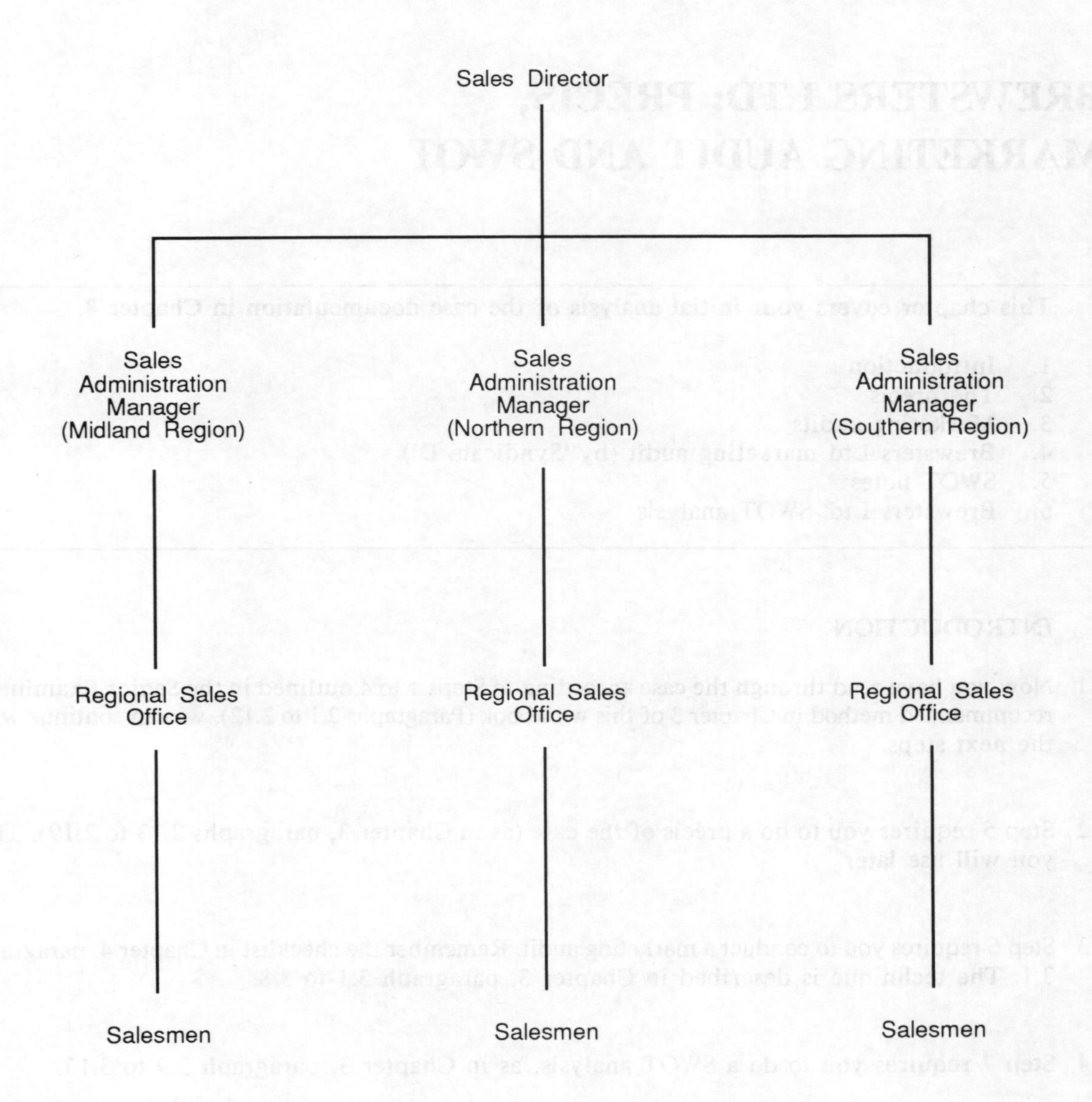

Chapter 9

BREWSTERS LTD: PRÉCIS, MARKETING AUDIT AND SWOT

This chapter covers your initial analysis of the case documentation in Chapter 8.

1. INTRODUCTION

1.1 Now you have read through the case according to Steps 1 to 4 outlined in the Senior Examiner's recommended method in Chapter 3 of this workbook (Paragraphs 2.1 to 2.12), we can continue with the next steps.

1.2 Step 5 requires you to do a précis of the case (as in Chapter 3, paragraphs 2.13 to 2.19). This you will use later.

1.3 Step 6 requires you to conduct a marketing audit. Remember the checklist in Chapter 4, paragraph 3.1. The technique is described in Chapter 3, paragraph 3.1 to 3.8.

1.4 Step 7 requires you to do a SWOT analysis, as in Chapter 3, paragraph 3.9 to 3.13.

1.5 These three steps are covered in detail in this chapter. To help you consider the case from a number of angles, you will be reading material drawn up by a number of notional 'syndicates'.

2. THE PRÉCIS

2.1 Complete your précis, and now compare it with the one which follows. In what ways do you think yours is better and/or worse that this somewhat rushed specimen? Has doing a précis enabled you to get a *better grip* on the case situation?

9: BREWSTERS LTD: PRÉCIS, MARKETING AUDIT AND SWOT

Brewsters Ltd: Précis (by Syndicate B)

2.2 *Candidates' brief*

David Downing - Marketing Director of Brewsters Ltd for six years - has a clear brief to develop longer term marketing strategy in a wider European context, competing for scarce resources both at company and group level.

2.3 *Brewsters Ltd*

(a) Brewsters Ltd represents the beer brewing interests of a large group (Leighlow Leisure plc).

(b) The Leighlow Group is a UK company involved in:

(i) the production and distribution of drinks;
(ii) the ownership and franchising of pubs, hotels and restaurants; and
(iii) the operation of a diverse range of leisure facilities.

(c) Its *mission* is to create value for shareholders, customers and employees by supplying products and services of high quality in all its businesses. It also has a high regard for the interests of general public and the environment.

2.4 *Environment - External*

(a) Brewsters Ltd owns the freehold of several thousand pubs and hotels. In 1989 the MMC (Monopolies and Mergers Commission) declared its finding that a complex monopoly existed and made recommendations to be put into effect by March 1992.

(i) No brewer to own more than 2,000 on-licensed premises including pubs and restaurants.

(ii) Tied tenants to be allowed to sell 'guest' draft beers and beers brewed by other than the pubs owners.

(iii) Tied tenants also to be free to competitively buy low alcohol beers, wines, spirits, cider and soft drinks.

(iv) No new loan ties, which oblige owners of so called 'free houses' to sell only one brewers products.

(v) Protection and security of tenure for tied tenants under the Landlord and Tenant Act.

(vi) Brewers to publish and adhere to wholesale price lists.

(b) *Social change* is radically altering British drinking habits. UK consumers have become discerning and more cosmopolitan in their outlook. Other trends are a move towards soft drinks, 'healthy' drinks, a preference for lighter, less alcoholic drinks. Also relevant are the increase in off license over the on-trade (pubs and bars), 'liberalisation' of niche products, demographic changes.

(c) *Advent of 1992.* The freeing of markets within the European community.

(d) *Current UK economic climate.*

(e) *Green issues*. Whilst cans predominate in the UK take home market, returnable bottles form the main medium in mainland Europe, strengthening the position of local brewers due to the need to have cost effective recycling networks.

Organisational change/sales force

2.5 There is a need for a professional sales force (perhaps with special account executives) as a result of greatly increased competition in the future (eg with guest beers).

2.6 Until now, Brewsters Ltd has been able to tell its tied trade what they should stock. The sales force's role has been more to maintain and develop *existing* business rather than seek new outlets. External trade has been negotiated by the brand or product group managers (through sales administration managers) whether for the home market or abroad.

Marketing orientation/organisation

2.7 Quality circles were recently extended to include white collar office staff as part of a total quality management programme. Some novel ideas have emerged from the office staff.

2.8 David Downing received authority from the MD to form a project team derived from all functions to investigate the viability of prospective new products for Europe in 1992.

Distribution

2.9 Exports are effected either direct or through distributors according to the nature of the product, the size and nature of the outlets (pubs/bars or retail shops) and logistics involved.

2.10 An export division is operated by the Group to handle the physical distribution aspects of all its companies.

2.11 For the British brewer, the key to the market is felt to be the distribution system.

2.12 The major options for foreign brewers seeking to enter a beer market would be as follows.

(a) Direct export using local wholesalers.
(b) Joint ventures with local companies.
(c) Licensing.
(d) Acquisition.

Product

2.13 The product portfolio is particularly in need of constant review in light of all the changes referred to above.

2.14 The question of whether to product beer under private or *own label* (eg for supermarkets) as well as under Brewsters' brands can also be considered.

2.15 Concepts of company, brand and product brand life cycles in addition to that of the product life cycle can be brought to bear.

2.16 David Downing is convinced that opportunities for developing strong European, brands exist for Brewsters, and is determined to investigate these fully.

Product adaptation

2.17 Brewsters have to decide whether to use standard formulations for their beer brands overseas or to adapt these to suit individual market tastes. Unlike the US, where beer is the same in most states, European beers in particular areas can be quite different. In Europe lager beers predominate.

2.18 Some companies prefer to position brands within niche markets such as those for really strong beers or those with a low alcohol content.

Promotion

2.19 Advertising restrictions vary. France has banned the advertising of alcohol on TV. The Spanish have doubled their TV rates for alcohol advertisements. In the UK advertising is governed by a code of practice.

3. MARKETING AUDITS

3.1 The next step is to conduct a marketing audit (allow about three hours). You will need to study the notes on in Chapter 3, paragraphs 3.1 to 3.8 of this Workbook plus the checklist in Chapter 4 paragraphs 3.2 and 3.3. Start with the checklist using this as a checklist to determine what information we have and do not have. You could tick those items we have and put a cross against those we don't have. The items with a cross could then form the basis of your marketing research plan. You could assume that some of the information crossed would readily be available within Brewsters organisation.

3.2 Now systematically work your way through the environmental audit to the marketing functions audit and the other functional audits (financial, production and personnel). What have you got? Did you find you had to make judgements - for example we have total sales as an index but not in £'s or units? Does your checklist show many more items crossed than ticked? How does your audit compare to the condensed version given on the following pages?

3.3 The models and analytical techniques provided by marketing authors are often based upon particular, average or typical situation and may need to be adapted by marketing managers for their specific decision-making purposes. Not all models and techniques are applicable. You need to select those most appropriate and be ready to adapt or modify these to suit the specific case study.

3.4 The marketing audit checklist applied to Brewsters Ltd is a good example. It is found wanting because (unusually) Brewsters Ltd's accounts are given as indexes rather than absolute figures. You could therefore have used the letter P to indicate that part of the information is given, rather than using the stark tick or cross to indicate all or nothing. You could also make the safe assumption that the indices are based upon absolute figures which would be readily available within the organisation.

3.5 You will notice that in their marketing audit, Syndicate D have added 'implications'. What do you think of their audit? Is the sequencing logical? Is it sufficiently comprehensive?

3.6 It is quite easy for people to panic a bit when they realise how little information they are given in a case study, on which to base their decisions. However, in real life we often have to take decisions based on inadequate information. The important thing is to recognise this and to make reasonable assumptions. Having created a marketing research plan to fill the information gaps you can then make decision 'subject to the research findings'. So, in the checklist below:

✓ means you have the information;
P means you have part of the information, or access to it;
x means you do not have the information.

Marketing audit checklist: available information

Internal information

3.7 (a) *Current position*

(i) *Performance*

P Total sales in value and in units
P Total gross profit, expenses and net profit
P Percentage of sales for sales expenses, advertising etc
✓ Percentage of sales in each segment
P Value and volume sales by year, month, model size etc
x Sales per thousand consumers, per factory, in segments
P Market share in total market and in segments

(ii) *Buyers*

x Number of actual and potential buyers by area

P Characteristics of consumer buyers, eg income, occupation, education, sex, size of family etc

x Characteristics of industrial buyers, eg primary, secondary, tertiary, manufacturing; type of industry; size etc

P Characteristics of users, if different from buyers

P Location of buyers, users

x When purchases made: time of day, week, month, year; frequency of purchase; size of average purchase or typical purchase x How purchases made: specification or competition; by sample, inspection, impulse, rotation, system; cash or credit

x Attitudes, motivation to purchase; influences on buying decision; decision making unit in organisation

√ Product uses - primary and secondary

(b) *Product*

(i) *Brewsters*

x Quality: materials, workmanship, design, method of manufacture, manufacturing cycle, inputs-outputs

x Technical characteristics, attributes that may be considered as selling points, buying points

P Models, sizes, styles, ranges, colours etc

√ Essential or non-essential, convenience or speciality

x Similarities with other company products

x Relation of product features to user's needs, wants, desires

P Development of branding and brand image

P Degree of product differentiation, actual and possible

√ Packaging used, function, promotional

x Materials, sizes, shapes, construction, closure

(ii) *Competitors*

x Competitive and competing products
P Main competitors and leading brands
x Comparison of design and performance differences with leading competitors
x Comparison of offerings of competitors, images, value etc

(iii) *Future product development*

√ Likely future product developments in company
√ Likely future, or possible future, developments in industry
P Future product line or mix contraction, modification or expansion

(c) *Distribution*

(i) *Brewsters*

P Current company distribution structure
P Channels and methods used in channels
x Total number of outlets (consumer or industrial) by type
x Total number of wholesalers or industrial middlemen, analysed by area and type

x Percentage of outlets of each type handling product broken down into areas
x Attitudes of outlets by area, type, size
x Degree of co-operation, current and possible
P Multi-brand policy, possible or current
x Strengths and weaknesses in distribution system, functionally and geographically
x Number and type of warehouses; location
x Transportation and communications
x Stock control; delivery periods; control of information

(ii) *Competitors*

x Competitive distribution structure; strengths and weaknesses
x Market coverage and penetration
x Transportation methods used by competitors
x Delivery of competitors
x Specific competitive selling conditions

(iii) *Future developments*

P Future likely and possible developments in industry as a whole or from one or more competitors

x Probable changes in distribution system of company

P Possibilities of any future fundamental changes in outlets

(d) *Promotional and personal selling*

(i) *Brewsters*

√ Size and composition of sales force
x Calls per day, week, month, year by salesmen
x Conversion rate of orders to calls
x Selling cost per value and volume of sales achieved
x Selling cost per customer
P Internal and external sales promotion
x Recruiting, selection, training, control procedures
x Methods of motivation of salesmen
x Remuneration schemes
P Advertising appropriation and media schedule, copy theme
x Cost of trade, technical, professional, consumer media
x Cost of advertising per unit, per value of unit, per customer
x Advertising expenditure per thousand readers, viewers of main and all media used
x Methods and costs of merchandising
x Public and press relation; exhibitions

(ii) *Competitors*

x Competitive selling activities and methods of selling and advertising; strengths and weaknesses

x Review of competitors' promotion, sales contests etc

x Competitors' advertising them, media used

(iii) x *Future developments* are likely in selling, promotional and advertising activities

(e) *Pricing*

(i) *Brewsters*

- P Pricing strategy and general methods of price structuring in company
- P High or low policies; reasons why
- P Prevailing pricing policies in industry
- x Current wholesaler, retailer margins in consumer markets or middlemen margins in industrial markets
- x Discounts, functional, quantity, cash, reward, incentive
- x Pricing objectives, profit objectives financial implications such as breakeven figures, cash budgeting

(ii) *Competitors*

- x Prices and price structures of competitors
- x Value analysis of own and competitors' products
- x Discounts, credit offered by competitors

(iii) *Future developments*

- x Future developments in costs likely to affect price structures
- x Possibilities of more/less costly raw materials or labour affecting prices
- x Possible price attacks by competitors

(f) *Service*

(i) *Brewsters*

- x Extent of pre-sales or customer service and after-sales or product service required (by products)
- x Survey of customer needs
- x Installation, deduction in use, inspection, maintenance, repair, accessories provision
- x Guarantees, warranty period
- x Methods, procedures for carrying out service
- x Returned goods, complaints

(ii) *Competitors*

- x Services supplied by competing manufacturers and service organisations x Types of guarantee, warranty, credit provided

(iii) x *Future possible developments* that might require revised service policy

(g) *Organisation.* This information is available.

External

3.8 *Environmental audit - national and international*

P Social and cultural factors likely to affect the market, in the short and long term

✓ Legal factors and codes of practice likely to affect the market in the short and long term

P Economic factors likely to affect market demand in the short and long term

x Political changes and military action likely to impact upon national and international markets

x Technological changes anticipated and likely to create new opportunities and threats

3.9 *Marketing objectives and strategies*

x Short-term plans and objectives for current year, in light of current political and economic situation

✓ Construction of standards for measurement of progress towards achieving of objectives; management rations that can be translated into control procedures

x Breakdown of turnover into periods, areas, segments, outlets, salesmen etc

x Which personnel required to undertake what responsibilities, actions etc when

x Review of competitors strengths and weaknesses likely competitive reactions and possible company responses that could be made

x Long-term plans, objectives and strategies related to products, price, places of distribution, promotion, personnel selling and service.

4. BREWSTERS LTD MARKETING AUDIT (BY 'SYNDICATE D')

Assumptions

4.1 (a) Brewsters Ltd manufactures alcoholic drinks in addition to owning the pubs.

(b) The figures quoted in all appendices are for the UK market and for Brewsters Ltd unless specifically stated to the contrary.

(c) The big six brewers keep 2,000 tied houses.

External environment

4.2 In the table which follows, the figures in the *Ref* column refer to the Appendix number in the case (if a number), or the text of the case itself (T) as given in Chapter 8.

Ref Chapter 8	*Information*	*Implications*
T (para 2.6)	MMC Rules • 2,000 maximum tied houses • Tied tenants can sell other beers • Tied tenants cannot be forced to sell B's soft drink • Legal rights of tenure for tenants • Published wholesale prices	
App 3 (para 3.3)	Environmental considerations • Global EC legislation within five years • national government power vs EC • 35% consumers are concerned • Government encouragement already in Germany and Denmark	Packaging implications - bottles for EC Constant MR process required for: • strength of national anti-advertising lobbies • information sources - FT, Economist, BOTB, Government EC experts
App 4 (para 3.4)	Water quality concerns	May become a necessity
App 5 (para 3.5)	Well established rules in UK advertising for alcoholic drinks	Know rules of game
App 5 (para 3.5)	No rules for soft drinks	
App 9 (para 3.2)	MMC pricing policy	20 year old monopolies may change
T (para 2.13)	1992 EC free market	Threat - EC competition in UK market Opportunities - easier penetration of EC markets
App 4 (para 3.4)	'Drink Drive' an important lobby	
App 5 (para 3.5)	EC rules on advertising	

Market data

4.3 This information relates to the market place

Ref Chapter 8	*Information*	*Implications*
T (para 2.12)	Rise in discernment/cosmopolitan taste Rise in health awareness Rise in preference for lighter drinks Rise in preference for low alcohol Less segmentation in drinking taste Rise in older age groups (demographics)	Soft drinks and low alcohol provide strategic opportunity Homogeneous drinking tastes leading to a rise in wine, cider and Perry sales?
App 1 (para 3.1)	Six brewers control 80% of market	View of UK market
App 2,3,4 (paras 3.2 3.3, 3.4)	Sophisticated products are a *new* area	Need for new image?
App 3 (para 3.3)	Lager market size (5m barrels for draught or premium). Both growing Bottled market is 360m units Target market is 4.5% of UK bottled market ie 20m units UK lager market is 1,620m pints The premium lager market in UK is growing flat rate by 12.5%	
App 8 (para 3.8)	Softs and minerals • bottled water growth (400% in UK) • also rising in Spain (30%) and Netherlands (11%)	Spain, Netherlands and UK are fastest growing
App 8 (para 3.8)	Low or non alcoholic beer is 1.5% UK beer market	
T (para 2.17)	Downning wants to enter EC with 'Euro-product'	
T (para 2.18)	Brewster's brands vs brew for own label?	Affects organisation of sales force etc
App 8 (para 3.8)	Global alcohol consumption per country • generally steady with small increase in former Eastern block	Small increases mean big volumes

Ref Chapter 8	*Information*	*Implications*
App 8 (para 3.8)	UK beer market • Size is 3,000m pints pa, split 50/50 beer to lager • UK beer market in decline by 2.5% pa • UK soft drinks consumption rising by 3.5% pa • Total UK alcohol slow decline (0.5% to 1% pa)	
App 8 (para 3.8)	EC/world beer market • Germany (combined) is the largest market • Denmark, France and UK less 'monopolised' than Netherlands and Canada	
T (para 2.17)	Brewster's beer/lager presence in EC: based on a UK formula or generic in all markets	Market research and test marketing

Customers

4.4

Ref Chapter 8	*Information*	*Implications*
App 2 (para 3.2)	The major market segment is the 25-40 age group	Target marketing More drinking at home
App 3 (para3.3)	Off-licence sales increasing	Desire for refreshing drinks
App 2 (para 3.2)	Hotter summers	Recognition that ale is into decline
App 2&3 (paras 3.2, 3.3)	Trend is generally away from strong alcoholic drinks - except premium lager	

Competition

4.5

Ref Chapter 8	*Information*	*Implications*
App 1 (para 2.1)	Top four brewers now control 60% of tied pubs	This oligopoly about to break. 21,900 pubs and restaurants to change ownership
App 8 (para 3.8)	Market shares of major overseas brewers	High entry cost

Sales data and sales force

4.6

Ref Chapter 8	*Information*	*Implications*
App 7 (para 3.7)	Declining external sales of soft drinks	Neglected area
	An increasing proportion of total group sales is in the UK	No international orientation of group
	Brewsters sales are 30% of Leighlow's turnover	
	Leighlow's leisure products have	Possible opportunities as joint ventures
	potential rise through more free houses	with other group businesses
	Soft drink sales a problem - falling in a growing market	Must find cause

Forecasting

4.7

Ref Chapter 8	*Information*	*Implications*
App 8 (para 3.8)	Beer is declining	A trend. Can it be reversed?
App 8 (para 3.8)	Wine, Cider and Perry increasing	A trend, or just a brief matter of fashion?

Product

4.8

Ref Chapter 8	*Information*	*Implications*
App 2,3,4 (paras 3.2 3.3,3.4)	Ideas for new products	Trend towards less alcoholic drinks, but premium lager segment is growing fast
App 4 (para 3.4)	Bottled water - high growth market, local supply (70% growth in 88/89)	(72% since 1985) Opportunity for diversification
App 4 (para 3.4)	Expansion opportunity	Range extension
Appx 8 (para 3.8)	Specialist British ales for export	Niche market, only
	Draught versus bottles issue	Must be bottled to sell to Europe
	Alcoholic and non/low alcoholic drinks are sold differently	Draught/packaged sales ratios are • Alcoholic 3:1 • Low and non-alcoholic/ alcoholic 1:3
	Market size information	Consumption per head
T (para 2.14)	Downing's portfolio needs reviewing	
T (para 2.25)	Product strategy based on brand life cycles	Branding is the *key* issue

Pricing

4.9

Ref Chapter 8	*Information*	*Implications*
App 9 (para 3.9)	Regional pricing structure	Cheaper in the North. Price war with competitors
T (para 2.6)	MMC rules - public wholesale prices	Pricing uniformity enforceable

Promotion

4.10

Ref Chapter 8	*Information*	*Implications*
App 1 (para 3.1)	Loss of sales at point of consumption in tied pubs	Need for creativity and persuasion to win over other non-tied pubs
App 1 (para 3.1)	Divestment	New decision making units (customers, distributors)
App 2 (para 3.2)	New market segment potential	Big push to new segments
App 3 (para 3.3)	Distinctive, premium product	Affects market mix
App 3 (para 3.3)	Topical creative platform	Campaign planning
App 5 (para 3.5)	Rules	Clues for advertising
App 8 (para 3.8)	Lagers are branded	Budgets and promotions strategies TV for ATL - 89 expenditure • £68m lager • £20.4m beer • £13.6m low alcoholic • £102m total spend • 2p/pint beer advertising • 4p/pint lager advertising • 40% budget is low alcohol

Distribution

4.11

Ref Chapter 8	*Information*	*Implications*
App 1 (para 3.1)	The proportion of tied house to free changes from 40/60 to 15/85	Loss of guaranteed distribution channel, but gain of access to more free pubs. Pubs bought by tenants. If Brewsters ceases brewing, it will become a retailer. If Brewsters abandons tied pubs, then brew only and sell to 'own label'.
App 2 (para 3.2)	Increase in off-licence sales	A way out of the distribution problem?
App 3 (para 3.3)	Bottles (lager) are a different size	Nature of distribution
App 3 (para 3.3)	Lager bottles may be bigger	A distribution problem?
App 3 (para 3.3)	Aiming for sales of 20m units which represents 5.5% of UK 1990 market in units - or 6% by volume	Budget planning

Organisation

4.12

Ref Chapter 8	*Information*	*Implications*
App 2 (para 3.1)	Divestment	
T (para 2.13)	Professional sales force needed	
T (para 2.15)	Quality circles company-wide	
App 6 (para 3.6)	Reducing personnel numbers	
App 10 (para 3.10)	Organisation that suggests production-orientation rather than market-orientation	Need for re-organisation of distribution and sales
App 10 (para 3.10)	Unclear whether well-defined marketing information system exists	
App 10 (para 3.10)	No evidence of export management	

Finance

4.13

Ref Chapter 8	*Information*	*Implications*
App 1 (para 3.1)	Divestment	Cash inflow frees capital resources
App 6 (para 3.6)	Profit margins improving	Better placed in declining market
App 6 (para 3.6)	Generally becoming more efficient	Improving ratios: capital employed per employee, profit and sales per employee, stock turnover, ROCE
App 7 (para 3.4)	Brewsters Ltd growing at the same approximate rate as group	Brewsters Ltd is reasonably secure within group

5. SWOT NOTES

5.1 The seventh step is the creation of a SWOT analysis - a task usually found quite enjoyable by most students. Allow two to three hours.

5.2 You will need to consult Chapter 3, Paragraphs 3.9 to 3.13 of this Workbook before tackling the SWOT.

5.3 Note, in one sense you are mixing the *analytical* and *decision taking* modes here, since you are required to decide whether a particular fact constitutes a strength, a weakness, an opportunity or a threat.

5.4 Most people go systematically and sequentially through the case study and the appendices, noting facts and allocating them to the four categories. However, you should also note the source of the fact (*ref*) and code it in the ways suggested in marketing audits in the previous pages.

5.5 If you are working on your own, it is worth noting and categorising all the facts however trivial. You can always decide to jettison the more trivial points later. However, to try to *enlarge* a sparse SWOT in the exam itself would be extremely time consuming.

5.6 It is usually found that one single syndicate will develop total lists of about thirty items. Another syndicate will have some but not all of these items and be able to add extra items. In this way an amalgamation of four syndicates' work will usually at least double the original list.

6. BREWSTERS LTD: SWOT ANALYSIS

6.1 Having done your own SWOT, please compare it with the rather comprehensive example which follows, noting that the group concerned saw fit to add the following codes.

(a) H, M, L indicate high, medium and low importance respectively.

(b) 'B' stands for Brewsters, 'L' for Leighlow and 'G' for the group.

(c) The function can be identified by M for marketing, F for finance, P for production and O for organisation.

Please look at this specimen critically - it is far from perfect but there are a total of over 90 items listed.

	Strengths	*Level*	*Chapter 8 para ref*	*Function*	*HML*
1	Group had an international physical distribution division	G	2.13	M	H
2	Brewsters has strong UK market position	B	2.3,3.1	M	H
3	Significant funds available	B	2.3	M/F	H
4	Brewsters already obtains 61% of T/O from external sales	B	3.7	F/M	H
5	Brewsters sited close to natural springs	B	3.4	M/O	H
6	UK has strong branding compared to EC	B	3.8(e)(i)	M	H
7	Strong management skills	B	3.6	O	H
8	British ales have specialist appeal in mainland EC	B	3.8(c)	M	M
9	Very strong advertising of lager in UK		3.8(g)	M	M
10	US and Australian lager brewed under licence in UK	B	3.8(g)	M	M
11	Group is environmentally 'aware'	B	2.22,3.3	P/O/M	M
12	Several new products exist	B	2.4	M	M
13	Downing has knowledge of market and authority from managing director for new product development	B	2.17	M/O	M
14	Brewsters has increasing sales and profit per employee	N	3.6(a)	F	M
15	Brewsters has good ROI and profit margin	B	3.6(a)	F	M
16	Financially sound	L/B	3.6	F	M
17	Group has several '000 pubs (and restaurants)	G	2.3	O/M	M
18	Part of a large, stable UK based group	G	2.2	O/F	L
19	Group has integrated range of products/services	G	2.2	O/M	L
20	Export distributors and direct sales already exists	B	2.13	M/O	L
21	Good existing distribution channels	L/B	2.3,2.4	M	L
22	TQM, Quality circles in place - and being extended	B	2.15	O	L
23	Brewsters the largest element of L group	G,B	3.7	F	L
24	Brewsters turnover increased steadily since 1987 and constitutes almost all Group growth (except 1990/1991)	G,B	3.7	F	L
25	Existing sales force	B	2.13	O	L
26	Recognition of declining ale sales (imported)	B	2.4,3.4	M	L

	Weaknesses	*Level*	*Chapter 8 para ref*	*Function*	*HML*
27	The sales force is not marketing orientated	B	2.13	M/O	H
28	The sales force has no experience of new business sales	B	2.13	M	H
29	Sales force is poorly organised for external sales	B	2.13	M/O	H
30	No real experience in European markets	B	2.13	M	H
31	Organisational structure	B	2.13	O	H
32	91% of group turnover is in UK	G	3.7	M	H
33	Current dependence on draught beers	B	3.9	M/P	H
34	Product portfolio inappropriate for a changing market	B	n/a	M/P	H
35	Lack of clear corporate objectives, strategy and marketing plan	B/G	2.8	O/M	H
36	Organisation - not marketing orientated and no export orientation	B	2.13	M/O	H
37	No marketing information system	B	3.10	O	H
38	Most British lagers are imitations of foreign beers	B	n/a	M	M
39	Not pushing soft drinks externally	B	3.7	M	L
40	Product development is a new area	B	2.14-2.16	P/M	L
41	Branding - many questions still open	B	n/a	M	L

	Opportunities	*Level*	*Chapter 8 para ref*	*Function*	*HML*
42	Tied tenants allowed to sell 'guest' beers	B	2.6	M/L	H
43	Expansion of pub/hotel franchising	B	2.8	M/L	H
44	Specialise in pub/hotels & divest brewing	G	2.8	M	H
45	Specialise in brewing & divest pubs/hotels	G	2.8	M	H
46	Increased off-licence market share	G	2.8	M	H
47	New drinking habits, wine etc	B	3.8	N	H
48	Development of Eurobrand lagers	B	2.21	M	H
49	Expanding market for premium lagers	B	3.3	M	H
50	Bottled water: rapidly expanding market especially UK	B	3.4	M	H
51	Bottled water sales in UK rose by 70% (1988-1989)	B	3.4	M	H
52	High beer consumption in many EC countries (eg Germany, Denmark, Belgium:(market development)	B	3.8(b)	M	H
53	High bottled water consumption in many EC countries Germany, Spain, Netherlands, UK	B	3.8(b)	M	H
54	European brand selection compared to UK	B	3.8(a)	M	H
55	Tendency towards 'healthy' drinks - growing market	B	2.12	M	M
56	Preference for lighter, less alcoholic drinks	B	2.12	M	M
57	To take American and Australian lagers brewed under licence and currently sold in the UK into EC	B	3.8(g)	M	M
58	Take advantage of environmental bandwagon	B	2.22	M/P	M
59	Growing concern over water quality	B	3.4	M/P	M
60	Branding: own label, brewer brand opportunities	B	2.18	M	L
61	Export of 'brown beers' as specialist niche products	B	2.20	M	L
62	The single market	B/L	2.17	O/M	L
63	New product development				
	- sparkling wine		n/a		
	- expanding low alcohol, light drinks market	B	3.8(b)	M	L
	- expanding premium lager market	B	3.8(g)	N	H
64	Tied tenants can buy soft drinks etc from cheapest supplier	B	2.6	M/L	L
65	Internationalisation of consumer markets (lager brands)	B	2.19	M	L
66	High wine consumption in many EC countries	B	3.8(b)	M	L
67	High carbonates consumption in many EC countries	B	3.8(b)	M	L

	Threats	*Level*	*Chapter 8 para ref*	*Function*	*HML*
68	Strong competition - home and abroad	B		M/P	H
69	From March 1992 less than 2,000 pubs, on-licence premises for brewers	B	2.6	O/M/L	H
70	Tied tenants allowed to sell 'guest' beers	B	2.6	M/L	H
71	March 1992 - foreign competition buying into UK market	B	2.24	M	H
72	Increased off licence market share	B	2.12	M	H
73	New drinking habits - declining beer market	B	2.12	M	H
74	Wines, cider & perry market will overtake beer market (which is declining) in 1996 in UK on trends	B	3.8(a)	M	H
75	Very little UK lager is exported	B	3.8(c)	M	M
76	UK beer imports (7% exports 2% in 1988)	B	3.8(a)	M	M
77	Preference for lighter, less alcoholic drinks	B	2.12	M	M
78	Pub/hotel outlets may become dominated by a few specialist operators	B	2.8	M	M
79	Brewing may become dominated by a few specialist brewers	B	2.8	M	M
80	Strong regional brands are going national	B	2.8	M	M
81	Internationalisation of world consumer markets (lager brands)	B	2.21	M	L
82	Consumer preferences move from alcoholic to soft drinks	B	2.21	M	L
83	Demographic changes (fewer young people)	B	2.21	M	L
84	Holland exports one third of its beer output	B	3.8(c)	M	L
85	Lager predominates in Europe (continental strong point)	B	2.19	M	L
86	Advertising of alcohol strictly controlled in some European countries (eg France and Spain)	B	2.23	M	L
87	European market - packaging issues - recyclable bottles	B	3.9	M	L
88	Advertising of alcoholic drinks is controlled in the UK	B	3.5	M	L
89	In France, Netherlands and Denmark the top four brewers have over 90% of the market	B	3.8(c)	M	
90	Over 50% UK beer exports go to USA and Eire (36% & 23%)	B	3.8(d)	M	L
91	Tied tenants can buy soft drinks etc from cheapest supplier	B	2.6	M/L	L

7. CONCLUSION

7.1 Doubtless, you might have thought of other issues, particularly in your SWOT analysis. Did you remember that not *all* the information in the case notes is relevant. The newspaper article, while giving you some detail of the cost structure of the tied trade, is not relevant to Brewsters Ltd's new product development, although it might help in deciding whether to abandon the tied house trade.

Chapter 10

BREWSTERS LTD: ANALYSIS OF APPENDICES

This chapter provides some hints for gaining further information from the appendices to the case study.

1. INTRODUCTION

1.1 The next step is to analyse and cross analyse the appendices. In the Brewsters case, in the format as published by the CIM, there are ten appendices. Approximately half the data is quantitative and half qualitative. Not all the data will be equally meaningful. Before conducting your analysis be sure to read Chapter 3 paragraphs 3.14 to 3.17 and use the format provided. You will need a clear head and two to or three hours to do a reasonable job.

1.2 Remember the format suggested on Chapter 3 paragraph 3.17 is a summary document. You will want to underpin this with working papers, perhaps containing graphs, pie-charts and financial analysis.

1.3 Now compare your summary sheets with those on the following pages. To what extent do they broadly agree? If they differ you are as likely to be right as the syndicate that produced them. The point is to give the difference proper consideration before rejecting or accepting it.

1.4 It may help you here to go through some of the appendices in a little more detail.

CASE APPENDICES - ANALYSIS/CROSS ANALYSIS

Appendix number	*What it is essentially saying*	*How does it help us?*	*Which other appendices or text can it be related to? (Chapter 8)*	*If so, what extra information* insights does this reveal?
1 (Ch 8, para 3.1)	Big 6 have 79% market share. $\frac{2}{3}$ tied houses to be divested. Brewer 5 is the most efficient.	Identifies potential opportunities and threats. Positions competitors. Advises strategic decisions.	Text: para 2.6 App: 3,7,8,9 paras 3.7,3.8,3.9	Ratio of internal vs external sales: four of the Big 6 have 60% market share. Costs of running 'owned' pubs.
2,3,4 (Ch 8, paras 3.2,3.3,3.4)	Staff believe in NPD opportunities. Concepts only, at this stage. Buying behaviour is overlooked. (casts doubts on NPD function)	Identifies potential product opportunities. Signals need for professional market research. Indicates need for legal and buyer behaviour research. Shows initiative/staff involvement.	Text: paras 2.16,2.17,2.18, 2.19 App: 5,8 paras 3.5,3.8	David Downing keen on European brand. Management support at top level. Legal constraints. Changes in consumer preferences.
5 (Ch 8, para 3.5)	Determines promotion parameters. Provides pointers for NPD.	Levels the UK playing field. Suggests need to check other European countries codes/laws.	Text: paras 2.21 to 2.23 App: 2,3,4,8 paras 3.2,3.3,3.4,3.8	Parameters for alcoholic new product concepts. Factor in determining drinks trends. Part of larger environmental trend.
6 (Ch 8, para 3.6)	Brewsters in a stable financial position. Steady growth. Borrowing position questionable.	Group funding possible. Outside group funding facilities cannot be assumed.	Text: paras 2.3,2.5,2.6 App: 7 para 3.7	Group commitment to shareholders. Loss of control over future performance. Brewsters positioning within group.

CASE APPENDICES - ANALYSIS/CROSS ANALYSIS

Appendix number	*What it is essentially saying*	*How does it help us?*	*Which other appendices or text can it be related to? (Chapter 8)*	*If so, what extra information insights does this reveal?*
7 (Ch 8, para 3.7)	Brewsters turnover growth is less than group in 1990/1991. Brewsters is key player within group. High proportion of Brewsters sales within group. Poor external performance in soft drinks. Group is dependent on UK.	Warrants group support. Group will expect continued growth despite poor market conditions. Room for improvement in exports.	App: 1,6,8 paras 3.2,3.6,3.8	Further quantifies future vulnerability. Indicates overall position and key areas. Majority turnover in external sales indicates a good brand/image. Brewsters appear to be less heavily dependent on tied outlets than some competitors.
8 (Ch 8, para 3.8)	UK beer consumption decreasing. Market breakdowns by product and country and large brewers. Exports. Brand distribution per bar/pub. Market trends. Advertising - beer/lager.	Provides scenario of UK market vs other countries. Indicates opportunities for NPD. Suggest potential costs of advertising new brands in UK. Indicates difficulties in expanding sales in mainland Europe.	App: 3.7,2,3,4,7 paras 3.2,3.3,3.4	Weakness in current product portfolio. Need for further research. Problems in obtaining continued growth. Advises market entry strategy.
9 (Ch 9, para 3.9)	Price is emotive issue. Pricing structure. Profitability of brewing. Advertising cost.	Advises marketing mix decision. Indicates need to manage PR. Constrains strategy.	Text: paras 2.5, 2.6 Apps: 1,8 paras 3.2,3.8	Potential factor in decreasing UK market trend. Price key issue in future free market.
10 (Ch 10, para 3.10	Brewsters not fully market-orientated. Selling is admin dominated. Sales organisation regionally structured.	Indicates urgent need for change so as to adapt to market. Need for increased sales force support. Advises market mix decisions.	Text: paras 2.1 to 2.13 App: 1,7 paras 3.1,3.7	Need to change sales force from order takers to order getters. Cultural change needed. Vulnerable against competitors with better salesforces.

2. APPENDIX 1

2.1 *Appendix 1.* You will note the total number of outlets differs between the two tables. This is only to be expected since they represent different years. Brewers will have acquired and divested outlets during this period. Remember the appendix only covers the six major brewers but you can calculate they had 79% of the beer market in 1988.

2.2 Did you total all the columns in the 1988 table and then add the two types of tied pubs together for each brewer? Did you then take the percentage of total outlets for each brewer and compare it to the market share? If so you should have found as follows:

Brewer	*% of outlets*	*% of market*
1	22	21
2	21	13
3	16	13
4	20	13
5	7	10
6	15	9

2.3 There is very little correlation between number of outlets and market share. The assumption has to be that turnover per outlet varies according to size and location. This has implications for divestment strategy. Perhaps brewers will wish to keep the larger urban/suburban outlets in order to maximise market share.

You should also have deduced from this appendix that 65% of the major brewers' tied outlets are to be divested. This implies a massive loss of control.

3. APPENDICES 2, 3 AND 4

3.1 *Appendices 2, 3 and 4*. The three product concepts appear to be aimed at quite different market segments. Only one could be classed as beer. Did you try to assess each of the three proposals?

3.2 'Charmonix du Monde' might depend heavily on image. This requires careful testing of its name, packaging, copy platform etc across a range of European countries. It would however, be relatively easy to produce a range of potential mixes for taste tests fairly quickly. 'Vronsky' or 'Minsk' is more problematic. Would Russian beer normally be associated with a premium quality? Would the copy platform be legal throughout Europe? Is 20 million units (representing about 6% market share) too ambitious a target? How long would it take to reach this target and at what cost?

3.3 'Effré' might be attractive from a corporate greening viewpoint but would certainly face a great deal of competition from established brands (particularly Perrier).

3.4 However, any doubts we have must be balanced by the fact that we, as David Downing, are convinced that opportunities exist for developing strong European brands. We must put aside any personal bias and objectively investigate viability. After all, you might not have personally liked the television series 'Dallas' but tens of millions of people across the world did and it was a huge marketing success.

4. APPENDIX 5

4.1 *Appendix 5.* Whilst a Code of Practice is a non-legal rather than a legal constraint, this appendix is a reminder of the need for extreme care as well as expertise when advertising alcoholic drinks in Britain. This applies to our major product (beer) and would also apply to concepts such as 'Charmonix du Monde' and 'Vronsky/Minsk'. The implications are that all European country targets would have to be vetted carefully. It would also suggest that an agency with wide European experience of products of a sensitive nature might have to be sought and briefed.

5. APPENDIX 6

5.1 *Appendix 6.* The financial accounts are usually the most troublesome for marketing students to analyse. Nevertheless, you are strongly recommended to do this stringently as a learning exercise, if necessary *with recourse to a textbook*. The less confident students tend to ask their company accountants for their views. Needless to say not all accountants agree between themselves on the meaning of particular sets of figures or ratios. What is a good or bad ratio can depend entirely on the nature of the industry.

5.2 You will also normally find some anomalies in the figures. Try not to let these bother you. They are not that important and would usually be explained in footnotes in the company accounts. However, reasons of confidentiality often cause these footnotes to be omitted.

5.3 You should have arrived at the following conclusions from this appendix.

(a) *Profitability ratios* are growing positively (net profit on capital employed, total assets and turnover).

(b) *Employee ratios.* These are measures of employee productivity, and are improving from the company's viewpoint. By indexing these (1987 = 100) we can see that growth in profit exceeds growth in average pay.

(c) *Efficiency ratios* have generally remained steady. The turnover/stocks ratio is rising and both the current ratio and the quick ratio have been constant over the past five years although both appear low against general norms.

5.4 *Financing ratios.* There is room for varying interpretations of the borrowing ratio but it is increasing. Equity gearing remains constant.

5.5 The overall picture is therefore quite healthy with a slight question mark over the future for borrowing. However, an assumption can be made that cash from the sale of tied outlets will be forthcoming in the short-term.

6. APPENDIX 7

6.1 *Appendix 7.* The group will be concerned that Brewsters Ltd's turnover relative to the group has declined in the last two years, and will be seeking profitable improvement.

6.2 Brewing does, however, remain the largest sales segment of the group. A high proportion of brewing sales are absorbed within the group, presumably by the pubs, hotels and restaurants.

6.3 The group is heavily dependent on the UK market and it can be inferred that Brewsters Ltd is too.

6.4 Since the text indicates a decline in beer sales and increased competition, the implications are that drastic short-term action will be needed simply for Brewsters Ltd to maintain its current market position.

7. APPENDICES 8 AND 9

7.1 *Appendix 8*. There is quite an amount of disparate data here not all of which appears terribly useful in itself.

7.2 However the indications are that expenditure on beer in the UK is falling, whilst expenditure on wines, fruit juices and mineral water is increasing. There are implications for the three new product concepts here. It is important to remember that the UK is part of Europe and you may wish to test these concepts in the UK area of Europe.

7.3 On the beer front East and West Germany lead the consumption table followed by Czechoslovakia. 'Vronsky/Minsk' *might* therefore do better in Eastern Europe (although the Russian name might conjure up unhappy memories of life during the Cold War). There are also possibilities for Brewsters Ltd to export existing products to these countries.

7.4 UK sales of bottles water have quadrupled between 1984 and 1992, reflecting increased concern with health. There are implications here for 'Effré'.

7.5 Although the six major UK brewers have nearly 80% of the UK market, heavier concentrations (based on the four largest brewers) occur in all the countries listed, notably France, the Netherlands and Denmark. Strong resistance can be expected if Brewsters Ltd attempted incursions into these markets.

7.6 Whilst UK exports of beer by country of destination are given for 1988, these are in percentages. The footnote to Appendix 8 (Chapter 8, paragraph 3.8(a)) of the case tells us that UK exports were only 2% of total consumption. This can be cross related with the text and the problems of distribution for British beers in mainland Europe. We can also see from Appendix 8 (Chapter 8, paragraph 3.8(d) and (e)) of the case that the number of brands per pub/bar is less in West Germany, France and Denmark than the UK indicating perhaps that it would be difficult for Brewsters Ltd to gain brand distribution in these countries. Finally Appendix 8 (Chapter 8 Paragraph 3.8(f)) shows that the UK consumption of all alcohol compares unfavourably with most other European countries both as an absolute and a trend.

7.7 As regards beer advertising in the UK, lager brands dominate expenditure. There are some useful figures tucked away at the bottom of the table on Appendix 8 (Chapter 8, paragraph 3.8(g)) which you may have missed.

7.8 *Appendix 9*. This indicates the sensitivity of the public to beer price increases and represents bad press for the brewers. The table in Appendix 9 (Chapter 8, paragraph 3.9) can be misleading. For example, the advertising expenditure at 3p should not be treated as 2% (3p of 150p) but rather as 6% from a brewers point of view (3p on 48p representing raw materials, production and distribution, advertising and profit).

8. APPENDIX 10

8.1 *Appendix 10*. If sales and marketing functions are both on an equal footing at director level then Brewsters cannot be said to be fully marketing orientated. It is more likely to be in the stage of transition from a production/sales orientation to a marketing orientation.

8.2 From a sales viewpoint, managers are entitled Sales *Administration* Managers implying that their role is seen more as an administrative function. Equally salesmen are stated to be order takers rather than order getters and they have so far not had to persuade tied outlets to stock the products. The sales role and the culture of the sales department will have to change radically in the short-term, otherwise Brewsters will lose a substantial amount of business.

8.3 David Downing has already shown concern about the lack of professionalism in the sales force. What steps need to be taken? We should consider training, recruitment, incentives and control. the more professional salesforce will require full support from other elements of the marketing mix and particularly the promotional mix.

9. CONCLUSION

9.1 This chapter provides you with a more detailed knowledge of the appendices. These contain nuggets of useful information. Often, as in the case of buyer behaviour, what is *not* stated can be as informative as what is.

Chapter 11

BREWSTERS LTD: SITUATIONAL ANALYSIS, KEY ISSUES, MISSION STATEMENT, BROAD AIMS, MAJOR PROBLEMS

This chapter covers the following topics.

1. Step 10: situational analysis
2. Step 11: six key issues
3. Steps 12 and 13: mission statements and broad aims

1. STEP 10: SITUATIONAL ANALYSIS

1.1 So much for contemplating your appendices. You must now turn your attention to the next step which is the situational analysis. You will need to read up on this in Chapter 3 paragraphs 3.8 to 3.18 and allow two to three hours. Before doing this however, you should re-consider/review your SWOT analysis, précis and marketing audit in light of the new insights gained from your appendix analysis and adjust these as necessary.

1.2 Remember your situational analysis, although wide ranging and time consuming, needs to be summarised on a half to full page of A4. Having done this you should find it interesting to compare this with your original précis, and with the following example submitted by 'Syndicate C'.

BREWSTERS LTD
Situational analysis
Syndicate C

Brewsters Ltd is a major, profitable player in the UK brewing and leisure-drinking industry with minimal presence in overseas markets.

The environment is characterised by changes ranging from severe short-term discontinuity, such as the sharp reduction in tied houses, to more gradual changes, such as those predicted for customer buying patterns, the growth of environmental concerns, and market liberalisation. there is a history of government intervention (for example, on alcoholic drinks advertising) therefore further change may easily arise. Changes in the market place will move demand away from traditional product lines, and away from traditional distribution channels.

As one of the top six, Brewsters Ltd sees its competitors facing the same threats and opportunities which are arising. In particular, it is likely that the company which best exploits the short term change in distribution channel ownership, will then be best placed (in terms of finance and market presence) to exploit the longer term changes. Brewsters Ltd products are strong and profitable, but the portfolio must be developed if market changes are to be exploited.

Weaknesses in the organisation (sales, product development) must be addressed. The strength of the group (in terms of financial resources) should enable this to be accomplished. There appears to be a management will to effect change.

2. STEP 11: SIX KEY ISSUES

2.1 Your next steps take you into decision making mode. You are asked to decide the key issues, using the notes provided in Chapter 3 paragraphs 4.1 to 4.3 of this workbook. This is the most important decision you will make, since the key issues will form the basis of your exam questions forecast. As it can get out of hand (eg you could put forward 47 key issues just to be on the safe side) you should limit yourself to a maximum of *six*. Bearing in mind that the exam paper will normally contain three questions, you can see the wisdom in limiting yourself to six key issues. When deciding key issues, look for clues not only in the case study itself, *but also in the Candidates' Brief*.

2.2 Try not to get carried away. By all means create a list of possible key issues, but then *reject* all those which are not key. You could use a *ranking technique* and you should 'parcel up' minor issues under a major heading eg:

4 Sales force effectiveness
6 Advertising constraints
8 Poor press relations (PR)

might then be parcelled up under the heading of *marketing communications* and allocated a ranking of 3.

2.3 You should only require an *hour* to *one and half hours* to do this. When you have finished you might like to compare your findings with those that follow based on a consensus of four syndicates of eight people.

BREWSTERS LTD: SIX KEY ISSUES

1 Divestment of tied outlets
2 Sales force professionalism
3 New product development
4 Marketing research
5 Market entry/distribution
6 Organisation

Notes

(a) The above issues are not mutually exclusive. In fact they are closely linked and overlap.

(b) Divestment of tied outlets has been given top priority since it is imminent (ie short term). This issue has to be addressed - it will not go away. It is also crucial. If we get it wrong our entire future is in jeopardy. Although of a short-term nature, these strategic decisions cannot be put off. For example:

(i) which outlets should we divest and which should we keep?

(ii) on what basis do we decide on turnover, profitability, location (distribution), the likelihood of keeping the business when divested, the price we can get etc?

(c) The professionalism of the sales force is also urgent and key because without it Brewsters Ltd:

(i) runs the risk of losing business (from formerly tied outlets) to competitors; and also

(ii) risks losing the window of opportunity to gain new business (in a declining market) from the outlets that competitors divest.

(d) New product development, marketing research and market entry/distribution are also interlinked. At the moment Brewsters has only concepts. Products will need to be developed for these concepts, based upon marketing research. If Brewsters Ltd needs to increase its presence in mainland Europe (owing to long-term decline and increased competition in the UK) then market research is needed not only to decide the best countries but also the marketing mix required, the method of market entry and the means of distribution.

3. STEPS 12 AND 13: MISSION STATEMENT AND BROAD AIMS

3.1 Let us now move forward to the next decision step, namely that of *creating a suitable mission statement*. Please refer to Chapter 3 paragraphs 4.4 to 4.8 for notes on this task which should take you about an hour. Although you will not normally be asked for a mission statement per se in the exam paper, it does of course provide a necessary setting and guide for our marketing plan. You will see in the case study, Chapter 8 paragraph 2.3, that the Leighlow group has a mission. Brewsters Ltd will have to take note of this when creating its own statement. In which ways should Brewsters Ltd's mission differ from that of the group?

3.2 When you have created a suitable mission statement please go straight on to the next step which is to *decide broad aims* (see notes in Chapter 3 paragraphs 4.9 to 4.14), bearing in mind that these should be consonant with rather than in contradiction of the mission statement. Again you will need about an hour for this decision. Do not set more than *four* broad aims otherwise you will confuse the issue. (Remember broad aims will need to be converted into quantified and timescaled objectives at a later stage.) Now compare your mission statement and broad aims with those of five syndicates given below.

BREWSTERS LTD

Syndicate	*Mission statement*	*Broad aims*
A1	Brewsters mission as an established major brewer is to maintain and develop its current position of strength by responsibly providing and developing quality services and products for a growing leisure market, both at home and abroad.	1 Continue to provide value for shareholders. 2 To continue to identify and satisfy consumer wants/needs with our products and services. 3 Develop and effective, pro-active sales and marketing function.
B1	To provide innovative and high quality drinks to an ever-changing international market, with respect for the environment	1 Comply with MMC regulations without loss of market share. 2 To develop and expand the business by anticipating and satisfying changing consumer tastes. 3 To develop a profitable export market. 4 To operate our business with respect for the environment.
C1	Building upon our existing successes, Brewsters aim to be a dynamic and innovative leader in the European drinks market, whilst meeting our customer needs, in a profitable and environmentally conscious way.	1 To become a marketing orientated company. 2 To increase market share in Europe.

Syndicate	*Mission statement*	*Broad aims*
D1	*Brewsters' five points to success* (a) Brewsters services the UK leisure industry by the production and distribution of beer and the provision of retail outlets. (b) We aim to maintain and expand our sales base during the period of tied house divestment required by the MMC. (c) We aim to develop our existing product/service base to extend our market coverage to the rest of Europe. (d) We aim to create value for shareholders, customers and employees by providing products and services of high quality in all our business areas. (e) We aim to operate with high regard to the public and environment.	1 Expand sales base into the rest of Europe. 2 Maximise long term profits from existing UK outlet. 3 Extend product portfolio to exploit European opportunities.
B2	To maintain the company's high profile in the UK market and to establish Brewsters as a top quality European name, known to be responsive to the changing needs of the market.	1 To make the company more marketing orientated through restructuring the salesforce/organisation. 2 To pursue a policy of NPD satisfying social and environmental trends in UK and Europe. 3 To seek out opportunities created by new legislation in UK.

3.3 We are now returning (for the last time) to analysis or at least some analysis mixed with decision. Your task is:

(a) to decide the six *major problems*;
(b) to identify alternative solutions;
(c) to evaluate those solutions;
(c) to select the best solutions.

You will need to read the notes in Chapter 3 Paragraph 4.15 to 4.18 and use the format provided.

11: BREWSTERS LTD: SITUATIONAL ANALYSIS, KEY ISSUES, MISSION STATEMENT, BROAD AIMS, MAJOR PROBLEMS

3.4 One more necessary discipline is to rank these six major problems in order. The reason this step has been left until now is that experience shows that if people get involved in specific and often minor problems too early on, they lose sight of the broader issues. Problem solution is also related to tactical as well as strategic planning. You will need to decide which are long-term and which need immediate action.

3.5 Students often get confused between *problems* and *key issues* which is quite natural because quite often they can be the same. However a key issue is not necessarily a problem. To be silly about it, what sort of toilet paper to have in the new office block may be a problem but it is hardly a key issue. Equally, marketing research may be a key issue, but might not be seen as a major problem.

3.6 You will need quite some time for this exercise, probably two to three hours. When you have finished you might like to compare your six major problems with those submitted by eight syndicates as given in the following table. Note how some of these are sub-elements of a larger problem. For example lack of marketing orientation (2) can be reflected in the marketing organisation (2), in the sales force organisation(2) which is not pro-active (13). Lack of marketing orientation is also indicated by a lack of marketing knowledge (6). Now is a very good time to clarify your thinking and get the priorities right. Also given for good measure is an example of a completed analysis sheet.

BREWSTERS LTD

Six major problems		*Rank order given by syndicates*							
	Item	*A1*	*B1*	*C1*	*D1*	*A2*	*B2*	*C2*	*D2*
1	Divestment (MMC), legislation	1	1	1	5	1	5	1	1
2	Competitor activity	2			2		3	4	
3	Salesforce/marketing organisation, lack of marketing orientation	3		4	4	3	1	2	
4	Distribution		2	6		5		5	5
5	Product portfolio		3			2	2	3	
6	Lack of marketing knowledge		4						
7	Export (4?)		5						
8	Packaging (4?)		6						
9	Lifestyle changes, social			3		4	6	6	3
10	Promotion, constraints			5	6				
11	Europe (4?), entry barriers, '1992'			2	1	6			4
12	Declining beer market				3		4		
13	Reactive rather than proactive								2

Try and decide which are *short term* and which are *long term*

11: BREWSTERS LTD: SITUATIONAL ANALYSIS, KEY ISSUES, MISSION STATEMENT, BROAD AIMS, MAJOR PROBLEMS

PROBLEM NO.	ALTERNATIVE SOLUTIONS	MAIN ADVANTAGES	MAIN DISADVANTAGES
1.0 Erosion of core business	1.1 Guest beers	1.1.1 Size of mkt	1.1.1 Cost of promotion
		1.1.2 Broaden recognition	1.1.2 Compare regions
		1.1.3	1.1.3 Distribution
	1.2 Training and incentives	1.2.1 Loyalty	1.2.1 Cost
		1.2.2 Retention	1.2.2 Personnel resources
		1.2.3 Increase in Professionalism	1.2.3
	1.3 Pricing incentives	1.3.1 Flexibility	1.3.1 Affects profits
		1.3.2 Penetration	1.3.2 Resistance to price difference
		1.3.3	1.3.3 Price war
	1.4 Broaden distribution	1.4.1 Inc. sales outlets	1.4.1 Distn network costs
		1.4.2 Mkt. awareness	1.4.2 Promotion costs
		1.4.3	1.4.3
	1.5 Tactical purchasing	1.5.1 Capitalise on distn n/work	1.5.1 Possible pay premium
		1.5.2 Build awareness	1.5.2 Old loyalties
		1.5.3 Economics of scale	1.5.3

PROBLEM NO.	ALTERNATIVE SOLUTIONS	MAIN ADVANTAGES	MAIN DISADVANTAGES
2.0 Organisation weakness	2.1 Recruit new sales people	2.1.1 Professionalism	2.1.1 Cost/time lag
		2.1.2 Mkt penetration	2.1.2
		2.1.3	2.1.3
	2.2 Re-organise salesforce	2.2.1 Limit cost	2.2.1 Retraining needed
		2.2.2 Value for money	2.2.2 Attitudinal
		2.2.3	2.2.3
	2.3 Marketing research	2.3.1 Quality information	2.3.1 Cost
		2.3.2 Allows positioning	2.3.2
		2.3.3 Awareness of mkg	2.3.3
	2.4 Adopt pro-active approach	2.4.1 Consumer focus	2.4.1 Managment of change
		2.4.2 Common objectives	2.4.2
		2.4.3 Optimise workforce	2.4.3
	2.5	2.5.1	2.5.1
		2.5.2	2.5.2
		2.5.3	2.5.3

PROBLEM NO.	ALTERNATIVE SOLUTIONS	MAIN ADVANTAGES	MAIN DISADVANTAGES
3.0 What to divest	3.1 Inept tenants	3.1.1 No loss of estate	3.1.1 Reducing mkt
		3.1.2 Retained loyalty	3.1.2 Lessening loyalty
		3.1.3	3.1.3 Competitive pricing
	3.2 Tied, managed	3.2.1 Recoup capital	3.2.1 Loss of control
		3.2.2 Reduce fixed costs	3.2.2 Reduction of fixed assets
		3.2.3	3.2.3
	3.3 Poor performers	3.3.1 Allows selectivity	3.3.1
		3.3.2 Recoup capital	3.3.2
		3.3.3	3.3.3
	3.4 Geographical selection	3.4.1 Targeting	3.4.1 Competition for area
		3.4.2 Pricing advert (beer)	3.4.2 Premium pricing
		3.4.3 Increased loyalty	3.4.3
	3.5 High/low ROCE outlets	3.5.1 Recoup more capital now	3.5.1 Finding buyers
		3.5.2	3.5.2 Loss of sales
		3.5.3	3.5.3

4. CONCLUSION

4.1 We are now in a position to develop our marketing plan.

4.2 By now, you should have a significant amount of information about the market and Brewsters Ltd's position within it.

Chapter 12

BREWSTERS LTD: OUTLINE MARKETING PLANS

This chapter covers the following topics.

1. INTRODUCTION: APPROACHING A MARKETING PLAN

1.1 We are now at the crunch decision stage namely that of drawing up a *complete* marketing plan starting with objectives, progression through strategy and tactics (including market research) and covering the organisational, financial and human resource aspects. You will also need to schedule, decide review and control mechanisms, and consider to contingency action. All these items are covered in the notes given in Chapter 3, paragraphs 4.19 to 7.4. You will need 15 to 18 hours to do a reasonably thorough job.

Remember that you will not be tested on your analysis in itself in the examination room. The purpose of your *complete* plan is to cover and prepare for all potential exam questions.

1.2 Experience shows that syndicates starting on the plan and working against time get bogged down on objectives for far too long, getting mixed up over corporate objectives and marketing objectives, and then between objectives, strategy and tactics. Tempers can get frayed and confidence lost. A technique we have successfully used to overcome this problem is to get syndicates to blitz through an *outline* plan first, taking a maximum of one hour to do this. You can then look at this outline to see that it is reasonably consistent and logical before committing yourself to detail. In this way you see the plan as a whole, whereas if you get straight into the detail you may never see the wood for the trees and never get to the end of your journey. What you are doing is creating a framework or a skeletal plan.

1.3 A useful analogy here is to consider a drawing or a painting. The artist does not normally paint a landscape by immediately painting leaves or blades of grass in great detail. He/she would consider first what proportion of the landscape is to be devoted to sky and what to land; whether the sky is to be cloudy and the land hilly; whether to depict some trees and meadows etc etc. Having then visualised the painting *as a whole* and put in the rough parameters, more detail would be added in the sure knowledge that it fitted into the setting. Consider the following two syndicates work after one hour.

Syndicate A *Syndicate B*

1.4 *Syndicate B* started with a head and went into great detail on the eye, debating how many eyelashes should be shown, their length, the position of the pupil, the shade of colour etc. They never completed the skeleton.

1.5 *Syndicate A* visualised their skeleton as a little girl. After one hour they produced a complete skeleton. they then split up to make best use of limited time, one pair to do the *detail* on the head, another pair the legs, a third pair the arms and a fourth pair the body. After a few more hours, they brought these parts together in the sure knowledge that they would fit.

1.6 If this syndicate had used division of labour without agreeing the skeleton first they might have produced a 'Frankenstein' monster, rather than the perfectly symmetrical little girl they had finished up with.

1.7 Please use this technique now. Produce an outline plan first taking only about one hour. Force it through, do not hover or vacillate over the detail. If it is only rough you can always adjust it later to gain better cohesion and consistency, before doing the detail.

1.8 Having done it, compare it with the very rough outline plans produced by five syndicates (C2, C1, D2, B1, AD in about the same time in the pages which follow. These may not be satisfactory but at least the syndicates got there and they all felt a lot better and more in command after the exercise, even though they realised a lot more work needed to be done.

2. POSSIBLE OUTLINE PLAN: C2

2.1 Objectives

(a) Retain the maximum number of outlets allowed by MMC (ie 2,000) as well as retaining 75% (by value) of divested outlets (short term).

(b) To gain 20% (by value) of trade related from competitors (short/medium term).

(c) To become a more marketing orientated company (medium/long term).

(d) To increase exports year on year by 50% for 5 years (medium/long term).

2.2 Strategies

(a) (i) Financial/profitability analysis.
(ii) Sell off low profit/high cost outlets.
(iii) Loan - retention of business.

(b) (i) New product development.
(ii) Active selling.
(iii) Market development.

(c) Sales and marketing, 1 director for each.

(d) Develop new export division:

(i) Germany and Belgium (2 years);
(ii) Rest of Europe (5 years +).

2.3 Tactics

(a) *Sales*

(i) Discounting.
(ii) Sell properties within group for redevelopment.
(iii) Retain existing distribution channel.
(iv) Profit from sale of divested properties to refurbish the 2,000 retained.
(v) More reps, key accounts, existing/new.
(vi) Brand loyalty.

(b) *Production*

(i) Premium lager production.
(ii) Draft market price: penetration pricing to be used.
(iii) Discounts (1st order).
(iv) TV advert of brand. PR events, competitions, sponsorship etc.
(v) Sales force training, recruit (from previous landlords).
(vi) Existing channels of distribution.

(c) *Organisation*

(i) Sales personnel to be controlled by marketing department.
(ii) Sales director - export director.
(iii) New sales manager to be appointed under marketing department.

(d) *Promotion*

(i) See above (export division).
(ii) International launch of premium lager.
(iii) Skim price policy.
(iv) Recruit international agents/distributors.
(v) TV ad, posters, balloon!

3. POSSIBLE OUTLINE PLAN: C1

3.1 Objectives

(a) To become a marketing orientated company within one year.

(i) Structure: organisation, people, salesforce.
(ii) Market and marketing research.
(iii) Develop marketing information system.
(iv) Total quality management to be used.

(b) To increase profitable market share in Europe.

(i) Split into departments for the UK, other EC, and non-EC markets.
(ii) More market research information about competitors is needed.

3.2 Strategy (based on Ansoff)

(a) UK

(i) Market development: existing products for new markets include own label brewing, and home drinking.

(ii) Product development: new products for existing markets to be developed.

(b) EC

(i) Market development. Existing products to be sold in new markets.
(ii) Diversification (inc UK). New products/new markets (eg mineral water).

(c) Non-European market penetration. The existing range of products in existing markets is to be sold in existing markets, supplemented by new products.

3.3 **Marketing mix**

(a) *Products*

(i) Eurobrands eg lager
(ii) Non-alcohol eg soft drinks

(b) *Services UK:* management services (after selling pubs off)

(c) *Price*

(i) High price to promote a perception of high quality.
(ii) Soft drinks must be more competitively priced (due to competition from established brands like Perrier).

(d) *Promotion*

(i) Different according to products and markets press
(ii) PR (launch)
(iii) Not TV
(iv) Reduce price on packaging
(v) Sensitive to country for drinks

(e) *Distribution UK*

(i) Outlets
(ii) Changing - review
(iii) Off-licencing

(f) Europe distribution. Further information is needed.

4. POSSIBLE OUTLINE PLAN: D2

4.1 **Mission statement**

To be a progressive high quality and environmentally aware company, catering for the changing needs of the drinks market within the UK and Europe.

4.2 **Broad aims**

(a) To maintain sales volume and market presence in the UK.
(b) To be a more integrated and marketing lead organisation.
(c) To exceed the market share of our main UK competitors in Europe.

4.3 **Objectives**

(a) For UK sales.

(i) Year 1 Maintaining the index of 160 whilst accepting a decline to a 13.5% profit margin.

(ii) Year 2 Increase the sales index to 170 and increase the profit margin to 15%.

(iii) Year 3 Increase the sales index by 15 points and increase the profit margin to 17%.

(b) Assuming that Brewsters export 5% of their total turnover, the aim is to increase this to 20% within five years.

(c) Have an integrated sales and marketing organisation within five years.

4.4 **Strategy**

(a) Marketing penetration (short term): UK and EC.
(b) Market development (medium term): UK (to external outlets).
(c) Product development (medium/long term): UK and EC.
(d) Diversification (medium/long term): EC only.
(e) Internal reorganisation:

(i) (short term): develop sales force;
(ii) (medium/long term): progressively integrate marketing and sales department.

4.5 **Tactics**

(a) *Product development*

(i) Market research
(ii) Marketing research
(iii) Develop
(iv) Test
(v) Launch in countries according to research

(b) *Organisation*

The production department to liaise with marketing.

(c) *Pricing*

(i) Niche markets, premium lagers so high-ish prices.
(ii) Existing market competitive pricing is more appropriate.
(iii) Implication for environmental packaging. This might raise prices.

(d) *Distribution*

(i) The tactics are based on the assumption that Brewsters produces only in the UK.
(ii) Products for the UK market distributed through existing channels.
(iii) Agents are used for distribution in Europe.

(e) *Communication*

(i) *Personal selling*

(1) Employ
(2) Train
(3) Motivate
(4) Control
(5) Personal sales staff

(ii) *Advertising*

(1) Poster
(2) TV (depending on research)
(3) Radio
(4) Press

(iii) *Public relations*

(1) Sponsorship
(2) Recycling, wildlife, forest

4.6 Financial implications

(a) *Internal*

(i) recruitment of staff
(ii) training of staff
(iii) sales of tied houses

(b) *Products*

(i) research
(ii) development
(iii) testing
(iv) launch (see promotion)

(c) *Production*

(i) (short term) using existing production facilities
(ii) (medium term) expanding production facilities

(d) *Price:* niche markets price - including revenue and profit

(e) *Promotion:* high expenditure to launch new high profile products

(f) *Distribution:* use local agents to keep initial costs low

5. POSSIBLE OUTLINE PLAN: B1

5.1 Mission statement

To provide innovative and high quality drinks to an ever changing international market, with respect for the environment.

5.2 Key aims

(a) Comply with MMC regulations without loss of market share.

(b) Develop and expand the business by anticipating and satisfying changing consumer tastes.

(c) Develop a profitable export market.

(d) Operate the business with respect for the environment.

5.3 Broad objectives

(a) Comply with MMC regulations without loss of market share.

(i) *Product:* re-package for off licence sales

(ii) *Price*

(1) Publish price list
(2) Maintain current price levels

(iii) *Promotion*

(1) Pull policy via TV and posters
(2) Push policy with reorganised sales force, features in the trade press
(3) Trade incentives, sponsorship

(iv) *Place*

(1) Off-licences
(2) Hotels

(v) A disposal strategy must be properly thought out.

(1) Research and rank on-licences.
(2) Overlay rank table with geographical location re distribution cost.
(3) Determine list of specific premises to be disposed of.
(4) Research prob profitability/finance important.
(5) Dispose of number of un-viable pubs.
(6) Re-structure personnel to fit.
(7) New organisation.

(b) Develop and expand the business by anticipating and satisfying changing consumer tastes.

(i) *Product*

(1) In 1992 research new product
(2) In 1993-1995 introduce new products in UK
(3) A brand image should be constructed

(ii) *Price:* A premium pricing policy should be maintained.

(iii) *Promotion:*

trade fair	
trade press	Push strategies
TV	
posters	Pull strategies
in-pub promotion	

(iv) *Place:* UK pubs off-licences/supermarkets.

(c) Develop a profitable export market.

(i) *Product:* introduce new international brands and product in environmentally acceptable packaging.

(ii) *Price:* a premium pricing policy will be pursued.

(iii) *Promotion*

(1) In 1992 market the appropriate promotion for each country should be researched.

(2) In 1993-1995 select and manage staged launch in Europe.

(3) An export sales force should be recruited.

(4) An export brand management team might be needed.

(iv) *Place:* joint venture with overseas bottling and distribution companies (low risk) is the option in the short term for distribution. For the long term is an overseas production capability (high risk) might be considered.

(d) Operate the business with respect for the environment.

(i) *Product:* packaging re-design

(ii) *Price:* bottle deposit funds

(iii) *Promotion*

(1) Tell the public about new packaging on TV and posters.
(2) Sponsor and support green orientated initiatives (useful in Europe).

(iv) *Place*

(1) Use waterways and canals for some distribution
(2) Horse drawn transport

(v) *Company:* production emission control

6. POSSIBLE OUTLINE PLAN: A1

6.1 Mission statement

Brewsters mission as an established major brewer is to maintain and develop its current position of strength, by responsibly providing and developing quality services and products for a growing leisure market, both at home and abroad.

6.2 Broad aims and objectives

(a) To continue to provide value for shareholders.

(b) To continue to identify and satisfy the consumers wants and needs without products and services.

(c) Develop an effective pro-active sales and marketing function.

6.3 Compliance with Monopolies and Mergers Commission (MMC)

It can be assumed that Brewsters have one year in which to sell 4,000 outlets. These can be divested as follows.

(a) 1,000 will be sold for property redevelopment.
(b) 1,000 will be leased and rented, with Brewster's beer as 'guest'.
(c) 1,000 will be sold to tenants outside a core region.
(d) 1,000 will be divested in a joint venture with a European partner(s).

6.4 UK market

(a) *Placement*

(i) Keep 2,000 of Brewsters own chosen outlets.
(ii) Develop external sales by 15%.

(b) *Product*

(i) Regional traditional brand bias (bitter) to be maintained and developed - increase sales by 10%?

(ii) Develop new non-bitter brands (dependent on MR) both locally and nationally.

(c) *Price*

(i) Discount to leased outlets on contractual basis.
(ii) Explore potential premium price brands.
(iii) A separate price policy should be pursued for Brewsters Ltd's own tied estate.

(d) *Promotion*

(i) Regional TV for brand awareness.
(ii) Point-of-sale material/promotion.
(iii) Not newspapers.
(iv) Posters and other regional BT.

6.5 Europe market

(a) *Placement*

(i) Aa joint venture with a local brewer in a selected country or countries using the brewer's outlets.

(ii) Test marketing.

(b) *Product:* research led, possible premium brand.

(c) *Price:* premium price/quality position if viable.

(d) *Promotion*

(i) Point-of-sale promotions.
(ii) Regional promotions (eg for regional brands).
(iii) Necessary market research.

6.6 Organisation

(a) Export sales and marketing department ('Euro-taskforce') to be set up.

(b) Internal marketing information system to be established.

(c) A pan-European advertising agency should be briefed.

(d) Split sales force into forces devoted to:

(i) Brewsters Ltd's own houses;
(ii) free houses.

(e) Retrain sales personnel.

(f) Recruit new sales personnel.

(g) Target markets more precisely.

(h) Undertake research and development and market research to re-assess Brewsters Ltd's capabilities.

6.7 Some quantified objectives are outlined below.

(a) Sales (based on 1987 = 100)

1991	*1992*	*1993*	*1994*	*1995*	*1996*	*1997*
160	165	170	180	190	199	215

(b) Target profitability (%)

1991	*1992*	*1993*	*1994*	*1995*	*1996*	*1997*
14.8	12.0	12.2	12.5	13.0	14.1	15.2

(c) Budget

	UK	*Europe*	*Total*
	£m	£m	£m
TV advertising	3.00	-	3.00
Point of sale advertising	0.50	0.75	1.25
Sales promotion	1.00	0.50	1.50
Public relations	0.25	0.05	0.30
Posters	1.00	-	1.00
Total	5.75	1.30	7.05

7. CONCLUSION

7.1 You will note the variety of outline plans submitted here. It can only be stressed that there is often no 'right' answer. Any plan for the future is inevitably a hostage to fortune.

7.2 However, a well considered plan is the best compass to help you navigate through the uncertainty of future market conditions, and, for that matter, in the examination.

Chapter 13

BREWSTERS LTD: DETAILED PLANNING

This chapter covers the following topics.

1. INTRODUCTION

1.1 What you must now do is to flesh out your *skeleton plan* with as many details as possible. Your complete detailed plan has to be your own. *Consultancy provided plans will be automatically failed.*

1.2 However, to help you a little in this your first practice we have included a few thoughts from syndicates which represent an *interim* stage between outline plans and the finalisation of individual syndicate members' plans. Obviously, these leave something to be desired but they might help to stimulate your thoughts. We feel sure you can improve on these and fill in the gaps. Do not neglect to go back to Chapter 3, paragraphs 5.1 to 6.8 to remind yourself of what is ideally required.

1.3 Having completed your detailed marketing plan, draw up your examination plan. All you need to do now is to practice writing in report style and read up on Chapter 6 again to prepare yourself for a mock examination.

1.4 When you are ready, allow yourself three hours and attempt the Brewsters actual exam questions given in Chapter 14.

1.5 After this you can self-mark your paper with the assistance of the Examiners Report and Marking Scheme which follow. We suggest you allow yourself a break before tackling your second practice case on Euro Airport Ltd.

2. AN EXPANDED MARKETING PLAN FOR BREWSTERS LTD (BY SYNDICATE C1)

2.1 Mission statement

Brewsters aim to be a major European producer and supplier of quality beverages which satisfy our customers' needs and increase the value of our shareholders' investments, with due regard for our social and environment responsibilities.

2.2 Aims

(a) Develop significant market share in Spain, France, Germany, Italy and UK.

(b) Develop a strategy consistent with MMC constraints, to establish a portfolio of owned outlets, working towards optimum profit and market share potential.

(c) Retain existing share of business in non-Brewsters outlets.

(d) Acquire significant share of business flowing through 22,000 untied houses.

(e) Identify changes in demand and develop/acquire products to satisfy customers needs in those areas.

2.3 Objectives

(a) UK market share to increase from 13% to 20% by 1994.
(b) To achieve 20% of business (by value) from Continental Europe by 1994.
(c) Maintain profit margin (14.8%).
(d) Achieve average sale value of outlets to £100,000 per outlet (total = £320m).

2.4 Strategy

(a) Obtain national coverage through highly visible, large, profitable outlets. Sell *and buy* as appropriate. All outlets to be managed.

(b) Reinforce existing brands.

(c) Establish sales relations with un-tied outlets.

(d) Develop new soft drink(s).

(e) Move some existing product into continental markets.

(f) Negotiate 'pub exchange' with continental owners.

2.5 Tactics

(a) Set up pro-active estates team.
(b) Research existing brands/markets and develop appropriate communications plan.
(c) Re-vamp sales structure, including business development focus and incentive scheme.
(d) Research soft drinks market to identify gaps in product line.
(e) Export the concept of British pub through franchise or ownership.

2.6 Controls

The following control measures can be introduced.

(a) Rate of sales, value of pub sales compared with target, cost of sales, achievement of targets in timescales.

(b) Monitor brand performance (volume, turnover, profit, customer attitudinal surveys).

(c) Monitor number of new opening rates of closure, new business against sales targets, adherence to published price, selling costs.

(d) Number of gaps identified, and ideas for filling the gaps.

(e) Number of new outlets opened, compared with target.

2.7 Budgets

(a) Total divestment and reacquisition costs (selling outlets and buying new ones).

(b) External questionnaires and surveys and specialist research will amount to £500,000.

(c) Set selling cost budget at 5% of targeted sales revenue.

(d) 'Product gap' market research is included in item (b), above.

(e) Cost of establishing franchised outlet not to exceed 50% of payment received by franchisee.

(f) Pub swaps should break even.

2.8 Contingency plans

(a) If outlet sales fall behind schedule:

  (i) close business in some outlets;
  (ii) reduce asking prices;
  (iii) finance deals for publicans;
  (iv) attempt to gain more time from MMC.

(b) If Leighlow Leisure takes the cash from sales of outlets:

  (i) review objectives;
  (ii) focus on UK only.

  (*Note.* The cash may not be at Brewsters Ltd's disposal.)

(c) If the decline in traditional beer consumption accelerates sharply:

  (i) set up alliances with other brewers;
  (ii) consider acquisitions;
  (iii) consider acquiring;
  (iv) consider joint ventures.

(d) If European entry strategy fails:

(i) distribute through supermarkets;
(ii) introduce other products;
(iii) abandon European ambitions.

2.9 Organisational implications

(a) One director (at board level) should be responsible for both marketing and sales.

(b) The export department will be strengthened.

(c) Organisation should focus on major customer accounts. Smaller accounts should be dealt with geographically.

(d) Establish a business development team, focused on continental business, to include an export department.

(e) Strengthen the product development team.

2.10 Financial implications

(a) Many costs (some unexpected) will be seen to arise from the MMC-inspired divestments and will cause one-off charges in the 1992 accounts.

(b) Divestment provides short term cash input and gives short term investment opportunity.

(c) Turnover/stocks ratio will improve as a result of lower stockholding. (Brewsters Ltd's owns fewer pubs, so its pub-based stockholding is reduced.)

(d) Credit period may extend significantly due to switch of business from owned outlets to un-owned outlets (and consequential invoice/payment delays).

3. A MARKETING RESEARCH PLAN

3.1 Objective

To define and clarify the problems facing Brewsters Ltd in terms of lack of information, to determine the appropriate sources and methods of obtention.

(a) *Primary:* direct contact with respondents
bespoke research

(b) *Secondary:* existing data

3.2 Primary methods

(a) Observation
(b) Interview/survey/questionnaire
(c) Experimentation
(d) Test marketing - sample procedure

3.3 Secondary sources

(a) Company reports/records
(b) Government statistics
(c) Press articles
(d) Market research agencies
(e) Other published research
(f) EC statistics

3.4 Information specification for marketing research plan

Area	*Some potential sources*
(a) *Consumption trends*	
Demographics	Government statistics, EC (Brussels)
Quantities by product item	LVA, Trade publications
Expenditure	Neilson
Geodemographics	CCN, CACI
(b) *Customer profiles*	
Existing customers/potential customers	UK/EC statistics
Who are they, how many?	Industry reports
What are their characteristics?	CAMRA
What is they buying behaviour?	Internal data
What are their likes/dislikes?	Market research surveys
	OTS, DTI, FT etc
(c) *Competitor analysis*	
Who, size where?	Internal sales force
Marketing mix details?	Competitors' literature/reports
Strengths and weaknesses?	Market intelligence
(d) *Phychographic analysis*	
Drinking habits by nationality	As above
Cross analysis by income/leisure	Primary data surveys
Lifestyle analysis	
Usage by lifestyle	
(e) *Physical distribution/required marketing mix*	
Available market entry, methods/costs	UK/EC statistics
European channels of distribution	Freight hauliers
European market players for joint venture	Market research agencies
Media availability/legal constraints etc	Primary data surveys

3.5 Marketing information system

(a) Brewsters' management do not currently have an efficient system to distill marketing information which will enable them to be pro-active and assist them in decision making, planning and control. There need to be personnel appointments made for such a system.

Initial resources of MIS	*Approximate cost of MIS*	*Timescale of MIS set up*
Manager	£40,000 salary + £40,000 support	4 months
Assistant	£20,000 salary + £20,000 support	4 months

(b) A commercial analyst should be seconded to this new unit.

(c) Hardware and software will be allocated from within the company.

3.6 *What are the benefits of an MIS to Brewsters Ltd?*

It will:

(a) provide regular quality information;
(b) prevent inertia;
(c) enable Brewsters Ltd to make pro-active decisions;
(d) turn data into useful information;
(e) provide information on the movements of the markets;
(f) be a mechanism for a continual audit of the business and its markets.

3.7 *How will the system work for Brewsters Ltd?*

(a) From the internal accounting system, the following financial data will be obtained.

(i) Sales figures
(ii) Stock levels
(iii) Receivable
(iv) Payables

(b) A proper marketing intelligence system will receive information:

(i) from the sales force;
(ii) from trade;
(iii) library system;
(iv) from other relevant press;
(v) by scanning industry and other relevant reports;
(vi) through analysing literature put out by competitors.

(c) The marketing research system will also manage specific research projects to answer requirements of management (eg entry into a specific market segment, test marketing).

(d) A marketing management/science system will feature:

(i) procedures to investigate such areas as price elasticity (eg effect of annual budget increases);

(ii) a bank of market and financial models;

(iii) forecasting models.

4. A DISTRIBUTION PLAN (BY SYNDICATE D1)

4.1 Objectives

(a) Divestment and acquisition activities to achieve a portfolio of 2,000 large, profitable, owned and managed outlets, on premium sites.

(b) Achieve 85% of UK 1992 sales revenue through un-tied outlets, and competitors' tied outlets.

(c) Distribution to be nationwide, except for areas of very low population density.

(d) Achieve 20% of Brewsters sales revenue from continental Europe by 1994.

4.2 Strategy

(a) To retain and build on the existing distribution network.
(b) Stick to central production, local warehousing and onward distribution.
(c) License another company to produce and distribute Brewsters' product on the continent.

4.3 Tactics

(a) Select outlets which best fit required potential for profit, location, visibility etc.
(b) Set service standards.
(c) Establish selection criteria to identify suitable partners.
(d) Analyse alternative distribution options.

4.4 Controls

(a) Compare measurement of individual tactical partners against standard criteria.

(b) Set and monitor delivery times, damage in transit, service standards, fulfilment, availability of products.

(c) The licensee's performance will also be measured.

(d) Compare costs of internal and external suppliers (vehicles, warehousing, rail etc), to assess whether some outstanding.

4.5 Budget

(a) There are no major changes, due to established distribution network.
(b) Licensees will be responsible for distribution in Europe.
(c) Potential income will arise from royalties (% of sales) from licensees.

4.6 Contingencies

(a) Failure to achieve targets: review scale of network.
(b) Failure to identify partners: review criteria; review strategy (eg own distribution).

4.7 **Organisational implications**

None as distribution network already exists.

4.8 **Financial implications**

(a) Increased costs will be incurred due to increased volume and outlets.
(b) Revenue from Europe may be slow to build up.

4.9 Furthermore, some analysis will be made of the distribution network.

(a) Divestment decisions will be based on net profitability, and on geographical location.

(b) Those outlets which are retained will be used for:

(i) distribution opportunities of *new products;*
(ii) the distribution of guest beer.

4.10 *An analysis of distribution channels*

CUSTOMER GROUPS IN THE UK

		Served by	
		Own transport	*Distributor*
Tied pubs		✓	
Free houses:	local	✓	
	distant		✓
Guest pubs: (ex tied)	local	✓	
	distant		✓
Supermarkets		✓	
Off-licences:	chain	✓	
	local	✓	
	distant		✓
Wholesalers:	local	✓	
	distant		✓
Distributors		Collect	

5. EUROPEAN MARKET ENTRY

5.1 A European market entry strategy (in brief) might include the following.

(a) *Product:* speciality English beer.

(b) Choice of markets:

(i) Long range objectives: all major European markets;
(ii) Short range objectives: select and launch in one selected market.

(c) *Method of entry*

Use a third part distributor, with bottling plant and existing distribution network to retain outlets eg pubs.

(d) *Distribution:*

(i) by bulk tanker (road/rail) UK brewery (to local bottling plant);

(ii) possibility of return load to cut costs and/or provide Brewsters with European produced product.

6. THOUGHTS ON MARKETING AND SALES REORGANISATION (BY SYNDICATE B2)

6.1 A number of the strategies mention sales organisation as being a factor in need of change. Here is a suggested change in the sales organisation.

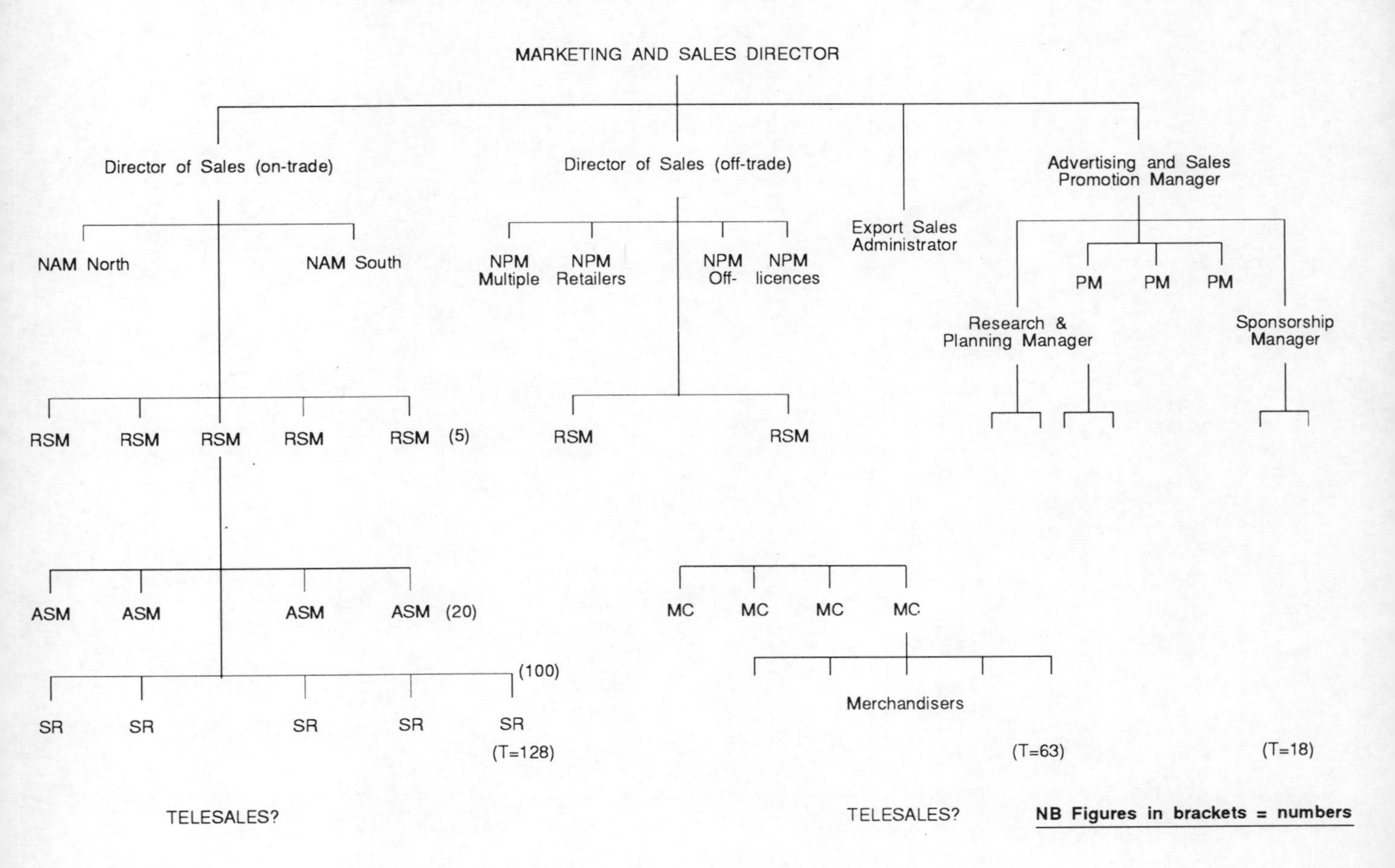

7. CONCLUSION

7.1 Now you are ready to take the exam.

Chapter 14

BREWSTERS LTD: THE EXAMINATION PAPER

This chapter covers the following topics.

1. The examination questions
2. Examiner's report
3. Illustrative marking scheme: question 1
4. Illustrative marking scheme: question 2
5. Illustrative marking scheme: question 3

BREWSTERS

THE EXAM QUESTIONS ARE ON THE NEXT PAGE

DO NOT LOOK UNTIL YOU ARE READY TO SPEND THREE HOURS ON DOING THESE AS A MOCK EXAM

1. THE EXAMINATION QUESTIONS

Question 1

Specify and *justify* the research needed to explore potential markets and to determine effective methods of market entry in order for Brewsters Ltd to adopt an improved strategic marketing position in Europe. (30 marks)

Question 2

Detail and schedule the specific actions required to establish the marketing and financial viability of the launch of Brewsters' conceptual new branded products aimed at the wider European market. (40 marks)

Question 3

Taking into account changes in the marketing environment, state clearly the steps needed to achieve a more professional selling and sales management strategy for the UK market. (30 marks)

2. EXAMINER'S REPORT

General comments

2.1 The worldwide pass rate shows a slight improvement over the previous year's December sitting, which is encouraging bearing in mind the increase in numbers attempting this paper.

This improvement in the pass rate was largely due to increases in the proportions of candidates who:

(a) adopted report format as instructed;

(b) applied exam techniques to answer all three questions adequately and to allocate time properly between questions;

(c) presented answers in a better standard of layout, structure and visual presentation.

2.2 However, too many candidates are still ignoring the actual questions set and adopting the 'write all you know' technique or presenting ill-fitting pre-prepared answers, identically worded to others in the group.

2.3 Overseas candidates in particular tend to spend far too much time on presenting detailed pre-prepared content pages, followed by over-lengthy lists of pre-prepared objectives and assumptions. The answer to each question then starts with extensive introduction and finishes with management summaries so that far too little time is devoted to the actual question asked. The result is usually answers which are far too superficial to pass.

2.4 Another practice which is causing some concern is that of *taking assumptions too far* and contriving by this means to considerably alter the questions in an attempt to bring these into line with pre-prepared answers. Such deliberately evasive techniques cannot result in a pass mark. It would seem that the weaker candidates will do anything to avoid answering the actual questions set.

2.5 With the above concerns in mind it is worth repeating some of the constructive advice given in previous Examiner's Reports.

(a) Candidates must therefore develop the ability to use their analysis *selectively* according to the specific questions set. Essentially this would entail *some* practice on an *individual* basis in adapting and extending analyses, so as to achieve a more flexible approach to the examination. Some *tuition centres* appear to be gambling on pre-prepared group analyses fitting the questions actually set, which they rarely will. In any case, this approach is entirely contrary to the intent and spirit of the subject, which is to develop individual marketing management ability to a professional standard.

(b) Candidates must also refrain from including overly detailed reference to textbook material, a knowledge of which is being tested in other Diploma papers. The subject of Analysis and Decision is testing the *application* of this knowledge to a practical situation and answers *must be case specific* rather than general treatises, in order to pass.

Question 1

2.6 Whilst some candidates demonstrated an excellent grasp of marketing research, others were unable to distinguish between the information needed:

(a) to explore potential markets; and
(b) then to determine effective methods of market entry.

Too few candidates attempted to justify the research specified. A four part answer was needed (specification and justification of research required on potential markets and market entry methods). Whilst frameworks for these exist in the recommended reading for the Diploma, answers needed to be case specific ie related to the formulation of an improved strategic position for Brewsters in Europe.

2.7 Weaker candidates also failed to structure their research and presented rambling essays. Some candidates insisted on simply describing the information that Brewsters Ltd already had, as given in the case study.

Question 2

2.8 Answers to this, the major question, were generally disappointing. Too many candidates failed to appreciate that the three proposed new products were still in the concept stage and therefore action was needed to develop actual products and put these through the appropriate screening processes to ascertain both their marketing and financial viability. Assumptions that these products were fully developed, had been thoroughly test-marketed and had already enjoyed a successful national launch in the UK were inappropriate. All three concepts were in fact variations on the theme of a potential pan-European brand so that separate treatments with regard to broad actions were unnecessary.

2.9 A three part answer was required, namely marketing actions, financial actions and their scheduling (in a timed and logical sequence). Unfortunately the vast majority limited their answers on financial viability to giving pre-prepared marketing plan costs. Candidates really do need to show a better appreciation of the financial implications involved in a potential major new product launch in overseas markets. This essentially means extending their horizons beyond marketing costs to total cost, capital required, projected returns on capital employed and pay-back periods, as a minimum. An assessment of financial risks is also appropriate with particular regard to fluctuations in exchange rates, foreign banking and legal restrictions etc. Marketing candidates needed to demonstrate their understanding that corporate objectives dictate that their proposed developments will be compared with other perhaps safer, quicker and more profitable opportunities.

Question 3

2.10 It has been hoped that this question would have been foreseen by all those candidates who had conducted a thorough analysis of the case. Clearly selling and sales management is still being under-valued. Candidates who thought that all that was required was organisational change were failed. This in itself would achieve nothing if the existing salesforce remained untrained in modern selling techniques. The essential problem was that the sales force were unprofessional order-takers and that in the new marketing environment they would be required to sell against competitors' sales forces. Some answers actually stated that the entire existing sales force would have to be replaced, rather than assessing individual potential and training needs, and only replacing people when necessary.

2.11 A typical answer listed the changes in the marketing environment but made no attempt to link these to specific changes in the sales force and its management. The examiner's hope that *timescales* and *cost indications* would accompany answer to this question proved over-optimistic. It appears that most examinees are happy to make proposals without any consideration of cost or implementation. Where organisational changes are recommended it is expected that suitable charts will be submitted in illustration, particularly when changes are being made in stages.

3. ILLUSTRATIVE MARKING SCHEME: QUESTION 1

3.1 Specify and justify the research needed to explore potential markets and determine effective methods of market entry in order for Brewsters Ltd to adopt an improved strategic marketing position in Europe. (30 marks)

Approach

3.2 A four part answer is needed (specification, justification, potential markets, methods of market entry). Whilst frameworks for these exist in the recommended reading for the Diploma, answers need to be case specific and related to strategy.

3.3 Research need to explore a potential market

Specification	*Justification*
1(a) 1 Total market sizes for Brewsters Ltd's products	To determine substantiality
1(a) 2 Competitors market shares	To help assess Brewsters likely share
1(a) 3 Market prices and costs	To determine viability (profitability)
1(a) 4 Critical success factors	To determine viability (marketability)
1(a) 5 PEST (or SLEPT) factors for each market	To determine the level of risk involved
1(a) 6 Barriers in each market	To assess ease of market entry
1(a) 7 Market growth/trends	To ensure longer term success
1(a) 8 Market gaps	To determine potential for Brewsters new products
1(a) 9 Market segments	To decide most attractive segments
1(a) 10 Competitors' positioning within segments	To determine appropriate marketing mix
1(a) 11 Competitors' positioning within segments	To help decide best channels of distribution
1(a) 12 Total distribution and marketing costs	To determine levels of investment needed
1(a) 13 ANO	
Suggest 1 mark per justified item	

3.4 Research needed to determine the methods of market entry

Specification		*Justification*
1(b) 1	Current means of distribution in the market	To establish the existing situation
1(b) 2	Evaluation of distribution effectiveness	To determine most effective method
1(b) 3	Distribution trends	To assess longer term viability
1(b) 4	Review of Brewsters resources	To confirm affordability and match
1(b) 5	Studies of competitors market entries	To avoid mistakes and learn from successes
1(b) 6	Legal constraints	To avoid possibility of legal action
1(b) 7	Attitudes of distributors to new entrants	To establish levels of resistance
1(b) 8	Costs of market entry	To assess cost-effectiveness
1(b) 9	Risk factors	To establish risk levels
1(b) 10	Likely lead times for various methods	To calculate speed of entry
1(b) 11	Levels of investment needed	To determine payback periods
1(b) 12	Marketing support ended	To establish viability and match
1(b) 13	Ease of market exit	Contingency planning
1(b) 14	ANO	
Suggest 1 mark per justified item		

4. ILLUSTRATIVE MARKING SCHEME: QUESTION 2

4.1 Detail and schedule the specific actions required to establish the marketing and financial viability of the launch of Brewsters' conceptual new branded products aimed at the wider European market. (40 marks)

Approach

4.2 The required answer is basically a new product development plan including screening and commercialisation applied to Brewsters' specific products. Packaging tests and the European complications are expected to be emphasised. A three part answer is appropriate namely marketing actions, financial actions and their scheduling.

Marketing (M) and financial (F) actions required in sequence (continued)	*Timings*
2.1 (M) Formation of project team and project management	January 1992
2.2 (M) Agree project brief, stages and go/no go criteria, scheduling etc	February 1992
2.3 (F) Initial cost assessments, stage by stage, absolute and cumulative	March 1992
2.4 (F) Funding and cashflow implications, initial budgets, project approval	April 1992
2.5 (M) Concept testing in Germany, Italy, France and the UK	May/June 1992
2.6 (F) Value analysis - this versus other potential projects	May/June 1992
2.7 (M) Develop prototype drinks, packaging and creative platforms - latter requiring agency briefs	July-September 1992
2.8 (F) Further costings, break-even analysis, capital investment assessments	July-September 1992
2.9 (M) Further marketing research in the selected European countries, both consumer and trade to establish degrees of product and creative platform acceptability; competition and the marketing mixes required	October-December 1992
2.10 (F) Forecasts of potential sales at various prices, C-V-P analysis, risk and payback assessments etc	December 1992 - January 1993
Suggest 2 marks per action scheduled but no pass if financial viability ignored	

Continued

Marketing (M) and financial (F) actions required in sequence (continued)			*Timings*
2.11	(M)	Finalise marketing mix including best methods of distribution (see answer to question 1). Formulate test market plans	April 1993
2.12	(M)	Test market in the selected countries to determine degrees of trial and repeat purchase plus acceptability of marketing mix	June 1993
2.13	(M)	Modify marketing mix and marketing plans as necessary	June 1993
2.14	(F)	Modify financial plans as necessary	June 1993
2.15	(M)	(Subject to satisfactory test market) Conduct full launches	September - December 1993
2.16	(M)	Modify marketing plans as necessary following full launches	September - December 1993
2.17	(F)	Modify financial plans as necessary following full launches	September - December 1993
2.18	(M & F)	Subject to satisfactory results, select further countries in the wider European market and proceed from 2.1 above	January 1994-1996
Suggest 2 marks per action scheduled but no pass if financial viability ignored			

5. ILLUSTRATIVE MARKING SCHEME: QUESTION 3

5.1 Taking into account changes in the marketing environment, state clearly the steps needed to achieve a more professional selling and sales management strategy for the UK market. (30 marks)

Approach

5.2 The starting point is the current situation ie the sales organisation chart and the fact that currently the salesforce tell rather than sell. An essential requirement is therefore that of professional sales training. With regard to sales management strategy, some restructuring is considered necessary coupled with a move towards relationship marketing. Within these tenets a fairly liberal approach can be taken with regard to the detail of the steps stated by the examinees. Scheduling of the steps together with their financial implications are considered necessary to grant a pass on this question.

Steps		*Timing*	*Est costs*
3.1	Conduct sales audit, internally and externally to identify current strengths and weaknesses of the sales operation versus competitors	January 1992	£3,000
3.2	Discuss implications of this audit with the Regional Sales Administration Managers (RASMs)	February 1992	-
3.3	Identify training necessary to convert the salesforce from the current tell-style to sell-style strategy	February 1992	£500
3.4	Draw up new job descriptions and person specifications incorporating the required changes. Discuss these in appraisal interviews with existing sales force members	March 1992	£500
3.5	Agree new selection criteria for future recruitment with personnel department	April 1992	-
3.6	Brief sales training agencies, obtain costed proposals and make selection	April 1992	£500
3.7	Appoint sales training manager and delegate the conducting of a continuous sales training programme using the services of the selected professional agency	April 1992	£35,000
		May 1992	-
Suggest 2-2½ marks per valid, costed and scheduled (timed) action. Allow re-organisation chart at 5 marks			

Continued

Steps	*Timing*	*Est costs*
3.8 Agree targets and actions with the RASM's with regard to the holding and development of existing accounts and the obtaining of new accounts	May 1992	£2,000
3.9 Change sales reporting and competitor intelligence to encompass continuous feedback on the changes in the marketing environment, so as to signal adjustments necessary to future selling and sales management strategy		
3.10 In discussion with RASM's identify and select existing and potential key accounts (eg multiple licensees) for the *planned* building up of long-tern relationships via a partnership approach to sales development strategies	June 1992	-
3.11 Appoint and train relationship managers for these key accounts (ideally from existing salesforce with accounts transferred)	July 1992 (ongoing)	£90,000 pa
3.12 Marketing management to provide support eg incentive schemes, consumer promotions for the building of these relationships	January 1993	£3,000
3.13 Conduct new sales audit to measure results of new strategy and determine future strategic action		
Suggest 2-2½ marks per valid, costed and scheduled (timed) action. Allow re-organisation chart at 5 marks		

6. CONCLUSION

6.1 How did you do in your mock exam? Not too bad but could do better? Do you think you would benefit by a second practice run? We are sure you would. Remember this is the one exam you really cannot afford to fail because you would have to start again from scratch, on an entirely new case.

6.2 Another good motivation for a second practice run is that once you have grasped the process you can apply it to any project you might be required to handle during your marketing career - that is a double bonus for your efforts.

Chapter 15

EURO AIRPORT LTD: CASE STUDY DOCUMENTATION

This chapter includes the case study information sent to candidates.
1. Candidates' brief 2. Euro Airport Ltd (EAL): text 3. Euro Airport Ltd: appendices

INTRODUCTORY NOTE

(a) The second practice case is Euro Airport Ltd which like Brewsters Ltd, students all over the world related to very well. The CIM received many compliments on it from tutors and students alike and the examination results showed a higher pass rate than in recent sittings.

(b) Now that you know the ropes try to enjoy the experience and relax a little more than during your first run.

(c) We will not repeat all the instructions detail we gave for Brewsters Ltd but will remind you of the essentials for each step/stage in panel form. Here we go then.

CONSULT THE GUIDANCE NOTES FOR THIS TASKS CHAPTER 3 PARAGRAPHS 2.1 TO 2.19
STEP 1 READ THE CASE **STEP 2 AFTER AN INTERVAL RE-READ THE CASE** **STEP 3 REFLECT ON THE INSTRUCTIONS AND CANDIDATES BRIEF** **STEP 4 THINK YOURSELF INTO THE ROLE AND THE SITUATION** **STEP 5 RE-READ THE CASE AND WRITE A PRÉCIS**
ALLOW YOURSELF BETWEEN 3 AND 6 HOURS FOR THIS TASK

15: EURO AIRPORT LTD: CASE STUDY DOCUMENTATION

1. CANDIDATES' BRIEF

1.1 You are Irma Bergmann, the recently appointed New Business Development Manager reporting to the Commercial Director of Euro Airport Ltd (EAL). This is a new position created largely by the threat of the loss of duty free sales. Also, an inherent part of the justification for this appointment is, however, a need for completely fresh thinking at a time of rapid change in the EC environment. EAL are wanting particularly to create a unified approach to the marketing of the airport as a whole and all applicants for vacant positions within both the Commercial and Operations divisions are being judged with this requirement in mind.

1.2 You therefore have considerable scope for development of your role in the longer term. You are young, talented and ambitious.

1.3 In putting forward your proposals it is necessary to be aware that other projects will be competing for scarce resources both at company and group level.

1.4 Following your initial assessment you will be required to make clear recommendations for future action.

1.5 This case material is based upon experience with an actual company. Alterations in the information given and in the real data have been made to preserve confidence. Candidates are strictly instructed not to contact companies in this industry.

2. EURO AIRPORT LIMITED (EAL): TEXT

2.1 Euro Airport Ltd (EAL) is a large airport situated in Europe which hosts most of the major airlines of the world. Although EAL owns substantial assets in the form of land and buildings only a small proportion of these are actually used by the millions of passengers who arrive and depart from the airport each year and whose expenditure at the airport constitutes a major proportion of its revenue. EAL is part of a group of related holdings but operates autonomously as a separate SBU (Strategic Business Unit).

2.2 The airport normally operates 24 hours every day and has over 25,000 employees including aircrews, air traffic controllers, security staff, cleaners, catering staff, baggage handlers, shop assistants and the management/clerical support staff.

2.3 EAL sees itself not only as an airport but also as a substantial retail shopping centre which incorporates shops, bars, restaurants and banks, most of which operate on a concession basis. This is an arrangement whereby a retailer is allowed to establish an outlet at the airport in return for a rent plus a percentage of the outlet's turnover. This large retail operation is extremely successful and the profits generated contribute considerably towards the very high costs of maintaining the runways and terminal buildings.

2.4 Like most airports, EAL is expanding in its effort to cope with the long term increase in demand for air travel by both the business and leisure segments and for airfreight services. However, expansion is constrained by environmental pressures. EAL has to conform to stringent safety standards and has to ensure that building developments blend naturally into the surrounding landscape insofar as possible. The containment of noise is another very difficult problem. These factors have given rise to what has become known as the 'not in my back yard' syndrome. Any attempts to extend runways or to increase the number of flights are strongly resisted by consumer protest groups which are particularly vociferous in the immediate vicinity of the airport.

2.5 The smooth operation of the airport is also interrupted by events outside its immediate control in the form of government interventions and industrial actions, not only in the home country but in countries throughout the world. However, undesirable though these hold-ups may be in causing customer dissatisfaction, they can actually result in more sales at the airport's retail outlets.

2.6 EAL is highly conscious of its responsibilities not only to its customers but to the community at large and seeks to be pro-active towards the increasing sensitivity of the environmental factors and within these, the 'green' issues, particularly those of conservation and anti-pollution. Very high levels of skills in forward planning, technological and environmental forecasting are needed in order to anticipate the nature and strengths of these uncontrollable variables several years ahead.

2.7 Particularly as a result of a commitment to quality, EAL has sought to establish a competitive advantage through the medium of design. This attempt to sustain a distinctive competence extends not only to buildings and landscapes but to all systems concerned with handling internal and external customers. More recently EAL has embarked on policies involving the concept of 'relationship marketing'. This concept in essence recognises the importance of building up long-term relationships with its customers, other people in the DMU (Decision Making Unit), with suppliers and with other publics such as local government, in a partnership type of approach.

2.8 A serious threat to EAL's future viability is the decision of the European Community Finance Ministers to take action to ban the practice of offering goods 'duty free'. These lower priced goods are a major attraction for passengers shopping at airports and revenue from sales of duty free goods contribute a considerable proportion of EAL's turnover and profits.

2.9 EAL is therefore actively identifying and considering alternative ways in which this potential loss in revenue and profit might be alleviated such as moving into the hotel business, joint ventures with other airports and developing non duty free sales.

2.10 Other opportunities for profitable development are felt to emanate from Eastern Europe's political changes and possible integration with providers of other transport services.

2.11 With these and other potential opportunities in mind EAL have recently created the position of New Business Development Manager reporting to the Commercial Director. Irma Bergmann, a former Merchandising Director of a prosperous chain of supermarkets operating nationally and internationally is to undertake this role with effect from 1 May 1992. Irma has a degree in European Business Studies, the CIM Diploma and is fluent in German, French and English.

2.12 Apart from her considerable expertise in buying and selling instore goods, Irma was consulted regularly with regard to new store sites and competitor acquisitions by her former company. Irma has already made a start on a marketing audit as part of her business development plan and found her freedom to develop business limited by a number of factors including the following.

(a) Customer perceptions of airports as being expensive places in which to shop or to eat and drink.

(b) Limited shopping time.

(c) Limited space for retail development.

(d) Some conflict between commercial and operational interests.

(e) Bad publicity regarding airports over exploiting a captive market.

(f) Difficulties in positioning caused not only by the proliferation of concessions, but also by the international nature of the airport's passengers.

(g) Changes in customer profiles eg the increasing proportion of Japanese in both business and leisure segments.

(h) Bureaucracy: the number of groups/departments to consult.

(i) Traffic congestion in the vicinity of the airport and difficulties in parking.

(j) Increase in security restrictions.

2.13 Irma also feels the need for new types of marketing research data in order to more effectively identify new product/service opportunities and new market segments/niches. She has been used to regularly receiving sophisticated data from retail audits, consumer panels, electronic point of sale systems, geodemographic surveys etc in her former position. This national and international data has not been seen as particularly relevant to EAL's retail concessions (concessionaires) in their limited geographical position, dealing with a diverse range of customers. However, Irma remains reasonably confident that some of the critical success factors relevant to her former business apply also to EAL and that she can make a considerable contribution to profitability in her new role.

2.14 She has been made aware by the Commercial Director that the most important indicators by which airport's commercial performance is measured are as follows.

(a) Sales turnover
(b) Sales per passenger
(c) Revenue
(d) Revenue per passenger
(e) Sales per square metre
(f) Revenue per square metre
(g) Profit
(h) Return on investment

2.15 There is of course a difference between the total value of sales made through the concessionaires and the revenue received by EAL. This revenue is only a share of retail sales made by the retail concession, plus a rent.

2.16 Airlines pay to use EAL's facilities to operate flights to and from the airport and for each departing passenger. These airline and passenger charges make up approximately 35% of total airport revenue, with commercial activities from retail concessions and other income making up the remaining 65%.

2.17 Airline passengers do therefore provide two sources of revenue for EAL:

(a) an airport charge for each departing passenger (paid by the airline); and
(b) that from goods and services purchased whilst at the airport.

2.18 A further source of revenue comes from expenditure made by people visiting the airport to meet or to bring passengers or for other purposes.

Market segmentation

2.19 *Passengers* segment into many categories but the major ones are:

(a) business/leisure;
(b) domestic/foreign;
(c) starting point/end destination;
(d) standard/transfer.

2.20 A transfer passenger is someone who arrives from another airport and transfers flights at the airport, for example, taking a local airport flight to EAL for transfer on to a long haul flight to America. Although it varies, transfer passengers can have more time to spend in the terminal but may have already bought duty free goods at their local airport or on their local flight. Transfer passengers can make up as much as 30 per cent of total traffic although this proportion is slowly decreasing as more regional airports lay on longer-haul flights. However, EAL are finding that airside transfers (passengers arriving by air and staying in the duty free area as opposed to landside transfers who arrive by coach and taxis and have to go through Passport Control to get to the duty free area) are spending more per head on duty free items than either landside transfers or standard, non-transfer passengers.

2.21 There are trends towards increasing proportions of leisure passengers, long haul passengers and female passengers.

Marketing research

2.22 Marketing research is regularly conducted to monitor passenger profiles and satisfaction levels with all operational aspects.

Competition

2.23 Competition is seen as emanating from two main areas:

(a) alternative forms of transportation ie car, coach, rail, boat;
(b) other airports, both domestic and international.

2.24 In addition the commercial sector must compete:

(a) for the passenger's *time*, against:

(i) check-in procedures;
(ii) security procedures;
(iii) airlines' embarking procedures;

(b) for the passenger's *spend*, against:

(i) airlines' in-flight sales;
(ii) High Street shops (indirectly).

Promotion

2.25 Promotion is carried out by EAL, by concessionaires and by makers of products sold on the airport. This takes many forms, including the following.

(a) On airport:

(i) illuminated signs;
(ii) posters;
(iii) trolleys;
(iv) leaflets to arriving and departing passengers;
(v) staff incentive campaigns;
(vi) shop sales promotion;
(vii) merchandising;
(viii) staff discounts;
(ix) point of sale displays.

(b) Off airport:

(i) railway posters;
(ii) national newspapers;
(iii) hotels;
(iv) radio;
(v) in the High Street branches of shops who have concessions at the airport.

(c) Regular airport, to create 'brand loyalty' amongst regular travellers.

(d) Users club.

2.26 With regard to the element of place, airports can be stressful and confusing for some passengers, and this can be aggravated by security measures, congestion and delays. All these can affect the moods of the passengers and their consequent inclination towards or against shopping or spending money. As far as possible therefore, attempts are made to make the commercial environments attractive, calm, spacious and logical.

2.27 Pricing policies are such that EAL guarantees any products/services bought at the airport are of equal or comparable price to their equivalent on the High Street. Exceptions include duty/tax free goods on which a specified saving is guaranteed and the 'Bureau de Change' where exchange rates are within one percent of the rates of a specified major bank.

2.28 The organisation or an airport as large as EAL is necessarily complex and tensions often arise between staff in the operations sections and those in the commercial sector. Some of these tensions can be seen to arise from a basic conflict of interests. The main objective of the commercial division is to satisfy customers needs for retail goods and services, during the time they are in the airport. The operations division's main objective is by contrast, to process passengers safely and efficiently from arrival at the airport, to the timely departure of their flight. Any activities which get in the way of this process can be regarded by operations personnel as counter productive, causing problems. Passengers tempted to linger in the airport's duty free shops might for example arrive late at their departure 'gate' and extra baggage means extra weight and storage. Operations personnel do not always appreciate that the purpose of generating income from commercial activities is to invest this in developing the airport generally. Both operations and commercial divisions need to learn that marketing the airport as a whole both to passengers and to airlines is a key element of the airport's mission.

3 EURO AIRPORT LTD: APPENDICES

No.	*Subject matter*
1	Services provided by the airport for its customers
2	Product/service range • share of income • share of space
3	Domestic and international terminals, passenger profiles
4	Commercial facilities, domestic and international terminals
5	Performance analysis • external and internal factors
6	Marketing research activities
7	SWOT analysis
8	Characteristics of main European airports
9	Ranking of charges for typical aircraft types • main European airports
10	Memo from commercial director to new business development manager
11	Extracts from newspaper articles/letters
12	Memo from commercial director to new business development manager
13	Organisation charts
14	Financial accounts
15	Memo from commercial director to new business development manager
16	Memo from public relations director to new business development manager
17	Survey of airport shoppers and their buying behaviour

3.1 **Appendix 1**

Services provided by the airport for its customers

(a) *Airline operators*

(i) Airline operators are provided with an internationally known airport with access to the centre of a large city in Europe, which attracts both tourists and business people. Many people want to fly there and the airline will therefore gain business because of this.

(ii) Use of modern facilities, offices, baggage handling machine etc.

(iii) Engineering and maintenance facilities.

(iv) Check-in desk and ticket office space.

(v) Fuel and filling facilities.

(vi) Hangar space.

(vii) Runway time.

(viii) Inflight catering facilities.

(ix) Use of staff leisure facilities.

(x) Strict security.

(xi) Strict safety regulations and controls.

(xii) An environment which will keep passengers informed and occupied.

(b) *Airline passengers*

(i) Regular flights enabling them to choose the one most convenient for them.

(ii) Direct flights to over 100 destinations worldwide.

(iii) Safety and security.

(iv) Well trained staff.

(v) Efficient passenger information service.

(vi) Porters, luggage trolleys.

(vii) Free transfer buses.

(viii) Information desks.

(ix) Facilities for the disabled.

(x) Cleanliness.

(xi) Shopping facilities.

(xii) Catering outlets.

(c) *Concessionnaires*

(i) Provided with a large number of potential customers.

(ii) Space in the terminals.

(iii) Support from EAL commercial department.

3.2 Appendix 2

Product/service range: share of EAL revenue and space

Product/ service	*Share of revenue* %	*Share of terminal space (inc store rooms kitchens etc)* %
Duty free tax shops	50.5	25.9
Catering	5.3	53.1
Banking/Bureau de change	5.8	3.0
Car rental	3.0	0.8
Hotel reservations	0.6	0.2
Payphones	0.6	1.3
Insurance	0.2	0.3
Bookshops	5.7	8.3
Specialist shops	3.5	6.0
Advertising	5.2	-
Car parks	19.4	-
Sundry	0.2	1.1

3.3 Appendix 3

Terminal passengers - differences between domestic and international terminals

	Domestic terminal %	*International terminal* %
(a) *Passenger type*		
Domestic business	43.5	27.4
Domestic leisure	28.8	20.7
Foreign business	12.4	26.9
Foreign leisure	15.3	25.0

	Domestic terminal %	*International terminal* %
(b) *Age*		
Less than 18	1.2	1.4
18 - 24	9.9	10.1
25 - 34	29.1	27.4
35 - 44	27.2	27.4
45 - 54	19.3	20.6
55 - 64	9.6	9.4
65 +	3.7	3.7
(c) *Sex*		
Male	69.6	69.9
Female	30.4	30.1
(d) *Socio-economic group (based on British JICNARS classifications)*		
AB	56.0	60.8
C1	29.9	30.3
C2	10.0	6.5
DE	4.1	2.4
(e) *Permanent residence in last 12 months*		
Domestic	72.3	48.0
Rest of EC	11.9	24.1
Rest of Europe	1.9	10.6
North America	7.5	8.5
Africa	1.8	2.5
Middle/Far East	2.3	3.9
Rest of the world	2.3	2.4

3.4 Appendix 4

Commercial facilities at EAL

Domestic terminal	*International terminal*
Bookshops	Bookshops
Clothes shops	Clothes shops
Sports shops	Fashion shops
Chemist	Chemist
Music shop	Music shop
Perfume shop	Luxury food shop
Fashion jewellers	Toy shop
Cosmetics shop	Luxury jewellers
	Shoe shop
	Novelty shop
	Cosmetics shop
	Duty and tax free shop
Waiter service restaurant	Catering outlets
Self service restaurant	Waiter service restaurant
Bar	Self service restaurant
Small catering outlets	Fast food restaurant
	Bar
	Small catering outlets
Car rental desks	Car rental desks
Hotel reservations desks	Hotel reservations desks
Telephones	Bureau de Change
Amusement machines	Telephones
Fax machines	Amusement machines
	Fax machines
Advertising sites	Advertising sites
• posters	• posters
• special displays	• displays

3.5 Appendix 5

Performance analysis

Performance can only be analysed by taking into consideration the following factors.

(a) *External factors*

(i) Inflation
(ii) Growth in consumer expenditure
(iii) Performance of overseas economies
(iv) Growth in passenger numbers
(v) Exchange rate changes
(vi) Changes in proportion of international passengers
(vii) Changes in taxation
(viii) Changes in passenger type
(ix) Competition
(x) Global changes in consumer tastes
(xi) Airline performance
(xii) Air Traffic Control delays
(xiii) Absolute ie actual prices received
(xiv) Price relative to alternative suppliers
(xv) Propensity to spend
(xvi) Foreign approval procedures (bureaucratic delays)

(b) *Internal factors*

(i) Concessionaires performances
(ii) Major redevelopment of terminals
(iii) Promotional activities
(iv) Changes in shop design and layout
(v) Contractual changes
(vi) Introduction of new product lines
(vii) Space allocated to commercial activities
(viii) Congestion in terminals and in individual shops
(ix) Terminal operational policies
(x) Design
(xi) Staff training and motivation

3.6 Appendix 6

Marketing research

Marketing research is regularly carried out to provide information on the following.

(a) Passenger profiles
(b) Attitudes towards shopping
(c) Domestic and foreign lifestyles
(d) Behavioural studies
(e) Airport facilities
(f) Duty free purchasing motivations
(g) Price/value for money perceptions
(h) Characteristics of specific nationalities eg Japanese
(i) Awareness and credibility of advertising campaigns
(j) Consumer needs and attitudes towards catering
(k) user profiles for specific outlets

3.7 **Appendix 7**

SWOT analysis (incomplete)

(a) *Strengths*

(i) Growth market
(ii) Captive market
(iii) Big High Street names/branding
(iv) High demand for commercial space
(v) High commercial growth
(vi) Many high income passengers
(vii) Customers can be easily identified, classified and targeted
(viii) Flexible - can change to meet changing consumer needs
(ix) Policy to give good customer service and value for money
(x) Centralised commercial function
(xi) Control over concessionnaires
(xii) Specialist operators
(xiii) Financial support from parent company
(xiv) Profitability
(xv) Increasing retail expertise
(xvi) Well known
(xvii) Good access links

(b) *Weaknesses*

(i) Image of airports as expensive
(ii) Limited time for shopping

(1) security measures
(2) length of check-in procedures
(3) congestion

(iii) Limited space for commercial development
(iv) Location of commercial facilities restricted by operational considerations
(v) Duty/tax free purchases limited due to import allowances
(vi) Organisation not commercially orientated
(vii) Staff not in a single location
(viii) Insufficient development land
(ix) High building cost
(x) Bureaucracy - number of groups to consult
(xi) Current ban on some night flights

(c) *Opportunities*

- (i) Market growth
- (ii) Passengers increasing
  - (1) frequency
  - (2) more leisure
  - (3) more long haul
- (iii) New technology (more information on customers, shopping trends)
- (iv) Arrivals duty free shopping
- (v) Proposed new terminal (commercial given equal priority at design stage)
- (vi) EC harmonisation (new commercial opportunities)
- (vii) Potentially strong brand name
- (viii) Additional capacity
- (ix) Transfer passengers

(d) *Threats*

- (i) Exchange rates (eg a weak dollar can result in fewer Americans travelling to Europe)
- (ii) More congestion
  - (1) additional security measures
  - (2) size of aircraft increasing
- (iii) Increase in cost of travel - may limit spending at airport
- (iv) Competition from airlines - duty free goods
- (v) Regulatory bodies
  - (1) Monopoly
  - (2) EC
  - (3) Legal
  - (4) Government
  - (5) Airports authorities
  - (6) Customs and Excise
- (vi) Economic recession
- (vii) Terrorism
- (viii) Vulnerability to media
- (ix) Decline in cigarette/tobacco market
  - (1) advertising restrictions
  - (2) health considerations
- (x) Competition (regional and European airports)
- (xi) Traffic congestion (on routes to the airport)

3.8 Appendix 8

Some characteristics of main European airports

	***Airport A**	*Airport B*	*Airport C*	*Airport D*	*Airport E*
Within ten miles of city centre	no	yes	yes	yes	no
Near a major tourist attraction	yes	no	yes	no	yes
Near a major business centre	yes	yes	no	yes	yes
Uncongested access routes	no	yes	yes	yes	no
Good passenger facilities	yes	yes	yes	no	yes
Relatively low risk from terrorism	no	no	yes	yes	no
Over 100 destinations	yes	yes	no	no	yes
Plans for major expansion/ development	yes	yes	yes	no	yes
Active marketing or airport	no	no	yes	no	no

*Airport A - EAL

3.9 Appendix 9

Ranking of charges, for typical aircraft types levied by the - main European airports

Destination	*Long haul route*	*Medium haul route*	*Short haul route*
Airport B	1	1	1
Airport E	2	2	3
Airport D	3	5	5
Airport A*	4	4	2
Airport C	5	3	4

1 = most expensive
5 = lease expensive

*Airport A = EAL

3.10 Appendix 10

MEMORANDUM

11 May 1992

From: Commercial director

To: New business development manager

This is simply to confirm our meeting last week when I asked you to become involved in the retail services for our new terminal for which we are expecting planning permission shortly.

I have enclosed drawings and other details of the proposed layout for this new terminal together with those of our existing terminals and would be interested to know:

(a) what you think of these proposals;
(b) whether you think we should make any changes.

You will also have to get involved with discussions with concessionaires to agree fine details in due course.

It is quite some time since we looked at our competitors in any detail and I would like you to conduct a survey of our major competitor airports, to confirm our relative strengths and weaknesses but more importantly to observe which elements of their retail mix appear to be doing well and to assess whether we have anything to learn from them.

Please feel free to call in for discussion as necessary before our next formal monthly management meeting.

PS. Our PR people want to do a feature on you for external publicity purposes, as well as our in-house magazine. Could you please contact Mrs Normal Bernhardt on this one.

3.11 Appendix 11

Extracts from newspaper articles and letters during November 1991

(a) EUROPE CLOSES DOOR ON DUTY FREE SHOPS

European Community Finance Ministers agreed last night to abolish duty free shopping within the community by July 1 1999.

The total turnover of duty free goods within the EC is estimated at £1.5 billion per year.

Britain has the EC's biggest duty free industry with shops at airports and on ferries accounting for c£1.0 billion annual turnover.

(b)

> *Sir*, Whatever Herr Peter Gundthardt may say it is not simply the British who spend heavily on duty free drink and tobacco. Few people of any nationality can resist a bargain, witness the queues of passengers at the Dubai duty free shops in the small hours in order to save a little money on a bottle of Scotch or French Brandy. Scandinavians throng the duty free shops at Mediterranean airports. Abolishing duty free goods within the EC will boost the takings of Cointrin airport (Geneva) at the expense of Satolas (Lyons): Zurich and Salzburg will benefit at the expense of Munich. Above all Morocco, Bulgaria, Turkey and Tunisia will flourish to the detriment of the EC summer holiday destinations. *Yours*, Henri Le Coin

(c)

> Evidence was uncovered this week that a concerted and coordinated effort is being made by lobbyists in Europe against further expansion in the number or size of airports. Envirnomentalists are planning to put pressure on the European Parliament against such expansions, on the grounds of destroying the green belt, polluting the atmosphere, creating more noise and exposing local communities to more danger from crashes and traffic congestion. Local communities are being urged to protest to their local political representatives on this issue.

3.12 **Appendix 12**

MEMORANDUM

21 May 1992

From: Commercial Director

To: New Business Development Manager

As you know the immediacy of the threat with regard to the abolishment of duty free shopping within the EC has lessened with the announcement of July 1st, 1999 deadline.

However, we had hitherto nurtured hopes that total abolition might not occur. In this sense our longer term strategic position has worsened.

We now definitely need new ideas on how to replace our duty free sales by other, at least equally profitable, business within existing space/buy time constraints. Since some of these ideas may require several years before they can be brought in practice, we need to start the process now rather than postpone it.

I would suggest that you take action to generate some viable ideas against the more obvious criteria, which can then be screened in a more sophisticated manner. I would ideally like to have your ideas for your next strategic review on June 30th.

3.13 Appendix 13

(a) *EAL: Corporate management*

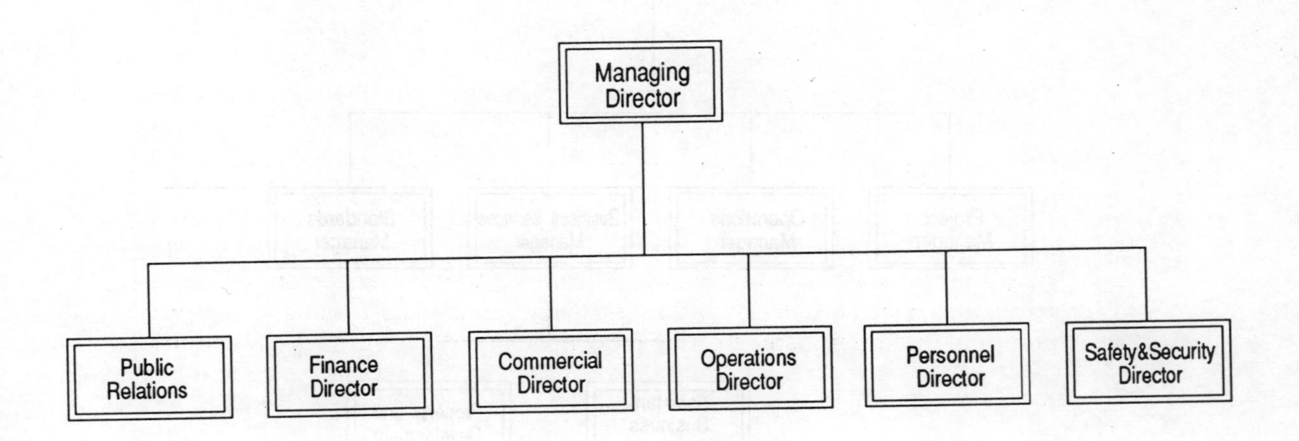

(b) *EAL operations management*

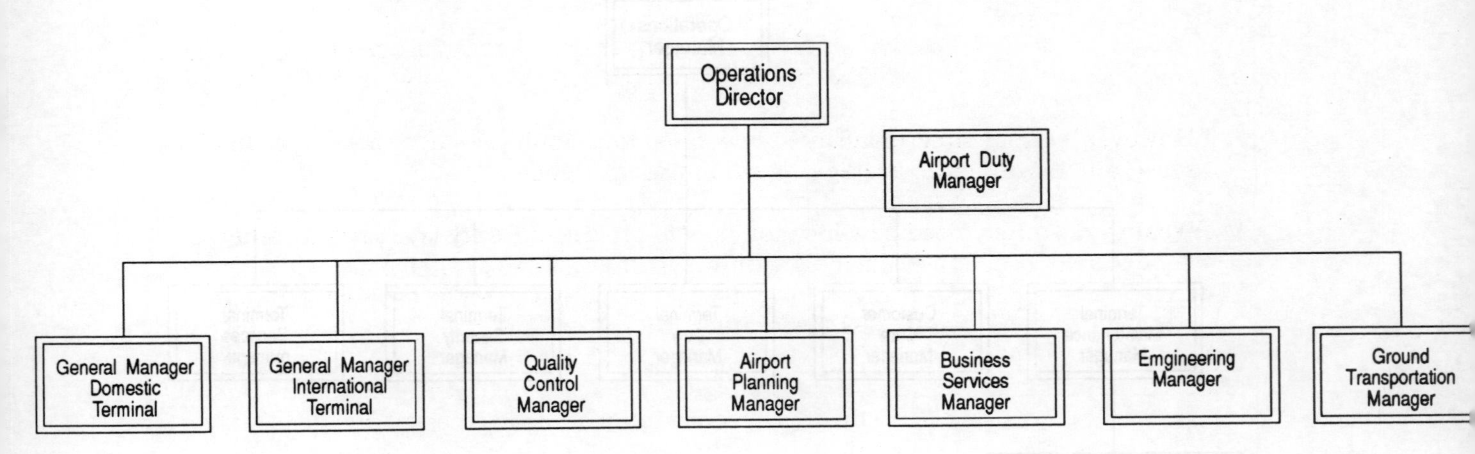

(c) *EAL terminal operations mangement (1)*

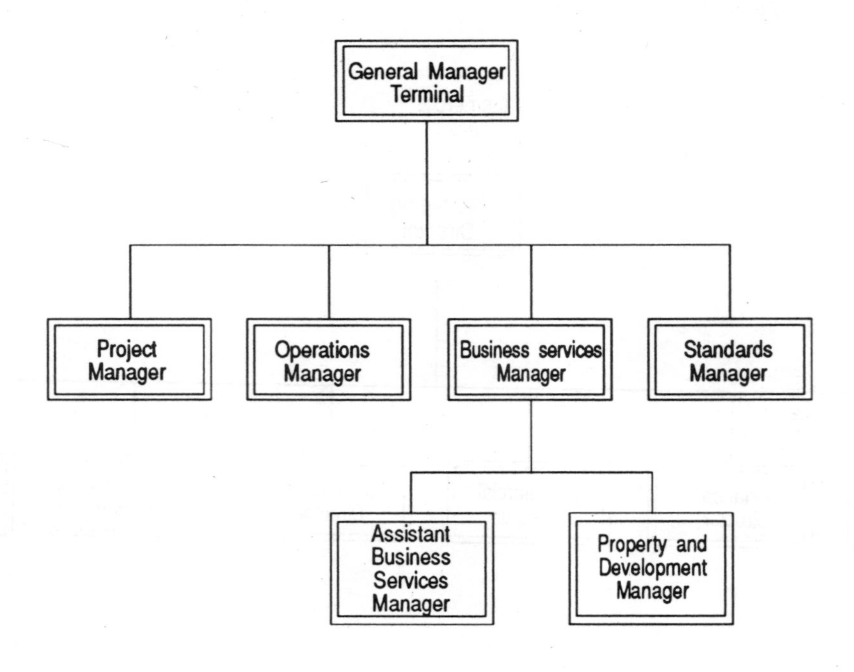

(d) *EAL terminal operations mangement (2)*

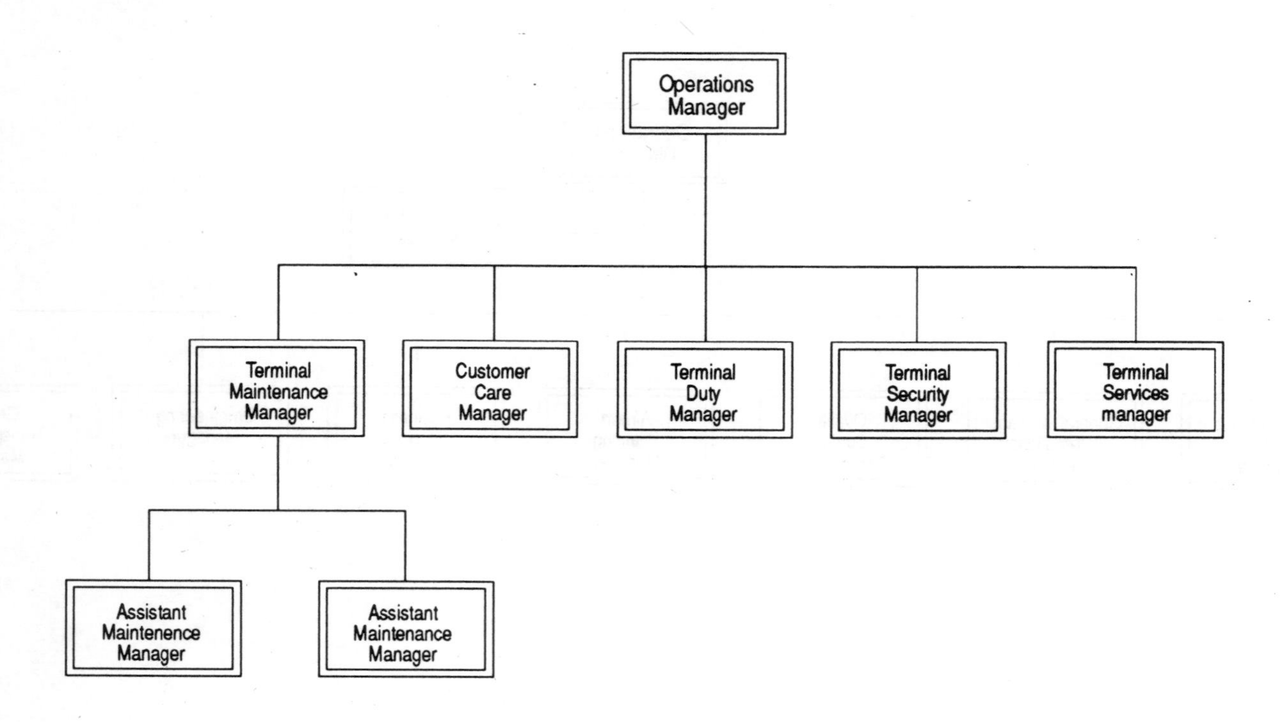

(e) *EAL Commercial management*

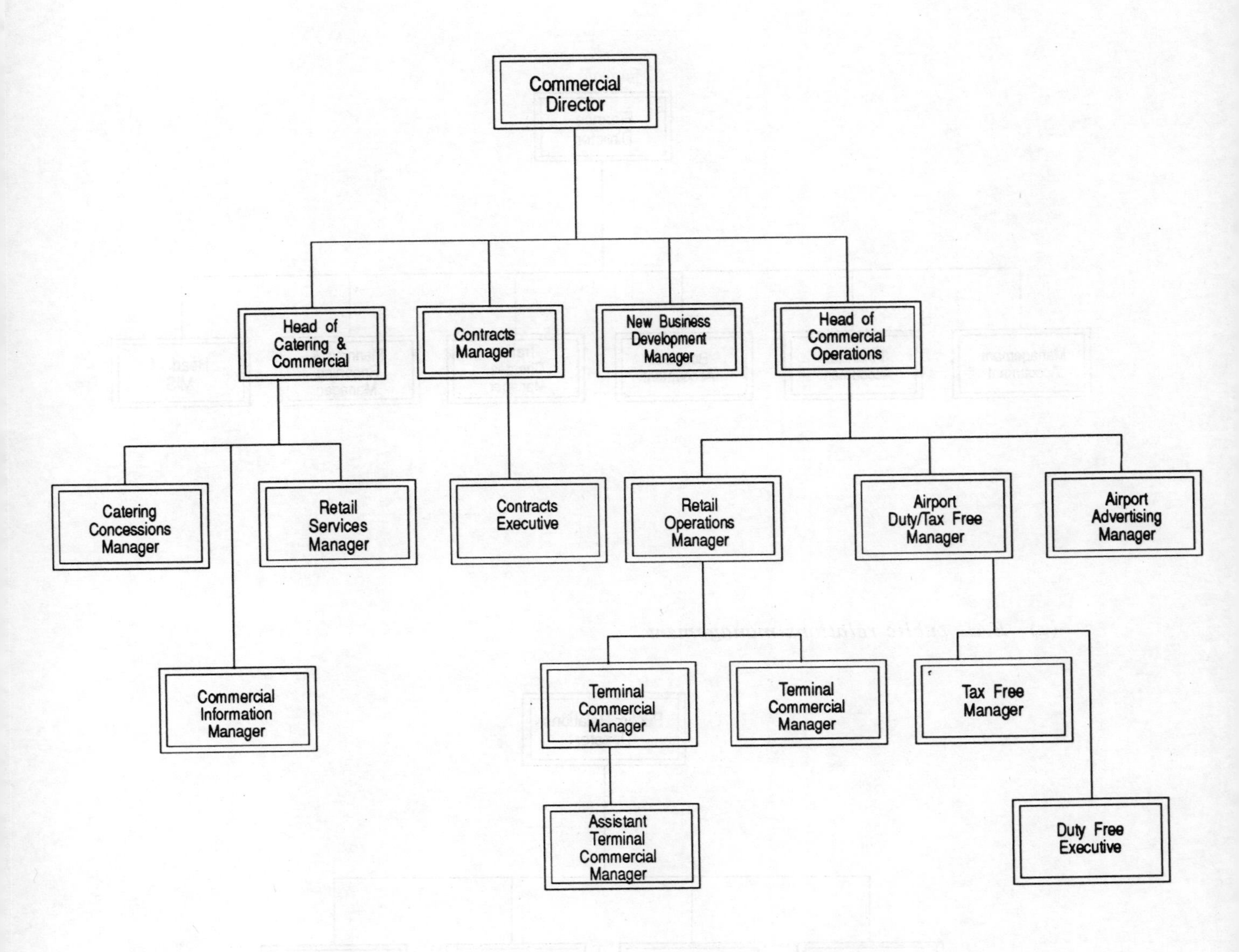

(f) *EAL financial management*

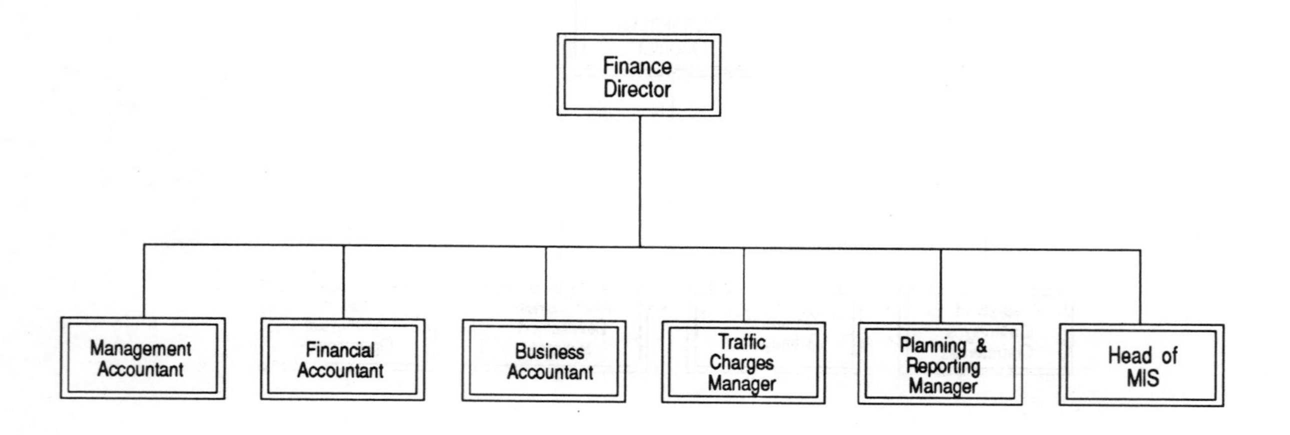

(g) *EAL public relations management*

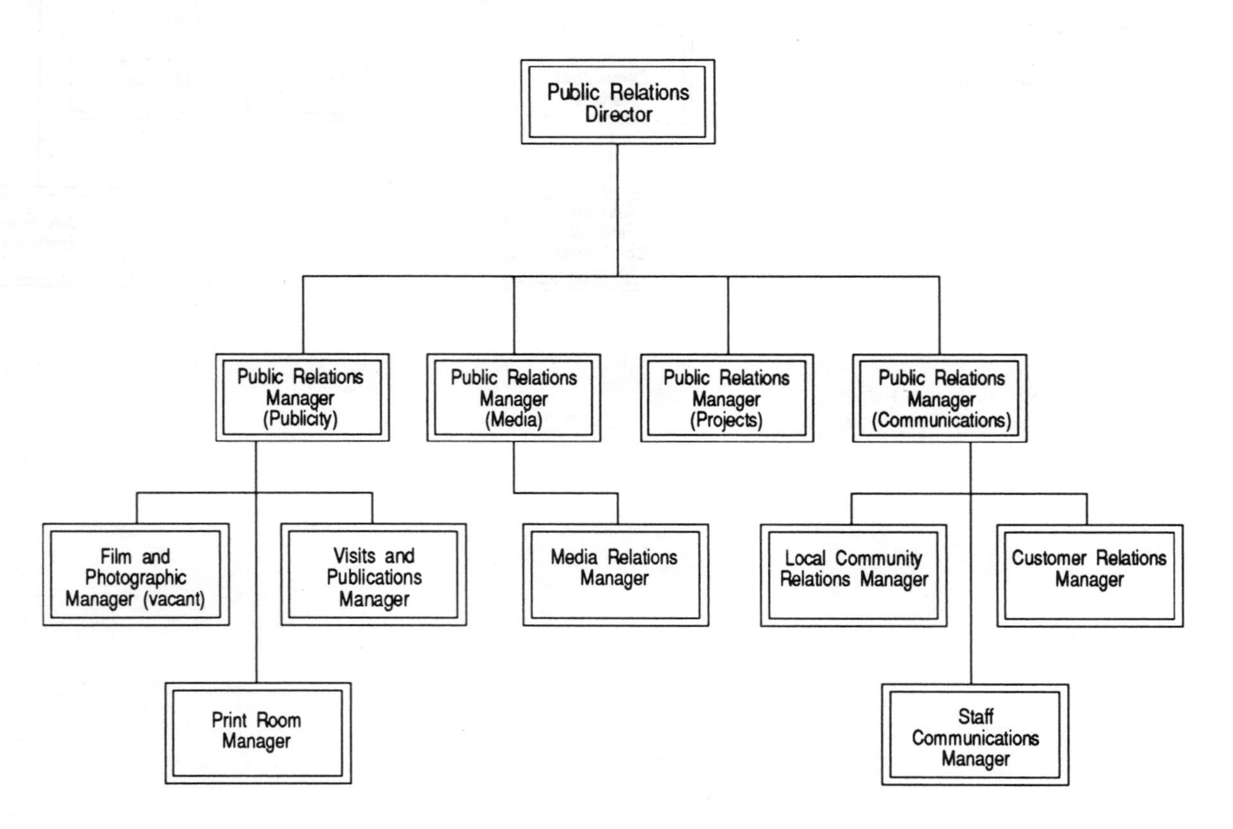

3.14 Appendix 14

Financial information

(a) EAL CONSOLIDATED FOR THE PROFIT AND LOSS ACCOUNT YEAR ENDED 31 MARCH

	1992	*1991*	*1990*	*1989*
	£m	£m	£m	£m
Revenue	220.30	199.50	171.95	154.30
Operating costs	129.65	124.35	134.50	114.20
Operating profit	90.65	75.15	37.45	40.10
Interest receivable	6.15	8.80	8.50	7.25
Profit on ordinary activities before taxation	96.80	83.95	45.95	47.35
Tax on profit on ordinary activities (current year tax charge)	33.40	3.25	20.50	22.10
Profit for the financial year	63.40	80.70	25.45	25.25
Dividends	-	(87.30)	(50.55)	(31.00)
Transfer from general reserve	-	6.60	25.10	5.75
Retained profit*	63.40	-	-	-

* In 1992 the directors did not recommend the payment of a dividend and the retained profit was transferred to reserves.

(b) EAL CONSOLIDATED BALANCE SHEET AS AT 31 MARCH

	1992	*1991*	*1990*	*1989*
	£m	£m	£m	£m
Fixed assets				
Tangible assets	653.15	667.85	562.25	387.20
Current assets				
Debtors	72.60	70.70	53.45	67.65
Creditors: amounts falling due within one year				
Trade	34.10	67.50	44.50	58.30
Other	32.55	32.65	20.65	19.00
Net current assets/(liabilities)	5.95	(29.45)	(11.70)	(9.65)
Total assets less current liabilities	659.1	638.4	550.55	377.55
Creditors: amounts falling due after more than one year	13.30	12.40	12.30	12.30
Net assets	645.80	626.00	538.25	365.25
Capital and reserves				
Called up share capital	190.10	190.10	190.10	190.10
Revaluation reserve	386.35	429.95	335.60	137.50
General reserve	5.95	5.95	12.55	37.65
Retained profit	63.40	-	-	-
Shareholders' funds	645.80	626.00	538.25	365.25

(c) SOURCE AND USE OF FUNDS STATEMENT (CONSOLIDATED) FOR THE YEAR ENDED 31 MARCH

	1992 £m	*1991* £m	*1990* £m	*1989* £m
Source of funds				
Profit for the financial year	86.80	83.95	45.95	47.35
Items not involving the movement of funds				
Depreciation	19.25	19.35	45.50	29.05
Loss on disposal of fixed assets	1.35	0.25	0.75	0.80
Funds generated by operations	117.40	103.55	92.20	77.20
Proceeds from disposal of fixed assets	0.15	0.15	0.30	0.30
	117.55	103.70	92.50	77.50
Use of funds				
Purchase of fixed assets	49.65	31.00	23.50	20.75
Dividends paid	32.60	57.95	47.30	31.00
Tax paid	3.25	20.50	22.10	8.45
	85.50	109.45	92.90	60.20
Movements in working capital				
Increase in debtors	1.90	17.25	(14.2)	21.75
Decrease in trade creditors	33.40	(23.00)	13.80	(4.45)
	35.30	(5.75)	(0.40)	17.30
	117.55	103.70	92.50	77.50

3.15 Appendix 15

MEMORANDUM

28 May 1992

From: Commercial Director

To: New Business Development Manager

Subject: Space Management

Further to memo dated May 21, as you are aware, one of the severe limiting factors to our commercial development is lack of space. In order to find ways of overcoming this problem, I would like you to head a working party, specifically designed to look at ways of ensuring the most efficient possible use is made of the space available to us, thus maximising revenue.

In addition to this, I would particularly like you to consider the extra 1,000 square metres that have been made available to us in the International Terminal, and to consider new businesses that may be suitable.

Following the group's next meeting, I would like a report on the following.

1 Products/services that can be sold from or can operate from small outlets.
2 Ideas for facilities that could be sponsored.
3 Creative ideas for efficient use of space.
4 Creative ideas for producing a high income per square metre.

3.16 Appendix 16

MEMORANDUM

31 May 1992

From: Public Relations Manager

To: New Business Development Manager

I understand from you chat with Norma Bernhardt that you have considerable experience of overcoming local community resistance to site development proposals, in your former position.

We are anticipating further strong protests from local political, environmental and consumer interest groups to our airport development plans and I would like to use your experience in drawing up some counter measures. I have spoken to your Commercial Director about this and he is quite amenable to your spending some time on this very important matter. Please ring my secretary to arrange an hour's preliminary discussion. Perhaps you could start by telling may how your former company tackled these sort of problems.

3.17 **Appendix 17**

Survey of airport shoppers and their buying behaviour: management summary

(a) Over 90% of visitors expect shops and catering facilities at an airport.

(b) About 80% rated duty free shops in their three most important facilities needed at an airport.

(c) Nearly 60% require self-service catering facilities.

(d) Although some 80% of those questioned said they wanted financial services only a quarter of these had actually used them when available.

(e) Airport shoppers are heavily weighted towards the higher social classes.

(f) American and Middle/Far Eastern passengers, although occupying a relatively small proportion of total passengers, nevertheless spend very heavily in gift and personal item outlets.

(g) Shoppers' profiles vary a great deal according to the nature of the concessionnaire. Some concessionnaires attract predominantly female shoppers (eg cosmetics/perfumes), some attract more males (eg socks/ties) and others have a predominance of younger shoppers.

(h) For all nationalities buying behaviour varies significantly according to whether the journey is outbound or homebound. Homebound overseas travellers spend much more heavily on gifts and duty free goods than outbound travellers.

(i) Generally speaking male shoppers are goal-orientated making planned purchases. Compared with females they buy rather than shop. Female shoppers are more inclined to look over all the merchandise and enjoy doing so when having the time.

(j) Stress reducing environments, logical layouts and clear signals have very positive effects on the amount of time and money spent on shopping in any locality, but particularly in airports. Fear of missing the flight and/or not hearing/seeing flight calls or alterations and confusion over gate locations - are all causes of stress which have negative effects on shopping behaviour.

Chapter 16

EURO AIRPORT LTD: PRÉCIS, MARKETING AUDIT, SWOT

This chapter covers the following topics.

1. Introduction
2. Sample précis
3. Marketing audit
4. SWOT analysis

1. INTRODUCTION

1.1 Compare your précis with the three specimens which follow each of which has its own strengths and weaknesses. Note the *lack* of structure in the first specimen, and the use of two different structures in the second and third specimens. Which do you prefer? Which gives you the best handle on the case? In which ways is your own précis better than or worse than these specimens? You should now be ready for your next analytical task.

2. SAMPLE PRÉCIS

2.1 *Sample précis 1*

(a) EAL is a large airport situated in Europe, which owns substantial assets of land and buildings, only small proportion of which are used by millions of passengers who pass through. A major proportion of revenue comes from these passengers. EAL is a part of a group but operates autonomously and hosts most major airlines in the world.

(b) EAL operates 24 hours a day and employs over 25,000 people. It has a diverse range of commercial outlets operating in a concession basis. This is extremely successful and profits generated contribute to the very high costs of maintenance.

(c) EAL is expanding but is constrained by environmental pressures and need to conform to stringent safety standards. New developments have to blend in and consideration of noise containment is a difficult issue.

(d) There has been considerable pressure from consumer protest groups at attempts to extend runways or increase number of flights. Other factors such as government interventions and industrial action both at home and abroad can cause problems but also present opportunities to increase sales at retail outlets.

(e) EAL is committed to quality through the medium of design both in terms of buildings, landscapes and all systems handling internal/external customers. EAL has recently embarked on 'relationship marketing' policies which recognises importance of long-term relationships with customers, suppliers and governmental sources.

(f) EC Finance Ministers' decision to ban 'duty free' goods is a threat as these contribute a considerable proportion of profits and turnover. Opportunities to develop alternative profitable ventures include diversification into hotel business, joint ventures and exploiting Eastern Europe's political changes.

(g) Irma Bergmann has considerable expertise in retailing including sitings and competitor acquisitions. The marketing audit has highlighted certain limitations to develop business; customer perceptions are that airports are expensive: there is limited shopping time and space for retail development. Other problems include bad publicity, difficulties re proliferation of concessions, the international nature of passengers, bureaucracy, traffic congestion and parking difficulties, and the increase in security restrictions.

(h) Although there is an MIS there is a lack of marketing research data to help identify new product/service opportunities and new market segment/niches.

2.2 *Sample précis 2*

(a) *Your role*

Irma Bergmann, recently appointed (1 May 1992) as New Business Development Manager of EAL. You are young, talented and ambitious!

Your CV includes: degree in European Business Studies; CIM Diploma; fluency in English, German and french; career experience as Merchandising Director of prosperous chain of supermarkets operating nationally and internationally. Experience includes buying and selling instore goods, involvement in decisions regarding new store sites and competitor acquisitions (Chapter 15, paragraphs 2.9 to 2.18). You are used to receiving a wide range of MR reports (Chapter 15, paragraph 2.13).

(b) *Type of company*

A large airport situated in Europe with over 25,000 employees. 35% of EAL's revenue is from airline and passenger charges and 65% from commercial activities (Chapter 15, paragraph 2.17). Half of this revenue is accounted for buy duty/tax free shops (Appendix 2: Chapter 15 paragraph 3.2). Total EAL revenue is £220m (Appendix 14: Chapter 15, paragraph 3.14).

(c) *Reason for your appointment*

The Single European Market, created with the aim of eliminating all internal barriers within member countries, threatens the future of duty free sales. Lobbying has been intense on this issue. Duty Free shopping within the EC is to finish 1st July 1999 (Appendices 11,12: Chapter 15, paragraphs 3.11, 3.12).

(d) *Scenario*

EAL is a complicated business. It needs to balance aircraft operations, passenger safety and revenue generation. Because of the impact of a major airport on the surrounding community there are substantial marketing communication issues. There are, in addition, 'green' factors concerned with the use of land, pollution etc.

EAL is the subject of competitive pressure. Other European airports vigorously attract airline business through a combination of lower airline and passenger charges and better facilities (runways, service bays, access etc). It is, in addition, subject to competition from regional airports (Appendices, 1,7,8,9 in Chapter 15 paragraphs 3.1,3.7,3.8, 2.9).

(e) *Major turning point* — The threat/actual abolition of duty free sales within EC countries.

(f) *EAL* — 65% of EAL's revenue is derived from commercial activities. Most of this revenue is derived from a concession system of running what is, in effect, a substantial shopping centre. EAL could be regarded as a medium for delivering customers. EAL is concerned with quality, the design of its buildings, and use of 'relationship marketing'.

2.3 *Sample precis 3*

(a) *Company*

(i) Large airport, situated in Europe. Part of large group, but operates as a strategic business unit.

(ii) EAL sees itself not only as an airport but also as a substantial retail shopping centre, with shops, bars, restaurants and banks.

(iii) EAL is considering expanding to cope with increases in demand for air travel.

(b) *Organisation*

(i) EAL employs over 25,000 people.
(ii) There is some conflict between commercial and operational interests.

(c) *Products and services* (see Appendix 1 of the case, Chapter 15, paragraph 3.1)

(i) Services are provided for three main groups: airline operators; airline passengers; concessionaires.

(ii) The airport is near major business centres and tourist attractions. It has good passenger facilities, over 100 destinations and has plans for major expansion/development. However, it is not close to the city centre. It has congested access routes. It carries a risk of terrorism and it is not actively marketed.

(iii) EAL guarantees any products/services bought at the airport are of equal of comparable price to their equivalent on the High Street (except duty free and Bureau de Change).

(d) *Financial aspects*

(i) EAL owns substantial assets in the form of land and buildings, although only a small proportion of these are actually used.

(ii) Shops etc operate on a concession basis whereby each operator pays a rent plus a percentage of turnover. Income generated (65%) goes towards the high costs of maintaining runways and terminal buildings. Other income sources are from airlines paying to use facilities to operate flights to and from the airport and for each departing passenger (35%).

(iii) The EC intends to ban duty free sales from 1 July 1999 (at the time of writing), which will have a considerable effect on turnover and profits, therefore need to identify other profitable alternatives for income generation.

(e) *Study of accounts* show apparently profitable, creditor/debtor ratio needs studying.

(f) *Profile and promotion*

(i) EAL is conscious of its responsibilities to customers and the community and seeks to be pro-active towards the increasing sensitivity of environmental factors, particularly conservation and anti-pollution. It also has a commitment to quality, and has sought to establish a competitive advantage through design (internal and external).

(ii) EAL has embarked on policies involving relationship marketing, building up long-term relationships with its customers, others in DMU and other publics (eg local government in a partnership approach).

(iii) Marketing research is regularly conducted to monitor passenger profiles and satisfaction levels with all operational aspects.

(iv) Many forms of promotion are used both within and outside the airport.
A marketing audit has commenced.

(g) *Constraints to growth*

(i) Consumer protest groups include: locals (not in my back yard syndrome); environmentalists are putting pressure on the European Parliament (various reasons see Appendix 11, Chapter 15, paragraph 3.11).

(ii) There is traffic congestion in the vicinity of the airport.

(h) *Irma Bergman*

(i) Appointed as New Business Development manager for EAL, Irma was formerly Merchandising Director of prosperous chain of supermarkets operating nationally and internationally. Irma has a degree in European Business Studies, the CIM Diploma and is fluent in French and English.

(ii) Irma has considerable experience in buying and selling instore goods, involved in decisions regarding new store sites and competitor acquisitions.

3. MARKETING AUDIT

CONSULT THE GUIDANCE NOTES FOR THIS TASK: CHAPTER 3 PARAGRAPHS 3.1 TO 3.8
STEP 6 CONDUCT A MARKETING AUDIT
ALLOW YOURSELF ABOUT THREE HOURS FOR THIS TASK

3.1 Have a thoughtful and critical look now at the marketing audit submitted by 'Syndicate B' below.

Marketing audit of EAL

3.2 *General*

Existing, patchy information needs to be augmented and integrated into a marketing information system (MIS). This is likely to require two staff to manage, and an annual budget of £100,000. Personnel should report to a new Director of Marketing.

3.3 *Market size/share*. **The following information is necessary.**

(a) Number of passengers, using headings in Appendix 3 (Chapter 15, paragraph 3.3), broken into domestic, EC, intercontinental.

(b) Number of airlines, flights broken down into domestic, EC, intercontinental.

(c) Cash values of (a) + (b) calculated by reference to average airport fees, average income per passenger from concessionaries.

(d) Market size and share broken down into products etc as in Appendix 2 (Chapter 15, paragraph 3.2).

3.4 *Market trends/forecasts*

(a) Keynote and other published market research reports on air travel (UK, EC and intercontinental).

(b) Surveys of travel agents' expectations, focus groups, 'Delphi' etc (possibly on a syndicate basis) should be conducted.

(c) Surveys of airline expectations as in (b) above are appropriate.

(d) Time series analysis of existing internal data, to provide a check against data revealed by primary research, would be helpful.

3.5 *Company strengths and weaknesses:* as in SWOT analysis (see below)

3.6 *Key features of marketing mix*

(a) Emphasis on quality, design, value for money.

(b) No active marketing of airport, some reactive PR, and concept of relationship marketing being developed.

3.7 *Competitor strengths and weaknesses*

(a) Need for extensive research due to lack of current data (Appendix 10, Chapter 15, paragraph 3.10), building on data in Appendices 8 and 9 (Chapter 15, paragraphs 3.8, 3.19). Requires desk research and visits to other airports.

(b) Need for desk research on other forms of transport (eg Channel Tunnel, Superferries, international railway services).

3.8 *Customer profiles, buying behaviours:* data in Appendices 3 and 17 (Chapter 15, paragraphs 3.3, 2.17) has to be augmented using:

(a) geodemographic surveys;

(b) customer panels (difficult considering customers are in a rush while at the airport, but Users Club members might be willing to attend separate panels;

(c) installation of EPOS (linked to airline tickets database?) at concessionaires (major financial implications - costs shared with concessionaries etc?)

(d) New research on *airline* buying behaviour, (especially price sensitivity), to enable critical success factors to be identified.

3.9 *Environmental factors audit*

(a) Sociological: trend to greater mobility development of niche markets.
(b) Legal: safety, duty free regulations.
(c) Economic: monitor recessions, economic cycle fluctuations.
(d) Political: currency and travel restrictions.
(e) Technological: bigger and quieter plans new technology allowing more efficient processing of passengers.

Comments

3.10 What do you think of it? *Not very good is it?* The first section on the market seems to be more like a marketing research plan than a marketing audit, doesn't it? Where is the marketing audit checklist (go back to Chapter 3) to support this? To what extent has the marketing research been justified? *The syndicate has prematurely moved into decision taking mode instead of remaining in analytical mode.* We hope you have not made this mistake. You shirk the marketing audit at your peril.

Now let us get on with this next analytical job.

4. SWOT ANALYSIS

4.1

CONSULT THE GUIDANCE NOTES FOR THIS TASK IN CHAPTER 3 PARAGRAPHS 3.9 TO 3.13
STEP 7 DO A SWOT ANALYSIS
ALLOW BETWEEN 2 AND 3 HOURS FOR DOING THIS

4.2 Let us have a look now at the SWOT analysis submitted by two syndicates, which follow in the next pages and see how these compare with yours.

(a) The SWOT submitted by 'Syndicate C' is certainly comprehensive but not all the items have been referenced and none of the items have been categorised.

(b) That submitted by 'Syndicate D' is by contrast not so comprehensive but more attempt has been made to categorise by function (M = marketing, F = finance, O = organisation). This syndicate has also categorised the items into degrees of importance (H = high, VH = very high, M = medium, L = low).

4.3 Add these two syndicates' work together with some sub-classification of the marketing items into the marketing mix, and it would be quite a good SWOT analysis for working purposes.

4.4 Euro Airport: SWOT analysis by Syndicate C

	Strengths (Syndicate C)	*Chapter 15*	*Reference*
1	Growth market	Para 2.7	(App 7)
2	Captive market	Para 2.7	(App 7)
3	Plans for expansion	Para 2.7	(App 8)
4	Design awareness/quality commitment		
5	High demand for commercial space	Para 2.7	(App 7)
6	High commercial growth	Para 2.7	(App 7)
7	Many high income passengers	Para 2.7	(App 7)
8	Easily identified target customers	Para 2.7	(App 7)
9	Flexible change-meet customer needs	Para 2.7	(App 7)
10	High street names/branding	Para 2.7	(App 7)
11	Control over concessionnaires	Para 2.7	(App 7)
12	Specialist operators	Para 2.7	(App 7)
13	Management decision-unified approach to marketing		
14	Pricing policy/guarantee		
15	Better debt management	Para 3.14	(App 14)
16	Improving liquidity	Para 3.14	(App 14)
17	Increasing strong sales margin	Para 3.14	(App 14)
18	Increasing ROCE-borrowing potential	Para 3.14	(App 14)
19	Low capital gearing	Para 3.14	(App 14)
20	Support from shareholders	Para 3.14	(App 14)
21	Large well known	Para 3.7	(App 7)
22	Financial support-parent company	Para 3.7	(App 7)
23	Profitability	Para 3.7	(App 7)
24	Increasing retail experience	Para 3.7	(App 7)
25	Good passenger facilities	Para 3.8	(App 8)
26	Good access links	Para 3.7	(App 7)
27	Over 100 destinations	Para 3.8	(App 8)
28	Near tourist attraction	Para 3.8	(App 8)
29	Near business centre	Para 3.8	(App 8)
30	Centralised commercial function	Para 3.7	(App 7)
31	Internal staff publication		
32	Low long haul charges	Para 3.9	(App 9)
33	Low medium hall charges	Para 3.9	(App 9)
34	Acknowledgement of policy on environment		
35	Recruitment of marketing professionals		
36	Long term relationship marketing		
37	Qualitative MR programs		
38	Substantial assets		
39	Regular airport users club		
40	Forward planning to counter		
41	Loss of duty free revenue		

	Weaknesses (Syndicate C)	*Chapter 15 reference*
1	Organisation not commercially oriented	Para 3.7 (App 7)
2	No active marketing	Para 3.8 (App 8)
3	Bad publicity regarding over-exploitation	Para 3.7 (App 7)
4	Limited space for commercial development	Para 3.7 (App 7)
5	Insufficient building land	Para 3.7 (App 7)
6	High building costs	Para 3.7 (App 7)
7	Changes in customer profiles eg Japanese	Para 3.7 (App 7)
8	Image of airports as expensive	
9	Duty free purchases limited	Para 3.7 (App 7)
10	Current ban on night flights	Para 3.7 (App 7)
11	Limited shopping time • security measures • congestion • length of check-in	Para 3.7 (App 7)
12	Difficulty in positioning caused by • proliferation of concessionaires • international nature of passengers	Para 3.7 (App 7)
13	Location facilities restricted operation	Para 3.7 (App 7)
14	Traffic congestion/difficulty in parking	Para 3.7 (App 7)
15	City location: over 10 miles away from town	Para 3.8 (App 8)
16	Staff not in single location	Para 3.7 (App 7)
17	Bureaucracy	Para 3.7 (App 7)
18	Conflict between commercial and operational	Para 3.7 (App 7)
19	Interests	Para 3.7 (App 7)
20	High short haul charges	Para 3.9 (App 9)
21	Assets turnover < 50%	
22	Underdeveloped facilities for concessionaires	
23	Stressed atmosphere	
24	Conflicts between commercial and operations	
25	Dependence on duty free sales	
26	Incomplete market research data - quantitative	
27	Passenger orientated research - lack airlines details	
28	Little room for expansion	
29	Need expertise to deal with environmental issues (PR department)	

	Opportunities	*Chapter 15 reference*	
1	Market growth	Para 3.7	(App 7)
2	EC Harmonisation		
	• new commercial	Para 3.7	(App 7)
	• opportunity	Para 3.7	(App 7)
3	Transfer passengers (Airside)	Para 3.7	(App 7)
4	Increasing passengers		
	• frequency	Para 3.7	(App 7)
	• more leisure	Para 3.7	(App 7)
	• more long haul	Para 3.7	(App 7)
5	New technology		
	• more information on customers	Para 3.7	(App 7)
	• shopping trends		
6	Arrivals: duty free shopping	Para 3.7	(App 7)
7	Proposed new terminal - commercial	Para 3.7	(App 7)
8	New commercial given equal priority at design stage	Para 3.7	(App 7)
9	Additional capacity	Para 3.7	(App 7)
10	Potentially strong brand name	Para 3.7	(App 7)
11	Integration with other transport modes		
12	Captive high income earners		
13	Capitalise on national products		
14	Pricing		
15	Airport - specific pysche of spenders (eg last minute buyers)		
16	Air traffic control delays		
17	Eastern Europe long term development		
18	Increase in Japanese market		
19	American Far East travellers		
20	Spend heavily: growth potential		

Threats (Syndicate C)	*Chapter 15 reference*
1 Competition • airlines (in flights) • regional airports • European airports • alternative transport	(Para 3.7 (App 7)
2 Economic recession (Domestic/international)	Para 3.7 (App 7)
3 Weak foreign exchange - US$	Para 3.7 (App 7)
4 More congestion • additional security • size of aircraft increasing	Para 3.7 (App 7)
5 Traffic congestion on routes to airport	Para 3.7 (App 7)
6 Travel cost increase may limit airport spend	Para 3.7 (App 7)
7 Regulatory bodies • monopoly • EC • legal • government • airport authority • Customs & Excise	Para 3.7 (App 7)
8 Vulnerability to media	Para 3.7 (App 7)
9 Decline in cigarette/tobacco market • advertising restriction • health considerations	Para 3.7 (App 7)
10 Changing patterns of travellers	
11 Natural phenomena (eg storm)	
12 High street shops	
13 Fewer transit passengers 35% (regional airport)	
14 Environmental pressures	
15 Social/economic developments	
16 Declining property value impact on assets value/borrowing	
17 Value reduced	

4.5 Euro Airport Ltd SWOT analysis by Syndicate D

No	*Importance*	*Strengths (Syndicate D)*	*Reference (Chapter 15)*	*Function*
1	H	Large international airport	Para 2.1	
2	M	Autonomy within group		
3	H	Wide customer base	Para 2.1	M/F
4	H	Most major airlines	Para 2.1	
5	L	Over 100 destinations	Para 3.1 (App 1)	
6	H	Well known	Asssumption	M
7	M	24 hour operation	Para 2.2	
8	H	Design	Para 2.7	
9	L	Security good		
10	H	Asset base	Para 2.1	F
11	H	Sound financial base - profitability	Para 3.14 (App 14)	F
12	VH	Appointment of Irma Bergmann	Assumption	O/M
13	M	Long term planning	Paras 3.1 to 3.17 and para 2.9	
14	M	Experience of personnel		
15	L	Location:		
		close to tourist attraction	Para 3.8 (App 8)	O/M
		close to business centres	Para 3.8 (App 8)	O/M
16	L	Specialist operators	Para 2.1	O
17	H	Active market recruitment	Candidates'Brief	O/M
18	H	Commitment to quality	Para 2.7	O/M
19	H	Relationship of quality to marketing policy	Para 2.7	O/M
20	M	Airport users club	Para 2.25	
21	H	Good customer/client knowledge	Appendices	
22	M	Regular marketing research	Para 2.22	
23	M	Retail centre		
24	H	Duty free shops - high income	Para 3.2 (App 2)	
25	H	High street names	Assumption	M
26	L	Controls concessionnaires		O
27	M	Increased retail expertise		O/M
28	H	Growth market	Para 2.4	F/M
29	H	Captive market		
30	H	High demand for commercial	Assumption	F/M
31	H	High income passengers	Para 3.3 (App 3)	F
32	H	Customer service/quality	Para 2.7	M

Key

M = Marketing	H = High importance
F = Finance	M = Medium importance
O = Organisation	L = Low importance

Para references denote paragraphs in Chapter 15, where you will find the case study documentation.

No.	Importance	Weaknesses (Syndicate D)	Reference (Chapter 15)	Function
1	L	High running/maintenance costs	Para 2.1 to 2.5	F
2	L	High development costs	Para 2.4	F
3	M	Congestion/terminals and shops		
4	H	Limited space allocation/development	Para 2.12	O
5	L	Over 10 miles from city centre	Para 3.8 (App 8)	M
6	H	Location restrictions ie noise etc	Para 2.12	O
7	M	Security problems		
8	H	Ban on night flights		O/M
9	H	Limited parking		F
10	H	Lack of airport marketing organisation	Para 3.13 (App 13)	M/O
11	L	Many departments		
12	L	Staff not in single location	Assumption	1O
13	M	Bureaucracy	Para 2.12	O
14	H	Depts conflicts of interest	Para 2.12	O
15	H	Expensive image	Para 2.12	M
16	H	Limited time for shopping	Para 2.12	M
17	L	Limit on duty free sales allowances		F
18	M	Stress/confusion of passenger		M
19	M	Difficulty in accurate merchandising (multi national customers)		
20	H	Difficulty in segmenting Customers		
21	H	Catering - 50% space + 5% revenue		

Key	
M = Marketing F = Finance O = Organisation	H = High importance M = Medium importance L = Low importance

Paragraph references denote paragraphs in Chapter 15, where you will find the case study documentation.

No	*Importance*	*Opportunities (Syndicate D)* *(4 P's + Ansoff)*	*Reference* *(Chapter 15)*	*Function*
1	H	Growth market	Para 2.4	F/M
		• Eastern Europe and CIS	Para 3.3 (App 3)	
		• Female	Para 3.3 (App 3)	6
		• Increased Japanese market	Para 3.3 (App 3)	
		• Visitors - extended exposure time	Para 3.3 (App 3)	
2	H	Freight increasing	Para 2.4	M/F
		Increasing passengers	Para 2.4	M/F
3	M	Development/growth international trade		
4	VH	Tourism/Business opportunities		
5	H	Proposed new terminal,	Para 3.15 (App 15)	M/O/F
6	H	Commercial/design		
7	H	Increase car park	Para 2.12	
8	H	Passenger profile changing	Para 2.12	M/F
9	H	More information on customers	Para 2.21	
10	H	EC harmonisation	Para 2.8	O
11	M	Reduced passport controls	Para 2.8	
12	M	New technology	Para 2.13	M/O
13	L	Flight delays increase retail trade	Para 2.5	
14	M	Increase duty free sales to non-EC passengers	Para 2.10	
15	H	Develop non-duty free sales	Para 2.9	
16	L	Transfer passengers (airside)	Para 2.20	M
17	H	Arrivals duty free	Para 2.20	M
18	H	Building of hotel on land - develop leisure industry	Para 2.9	
19	H	Development of site - extra space	Para 3.15 (App 15)	
20	H	Potentially strong brand	Assumption	
21	H	Develop public relations - environmental issues		
22	L	Increase selling of advertising space		
23	M	Joint ventures • with other means of transport • with other airports, particularly Eastern Europe	Paras 2.3, 2.23	
24	H	Place: • Terminal enlargement • Fax/telephone • Travel agents • Direct bookings • T/A data base • Local business incentive packages	Para 3.8 (App 8)	

No	Importance	*Opportunities (Syndicate D) continued (4 P's + Ansoff)*	*Reference (Chapter 15)*	*Function*
25	H	Price:		M/F
		• Wide promotional media	Para 2.17	
		• Air travel pricing	Para 3.9 (App 9)	
		• Price advantage	Para 3.9 (App 9)	
		• Adjacent tourist market	Para 3.8 (App 8)	
		• Competitive pricing	Para 2.27	
26	H	Promotion:		
		• Internal - POS	Para 2.17	M
		• External - T/A, Direct Mail etc	Para 2.17	M
27	H	After sales:		
		• Database marketing/servicing		M
		• Loyalty		
		• Confidence		
		• Repeat purchase		
		• Guarantee		
		• Money back		

Key	
M = Marketing F = Finance O = Organisation	H = High importance M = Medium importance L = Low importance
Para references denote paragraphs in Chapter 15, where you will find the case study documentation.	

No	Importance	Threats (Syndicate D)	Reference	Function
1	M	Increased risk of terrorism	Para 2.24	O
		• Increased security procedures		
2	M	Congestion	Para 2.12	
		• Security		O
		• Size of aircraft/including passengers		O
3	L	Increased cost of travel		F
4	H	Traffic congestion	Throughout	
5	H	Environmental pressure issues/groups	Para 2.5	
6	L	Air traffic controllers' strikes	Para 2.4	O
		• Industrial action		
7	M	Competition/airlines	Para 2.24	M
8	L	Alternative forms of transport	Para 2.23	
9	L	Price relative to alternative suppliers	Para 2.12	
10	H	Vulnerability to media	Para 3.11 (App 11)	
11	H	Bad publicity	Para 2.12	M
12	H	Airline in-flight sales	Para 2.24	
13	H	Loss of duty free shops	Para 2.8	
14	H	Importance of duty free	Para 3.2 (App 2)	
15	L	Decline in cigarette/tobacco and drinks markets	Assumption	M/F
16	L	Exchange rates	Assumption	F
17	M	Economic recession	Assumption	F
18	L	Sensitivity to European trends	Assumption	
19	L	Inflation/tax changes	Assumption	
20	M	Regulatory bodies		
21	M	Foreign approval procedures		
22	M	Fewer transfers	Para 2.20	
23	M	Competition from non EEC countries	Para 3.11 (App 11)	
24	M	Advertising restrictions on alcoholic drinks/cigarettes	Para 3.7 (App 7)	

Key	
M = Marketing F = Finance O = Organisation	H = High importance M = Medium importance L = Low importance
Para references denote paragraphs in Chapter 15, where you will find the case study documentation.	

5. CONCLUSION

5.1 Check how your SWOT compared, and proceed to the next chapter.

Chapter 17

EURO AIRPORT LTD: ANALYSIS OF APPENDICES

This chapter covers the following topics.
1. General analysis of tables and memoranda in the appendices
2. An accountant's view of EAL's accounts: Appendix 14

1. GENERAL ANALYSIS TABLES OF TABLES AND MEMORANDA IN THE APPENDICES

CONSULT THE GUIDANCE NOTES FOR THIS TASK IN CHAPTER 3 PARAGRAPHS 3.14 TO 3.17
STEP 8 CONDUCT ANALYSES/CROSS ANALYSES OF THE APPENDICES
ALLOW ABOUT 2 TO 3 HOURS FOR THIS JOB

1.2 Having done your own analyses, you can now compare them with the specimens which follow. In the tables which follows, the appendices are analysed as references to other parts of the case where this is relevant.

Appendix (Chapter 15)	*What it is essentially saying*	*How does it help us?*	*Which other appendices or text can it be related to? (Chapter 15)*	*If so, what extra information insights does this reveal?*
1 (para 3.1)	Wide range of services provided Broad customer types	Provides product range and high level market segmentation	Para 2.12, 2.13 App 2,7,10,15,17 (paras 3.2,3.7,3.10,3.15,3.17)	Can identify areas of weakness/ strength and potential opportunity Passenger perception of airport
2 (para 3.2)	Gives share of revenue and share of space for a range of services provided	Reveals large variation in efficiency in these terms, suggesting possible room for improvement. See chart appended	App 1,4,6,7,10,11,12,15,17 (paras 3.1,3.4,3.6,3.7,3.10, 3.11,3.12,3.15,3.17)	Space gained from duty free, new terminal and 1,000 sq m needs to be used against these efficiency measures
3 (para 3.3)	Consumer profile of our passengers contrasting domestic and international	Market identification Market segmentation Competitor comparisons	Para 2.22 App 4,6,7,9,11,14,17 (paras 3.4,3.6,3.7,3.9,3.11, 3.14,3.17)	Which customers are highest spenders on what sorts of goods and services so that we can tailor our marketing mix and maximise our revenue
4 (para 3.4)	Commercial facilities at domestic and international terminals	Can compare the terminals Domestic terminal has not duty free International terminal has more luxury outlets	App 2,3,6,7,9,11,14,17 (paras 3.2,3.3,3.6,3.7,3.9, 3.11, 3.14,3.17)	To analyse revenue generating potential by facility and tailor retail mix accordingly
5 (para 3.5)	Factors governing performance - split into internal and external	Tells us that EAL work in a complex and changing environment. Suggest areas for future planning Indicates performance measures/controls	App 7,8,11,15,16,17 (paras 3.7,3.8,3.11,3.15, 3.16,3.17)	Identifies areas for SWOT analysis and the marketing audit

CASE APPENDICES - ANALYSIS/CROSS ANALYSIS

Appendix (Chapter 15)	*What it is essentially saying*	*How does it help us?*	*Which other appendices or text can it be related to? (Chapter 15)*	*If so, what extra information insights does this reveal?*
6 (Para 3.6)	Marketing research Information available	Gives general areas covered by MR - can omit these from MR plan	App 7,8,11,16,17 (paras 3.7,3.8,3.11,3.16,3.17)	By default. Indicates areas where further MR is needed
7 (Para 3.7)	SWOT analysis incomplete	Future marketing planning	Most of case's text App 8,14 (paras 3.8,3.14)	Consolidates information and confirms areas for action
8 (Para 3.8)	Some characteristics of EAL versus other main European airports	Establishes our positioning Supplies further strengths and weaknesses	Paras 2.1 to 2.8 App 6,7 (paras 3.6,3.7)	Relative advantages for exploitation. PR planning
9 (Para 3.9)	League table of airport charges for long, medium and short haul routes	Establishes our price positioning	Paras 2.17 and 2.18 App 3,4,6 (paras 3.3,3.4,3.6)	Competitor analysis for marketing planning. Need to compensate price weaknesses Mr to establish importance of price
10 (Para 3.10)	Irma's involvement in new terminal, competitor surveys and importance in organisation	Gives insights into future plans Establishes Irma's authority	Candidates' brief Paras 2.9 to 2.14 App 8,12,13,15,16 (paras 3.8,2.13,3.13,1.15,3.16)	Company have high expectations of Irma. Need to set priorities and schedule
11 (Para 3.11)	Decision of EC to abolish duty free by July 1st 1999 Potential effects on other airports Anti-airport expansion lobby	Indicate potential resistance to development plans	Paras 2.5 to 2.12 App 2,6,7,8,10,14,15,16 (paras 3.2,3.6,3.7,3.8, 3.10,3.14,3.15,3.16)	Strong PR policy needed MR needed
12 (Para 3.12)	Telling Irma to work on generating viable ideas	Suggests likely exam question Company recognises problem Need to find new profitable business	Paras 2.9 to 2.12 App 2,4,6,7,11,17 (paras 3.2,3.4,3.6,3.7,3.11,3.17)	Commercial director looking to Irma for solutions. Although long term company want to start planning now.

CASE APPENDICES - ANALYSIS/CROSS ANALYSIS

Appendix (Chapter 15)	*What it is essentially saying*	*How does it help us?*	*Which other appendices or text can it be related to? (Chapter 15)*	*If so, what extra information insights does this reveal?*
13 (Para 3.13)	Organisation charts show highly complex multi-layered organisation. Apparent anomalies in responsibilities	Helps to explain the conflict between Opns and Commercial. Confirms that EAL are not yet fully marketing oriented	Para 2.12 (4 and 8) App 5,10,12 (paras 3.5,3.10, 3.12)	Organisational bureaucracy and conflict could constrain Irma's plans to develop new profitable business
14 (Para 3.14)	Company accounts last 4 years indicate reasonably healthy financial position and growth	Provides re-assurance for future plans and challenge to sustain improvement	App 10,15 (paras 3.10,3.15)	Sufficient ability to generate funds for expansion - see accountants view of these accounts appended
15 (Para 3.15)	That 1,000 sq m of extra space is available to us in the International terminal	Opportunity to develop new business Confirms Irma's position - she is to head up working party	App 3,4,12,7 (paras 3.3,3.4,3.13,3.7)	Re-inforces possibility of exam question on this area and need for competitor research
16 (Para 3.16)	That Irma has experience in handling NIMBY syndrome which is valued by PR Director	Adds to Irma's position and worth Widens her potential contribution to future marketing strategy	Paras 2.26 to 2.28 App 7: Threats 8,11 (paras 3.2,3.3,3.4,3.6,3.15)	Numerous strong protest groups are threat to future expansion
17 (Para 3.17)	Airport shoppers buying behaviour and profiles differ	Suggests difficulty in positioning and need for market segmentation	Paras 2.24 to 2.28 App 2,3,4,6,15 (paras 3.2,3.3,3.4,3.6,3.15)	Opportunities to gain profitable new business from existing customers via segmentation strategies

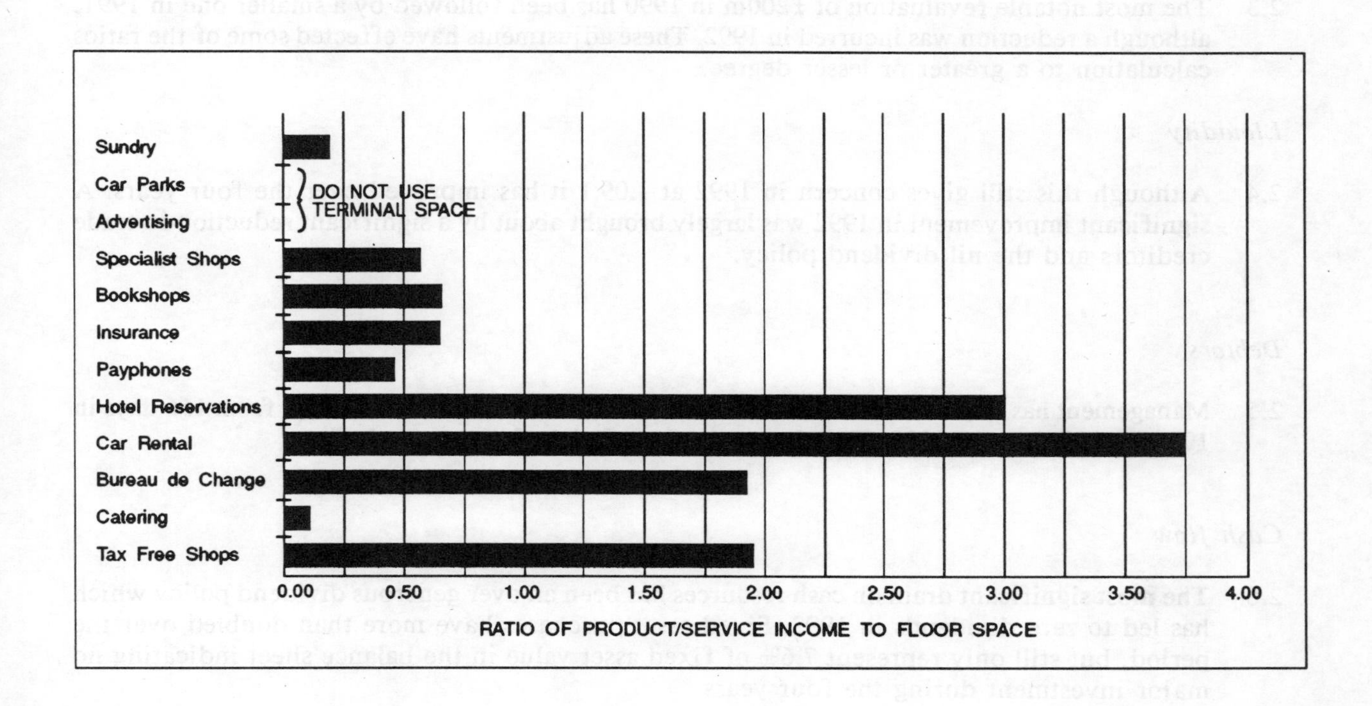

The above needs augmenting with data on costs in order to calculate profitability.

2. AN ACCOUNTANT'S VIEW OF EAL'S ACCOUNTS: APPENDIX 14

Summary

2.1 EAL has increased return on net assets from 12.96% in 1989 to 14.99% in 1992. This has largely been achieved through improved sales margins. A precarious liquidity position has been improved from 1:0.88 to 1:1.09 between 1989 and 1992. The company has pursued a generous dividend policy between 1989 and 1991 although the announcement of zero dividends in 1992 indicates the company has come to special arrangements with shareholders possibly with a view to retaining earnings for future growth.

Profitability: (ROCE)

2.2 A fall from 12.96% in 1989 to 8.54% in 1990 was brought about by profit margins falling from 30.69% to 26.72% and asset turnover falling from 0.42 to 0.32 during the same period. The latter was particularly affected by some £200m asset revaluation during 1990. Since this blip, ROCE has recovered to 17.99% in 1992 due to drastically improved sales margins, 43.94% in 1992 largely achieved through operating costs being reduced from 78% of sales in 1990 to 59% in 1992. This indicates notable achievements on cost efficiency.

Revaluation of assets

2.3 The most notable revaluation of £200m in 1990 has been followed by a smaller one in 1991, although a reduction was incurred in 1992. These adjustments have effected some of the ratios calculation to a greater or lesser degree.

Liquidity

2.4 Although this still gives concern in 1992 at 1.09:1 it has improved over the four years. A significant improvement in 1992 was largely brought about by a significant reduction in trade creditors and the nil dividend policy.

Debtors

2.5 Management has improved drastically in this area with the reduction of 37 days from 156 days in 1989 to 119 days in 1992. This has had a beneficial effect on cash flow.

Cash flow

2.6 The most significant drain on cash resources has been an over generous dividend policy which has led to zero dividends in 1992. Fixed asset purchases have more than doubled over the period, but still only represent 7.6% of fixed asset value in the balance sheet indicating no major investment during the four years.

Tax

2.7 A significant tax adjustment in 1991 profit and loss account signifies overpayment in previous years. This helped the cash flow situation in 1992.

Dividend

2.8 The dividend cover between 1989 and 1991 was consistently less than unity indicating an extremely generous policy possibly looked on favourably by shareholders. However, a critical cash flow and liquidity position in 1992 has partially been avoided by a zero dividend policy. This would have been agreed by shareholders although one would imagine the company's~share price has suffered as a result.

2.9 FIXED ASSETS

	£m		£m
1988-1989			
Opening balance	396.60	Depreciation	29.05
Purchases	20.75	Sales	1.10
		c/d 31/3/1989	387.20
	417.35		417.35
1989-1990			
B/d 1/4/1989	387.20	Depreciation	45.50
Purchases	23.50	Sale	1.05
Rev	198.10	c/d 31/3/1990	562.25
	608.80		608.80
1990-1991			
b/d 1/4/1990	562.25	Depreciation	19.25
Purchases	31.00	Sale	0.40
Rev	94.35	c/d 31/3/1991	667.85
	687.60		687.60
1991-1992			
b/d 1/4/1991	667.85	Depreciation	19.25
Purchases	49.65	Sale	1.50
		Rev	43.60
		c/d 31/3/1992	653.15
	717.50		717.50

2.10 *Dividends*

		£m
Year to 31 March 1989:	Accrued (P & L)	31.00
	Paid out (Source & Apps)	(31.00)
		-
Year to 31 March 1990:	Accrued (P & L)	50.55
	Paid out (Source & Apps)	47.30
Carried down		3.25
Year to 31 March 1991:	Brought down	3.25
	Accrued (P & L)	87.30
	Paid out (Source & Apps)	57.95
Carried down		32.60
Year to 31 March 1992:	Brought down	32.60
	Accrued (P & L)	-
	Paid out	32.60
Owing at 1/4/1992		NIL

There will still be a cash outflow of £32.6m in the year to 31 March 1992.

2.11 *Profit ratios*

	1992	*1991*	*1990*	*1989*
(a) ROCE (Profit before tax / Capital employed)	96.80 / 645.80	83.95 / 626.00	45.95 / 538.25	47.35 / 365.25
	= 14.95%	= 13.41%	= 8.54%	= 12.96%
(b) Profit Margin (Profit before tax / Sales revenue)	96.80 / 220.30	83.95 / 199.50	45.95 / 171.95	47.35 / 154.30
	= 43.94%	= 42.08%	= 26.72%	= 30.69%
(c) Asset turnover (Sales revenue / Capital employed)	220.30 / 645.80	199.50 / 626.00	171.95 / 538.25	154.30 / 365.25
	= 34.11%	= 31.87%	= 31.95%	= 42.24%
(d) Operating cost as percentage of revenue	59%	62.3%	78%	74%

2.12 *Solvency ratios*

(a) Liquidity ratio	72.60 / 66.65	70.70 / 100.15	53.45 / 65.15	67.65 / 77.30
	= 1.09	= 0.71	= 65.15	= 77.3
(b) Debtors' ageing	72.60 / 220.30	70.70 / 199.50	53.45 / 171.95	67.65 / 154.30
	= 119 days	= 128 days	= 112 days	= 156 days

3. CONCLUSION

3.1 It is now time to move to the next two steps.

Chapter 18

EURO AIRPORT LTD: SITUATIONAL ANALYSIS, KEY ISSUES, MISSION STATEMENT, BROAD AIMS, MAJOR PROBLEMS

This chapter covers the following topics.

1. Introduction
2. Situational analysis (by Syndicate D2)
3. Situational analysis (by Syndicate C2)
4. Situational analysis (by Syndicate B1)
5. Decide key issues
6. Mission statements and broad aims
7. Major problems

1. INTRODUCTION

1.1 It is now time to move on to the next two steps.

CONSULT THE GUIDANCE NOTES IN CHAPTER 3, PARAGRAPHS 3.18 TO 3.28
STEP 9 RECONSIDER YOUR PRÉCIS, MARKETING AUDIT AND SWOT ANALYSIS **STEP 10 CONDUCT A SITUATIONAL ANALYSIS**
ALLOW BETWEEN 2 AND 3 HOURS FOR COMPLETING THESE STEPS

1.2 When you have completed your situational analysis please compare it with the three specimens which follow.

1.3 It is interesting to note the three treatments which are given in decreasing order of complexity. Syndicate B1's is extremely succinct. Do you find it more or less helpful than the others? Do you agree with it?

Remember, this is something you will need to consult in the exam.

2. SITUATIONAL ANALYSIS (BY SYNDICATE D2)

2.1 *External factors*

(a) Economic

(i) Inflation
(ii) Growth in consumer expenditure
(iii) Performance of overseas economies
(iv) Exchange rates
(v) Changes in taxation
(vi) Propensity to spend

(b) Political/legal

(i) Foreign approval procedures
(ii) Changes in taxation
(iii) Abolishing duty free tax
(iv) EEC regulations
(v) Government intervention
(vi) Industrial actions
(vii) Threat of terrorism
(viii) Laws on safety, security and noise

(c) Socio-cultural

(i) Growth in passenger numbers
(ii) Changes in passenger types
(iii) Propensity to spend
(iv) Global changes in consumer tastes
(v) Customer perceptions
(vi) Changes in demographics
(vii) Increase in business travel

(d) Technological

(i) Airline performance
(ii) Air traffic control delays
(iii) Retail point of sale
(iv) Advances in IT and communication processors

(e) Competition

(i) Price relative to alternative suppliers
(ii) Other types of transport
(iii) Other airports

(f) Environment

(i) Noise pollution
(ii) Building design
(iii) Air pollution
(iv) Use of land
(v) Traffic congestion

2.2 *Internal factors*

(a) Sales and finance

(i) Strong assets (land and building)
(ii) Sufficient funds
(iii) Group support
(iv) Profitability
(v) Revenue £220 million
(vi) 35% revenue airline and passenger charges
(vii) 65% concessions and other income
(viii) Dependent on EEC duty free goods

(b) Price

(i) Airline
(ii) Competitively priced on long and medium haul route, expensive on short haul
(iii) Airline passengers
(iv) Competitively priced in retail shops (comparable to high street prices)

(c) Product

(i) Extensive product/service range for all customers

(d) Promotion

(i) Not perceived as actively promoting
(ii) Conduct on-off airport and regular airport users Club
(iii) Large PR department

3. SITUATIONAL ANALYSIS (BY SYNDICATE C2)

3.1 External

(a) Current recession
(b) Long term increase in demand for air travel
(c) Competition from alternative forms of transport and other airports
(d) Larger planes, greater safety and more information available on customers and shopping trends
(e) Abolition of duty free sales in 1999
(f) Increasing involvement environmental pressure group and lobbying
(g) Increasing legislation to protect environment

3.2 Internal

(a) EAL strives to offer a quality service
(b) It offers a wide range of these services with opportunities to improve and expand further
(c) Wide range of promotion forms but no plan
(d) Competitive pricing for long and medium haul routes but relatively expensive for short haul.
(e) Captive market
(f) Near tourist attraction and major business centre
(g) Marketing research regularly carried out, but gaps

(h) Complex organisational structure, emphasis on operational departments, but no marketing
(i) Financial generally healthy

4. SITUATIONAL ANALYSIS (BY SYNDICATE B1)

4.1 EAL is a major European Airport which has substantial assets, and has achieved profitable growth.

4.2 We need to establish substantial marketing activity to determine our customers' needs, with a view to maximising revenue and profit from airlines and passengers, and with a view to establishing the viability of the new terminal.

4.3 We need a PR/Marketing communications plan to offset potential opposition to the new terminal In the longer term (five to seven years) we need to replace duty-free sales with a profitable new business. Internal marketing is needed to inform and motivate the workforce, and to improve team work

5. DECIDE KEY ISSUES

5.1 You are reminded that the next step is probably the most important one since it has the most bearing on the likely exam question areas.

READ THE GUIDANCE NOTES FOR THIS STEP IN CHAPTER 3 PARAGRAPHS 4.1 TO 4.3
STEP 11 DECIDE THE KEY ISSUES
ALLOW AND HOUR TO ONE AND A HALF HOURS TO DO THIS

5.2 You are also reminded to limit these to a *maximum of six* and that you might like to construct a list of candidate key issues which could then be ranked, as a way of doing this exercise.

5.3 Remember also the technique of parcelling up several minor issues into one major issue as described in Chapter 3 paragraph 4.1

5.4 Now that you have completed this crucial exercise, please compare your conclusions with those produced by six separate syndicates as given on the next page.

5.5 **EURO AIRPORT LTD - KEY ISSUES**

Syndicate A1 1 Duty free changes 2 Environmental pressures 3 Development of fully integrated marketing organisation 4 Commercial vs operations conflict 5 Communication/access to airport	*Syndicate C1* 1 Duty free abolition 2 Relationship MKG - internal/external 3 New terminal and space utilisation 4 Environmental issues 5 MR/MIS 6 Organisation
Syndicate A2 1 1999 - loss of duty free 2 New terminal 3 Communications - internal/external 4 Environmental issues 5 Competition	*Syndicate B2* 1 Duty free abolition 2 Environmental issues - space etc 3 Internal organisational conflict 4 Competition ↑ 5 Poor image 6 Changes in customer demographics
Syndicate C2 1 Loss of duty free 1999 2 Lack of marketing orientation 3 Space constraints 4 Environmental lobbying 5 ↑ Competition 6 Customer profile change	*Syndicate D2* 1 Abolition duty free 2 Commercial vs operations conflict 3 New terminal 4 Marketing orientation 5 Changes in customer profile/bb 6 Re-definition of retail/service mix

Note the very high degree of unanimity.

Let us now move forward again to the next two steps.

6. MISSION STATEMENT AND BROAD AIMS

PLEASE CONSULT THE GUIDANCE NOTES IN CHAPTER 3 PARAGRAPHS 4.4 TO 4.14
STEP 12 DEVELOP A MISSION STATEMENT **STEP 13 DECIDE BROAD AIMS**
ALLOW ABOUT AN HOUR FOR EACH OF THESE STEPS

6.1 Remember that there should be consistency between your mission statement and your broad aims, also that you should try to limit the latter for four bearing in mind the need to convert these into quantified and time-scaled objectives at a later stage.

6.2 Having completed these two steps you can now compare your results with those of seven separate syndicates given on the following pages.

6.3 Did you find your broad aims were similar to any of these?

(a)

Syndicate A1

Mission

As an established major airport, EAL aims to safely, securely and profitably develop and maintain its service base to meet all our varied customer needs with maximum environmental consideration.

Broad aims

1 To become the airport of first choice as a gateway for international and domestic groups.

2 To expand and develop our retail experience.

3 To deliver a more positive image as a provider of environmental products and services at reasonable prices.

4 To reduce dependence on space as a prime determinant of profitability.

5 To create an integrated function responsible for co-ordinating marketing.

6 To continue to maintain and develop our policy of relationship marketing.

(b)

Syndicate B1

Mission

As the most innovative airport and retail centre at the heart of Europe, our mission is to develop our business into the most profitable, safe and enjoyable travel experience in the world.

Broad aims

1 To improve the profitable employment of all available space.

2 To find and implement profitable replacement services to offset loss of EC duty free revenue.

3 To evolve an organisation structure which will ensure the efficient and profitable transfer of customers.

4 To ensure all future development is in consideration of the environment and meets public approval.

(c)

Syndicate C1

Mission

EAL aims to be the airport of first choice for all users, investors and employees; whilst at the same time being aware of and assisting, rather than adding to, environmental problems

Broad aims

1 To become a more marketing-oriented and integrated company.
2 To maximise and develop existing and new sources of income.
3 To maintain and develop a high standard of customer care and security.
4 To develop business strategies which are sensitive to community and environmental needs.

(d)

Syndicate D1

Mission

To provide excellent facilities for the domestic and international air travel industry including services for airline operators, airline passengers, air freight and retail concessionnaires. EAL seeks to profitably develop its current business to cater for the increasing demand for air travel, whilst having due regard for the environment, the community and the safety/security of its customers.

Broad aims

1 To replace duty free sales with other equally or more profitable business.

2 To reduce internal departmental conflict and become more marketing orientated.

3 To manage effectively external environmental pressures.

4 To develop policies of relationship marketing and quality design.

5 To use efficiently the limited space and resources to increase profitability.

6 To continue to provide quality services to all customers.

(e)

Syndicate B2

Mission

To be the number one international airport by providing maximum service satisfaction to all our customers trough a unified approach to quality, with consideration for the environment.

Broad aims

1 To be the number one international airport.
2 To develop alternative sources of revenue.
3 To be unified in our commitment to the customer.
4 To be environmentally responsible.

(f)

Syndicate C2

Mission

To provide a wide range of high quality services to all our customers by drawing on the skills and expertise of our workforce, whilst remaining environmentally sensitive

Broad aims

1 To reduce the impact of the loss of duty free sales.
2 To be marketing orientated.
3 To maintain profitable growth.
4 To be environmentally sensitive.

(g)

Syndicate D2

Mission

To be the European market leader providing quality services and facilities by responding to the changing needs of our passengers, airlines and concessionnaires in a profitable and environmentally conscious way

Broad aims

1 To replace the revenue from lost duty-free sales.
2 To be a more integrated and marketing led organisation.
3 To achieve long-term growth and profitability.
4 To be sensitive to environmental issues.

6.4 We are now on the way back to analytical mode.

7. MAJOR PROBLEMS

CONSULT THE GUIDANCE NOTES GIVEN IN CHAPTER 3 PARAGRAPHS 4.15 TO 4.18
STEP 14 IDENTIFY AND ANALYSE MAJOR PROBLEMS
ALLOW BETWEEN TWO AND THREE HOURS TO DO THIS TASK

7.1 **Remember to restrict yourself to six major problems in rank order.**

7.2 **Do not worry if your major problems relate closely with the key issues. This is quite usual.**

7.3 **Having done this, you can now compare your ranking with those of seven syndicates provided below.**

7.4 **EURO AIRPORT CIM CASE - PROBLEM ANALYSIS**

Item		*Rankings*						
		A1	*B1*	*C1*	*D1*	*B2*	*C2*	*D2*
1	Loss of duty free sales	1	1	3	1	1		1
2	Organisation/conflict	2	2	1	2	6	2	2
3	Security/safety	3		5			6	
4	Environmental issues	4	4	4		2	4	3
5	Communications/access/traffic congestion	5		6	5		5	
6	Increased competition	6	3			4	3	6
7	Space management			2		3		4
9	Poor image				6	7		
10	Changing customer profiles					5		5
11	Retail mix						1	

There is a high degree of unanimity here - as indeed with the key issues and broad aims. Make your mind up individually and identify which are more short-term and which are longer-term.

8 CONCLUSION

8.1 **Once you have decided what the major problems are, you are ready to move forward to your plan.**

Chapter 19

EURO AIRPORT LTD: MARKETING PLANNING

This chapter contains the following plans.

1. Introduction
2. Sample outline plan (by Syndicate B1)
3. Sample outline plan (by Syndicate A2)
4. Sample outline plan (by Syndicate C1)
5. Detailed plan
6. Space management plan
7. Possible opportunities for developing business
8. Environmental issues

1. INTRODUCTION

1.1 We strongly recommend you now re-read the notes provided for the Brewsters' practice run, and that you opt to produce an *outline* plan before developing this into the complete *detailed* marketing plan required as follows.

CONSULT THE GUIDANCE NOTES GIVEN IN CHAPTER 3 PARAGRAPHS 4.19 TO 6.8
STEP 15 DEVELOP QUANTIFIED, TIMESCALED OBJECTIVES **STEP 16 CONSIDER ALTERNATIVE STRATEGIES. SELECT THOSE MOST APPROPRIATE** **STEP 17 DRAW UP DETAILED TACTICAL PLANS COVERING THE MARKETING ORIENTATION** **STEP 18 DRAW UP A MARKETING RESEARCH PLAN** **STEP 19 CONSIDER ORGANISATIONAL ISSUES, CHANGES AND MARKETING ORIENTATION** **STEP 20 CONSIDER ORGANISATIONAL CULTURE AND NEED FOR INTERNAL MARKETING** **STEP 21 DETERMINE THE FINANCIAL/HR RESOURCE IMPLICATIONS OF YOUR PLANS** **STEP 22 ASSESS COSTS AND DRAW UP INDICATIVE BUDGETS** **STEP 23 DRAW UP SCHEDULES GIVING TIMINGS/SEQUENCE OF ACTIONS** **STEP 24 SPECIFY REVIEW PROCEDURES AND CONTROL MECHANISMS** **STEP 25 DRAW UP OUTLINE CONTINGENCY PLANS** **STEP 26 REVIEW YOUR COMPLETE MARKETING PLAN**
YOU WILL NEED BETWEEN 15 AND 18 HOURS TO DO THIS MAJOR TASK

1.2 Having completed your outline plan you might like to compare thoughts with the syndicates whose first attempts follow - namely syndicates B1, A2, C1.

1.3 Please then flesh out your own outline plan into more detail before looking at the developments offered by other syndicates.

1.4 At this point we need to advise that whereas a complete marketing plan is intended to cover you for all eventualities, it cannot of course provide *all* the detail that might be needed for a specific examination question. You will therefore have to add detail as required in the examination itself. Moreover, the CIM reserves the right to introduce additional material to you in the examination hall.

1.5 However, in anticipation of examination questions signalled in the case study some syndicate will prepare extra materials on, say, organisation or financial implications.

(a) You will find specimens of such further attempts in the more fleshed out plan of syndicate A who have recognised EAL as being essentially in *service marketing* and who have therefore submitted a '7P' marketing mix.

(b) Syndicate C3 anticipated a question on space management and put some extra thoughts down on this.

(c) As an example of lateral or creative thinking please have a look at the flow chart provided by syndicate D2.

(d) Finally, you will find a submission on environmental issues by syndicate B2 in anticipation of a question on this aspect.

1.6 You must now get your preparations finalised for second mock exam before turning to the exam paper which follows in the next chapter.

2. SAMPLE OUTLINE PLAN (BY SYNDICATE B1)

2.1 Mission statement

As an established major airport and retail centre, EAL aims to safely, securely and profitably develop its high quality service base to cater for increasing demand and our varied customer needs, whilst continuing to be environmentally considerate.

2.2 Objectives

(a) To increase overall turnover to £300m by 2003.
(b) To become fully marketing orientated within five years.
(c) To increase awareness and improve perceptions of our services within 12 months.

2.3 **Strategy**

NEW PRODUCTS	DIVERSIFICATION 1 New hotel 2 Exhibitions/conference facilities 3 Leisure facilities 4 New visitor centre	PRODUCT DEVELOPMENT 1 New terminal 2 Improved transport links to airport 3 Improving existing facilities eg signage 4 Improve car parking
EXISTING PRODUCTS	MARKET DEVELOPMENT 1 Improve MIS 2 Increase number of flights 3 Attract more customer groups eg Japanese	PENETRATION 1 Restructuring of concessionnaires 2 Pricing policies 3 Promotion: salesforce, advertising PR 4 Efficient use of space 5 Review company organisation 6 Exploit duty free while it lasts

3. **SAMPLE OUTLINE PLAN (BY SYNDICATE A2)**

3.1 **Objectives**

1 To increase revenue excluding duty free by 15% pa until 1999
2 To improve sales margin to 50% by 1999
3 To achieve 40% of revenue from new markets/products by 1999

Year	*1992*	*1993*	*1994*	*1995*	*1996*	*1997*	*1998*	*1999*
Non duty free revenue	109	125	144	166	191	219	252	290

3.2 **Product**

(a) Tailor services offered through the use of market segmentation to attract growing sectors and high spenders (eg women, Far East, Americans).

(b) Develop hotel/conference facilities as a joint venture outside the terminal with a free shuttle service to airport.

(c) Restructure space allocated to catering to introduce fast food outlets wherever possible. This will free space for other revenue providers.

(d) Expand the number of destinations, and the number of flights to boom areas.

3.3 Price

(a) Keep revenue split at 65/35 between commercial revenues and airline charges to avoid over reliance on retailing, and to encourage the active marketing of the airport. The price should be justified by additional services, increased traffic.

(b) Rent received from retail space can be increased, providing this will not cause prices to rise above High Street levels. This could be negotiated using EAL's commitment to increase sales per passenger and active marketing of airport.

3.4 Place

(a) Airport layout is very important to minimise stress, and puts passengers in the right frame of mind for shopping.

(i) Well signposted (multilingual signs)
(ii) Spacious
(iii) Rendez-vous points
(iv) Information desk
(v) Adequate notice boards, arrivals, departures
(vi) Clear announcements - multilingual
(vii) Easy access to luggage trolleys
(viii) Adequate toilet/wash room facilities
(ix) Facilities for children

(b) Passengers buy more when they begin the homeward journey - offer suitable retail mix at international departure gates.

(c) Modify facilities at domestic terminal to cater for the 'non-travelling' shopper.

(d) To help with congested access offer a free bus service from train stations, local business centre, tourist attraction, nearest town.

3.5 Promotion: selling

(a) Customer care training is needed for all staff (ie who are your customers? How can you meet their needs more effectively?)

(b) Install a system to monitor EAL's retail mix (Irma's experience will help decide which is most appropriate) eg EPOS (Electronic point of sale bases). Also:

(i) conduct retail audits;
(ii) set up consumer panels;

(iii) customer satisfaction surveys.

(c) Passengers must be put in a frame of mind to buy.

(i) Goods should offer value for money.
(ii) Customers should be well informed about choice/range of shops.
(iii) No pressure should be put on browsers.
(iv) Avoid queues.
(v) Notice boards and announcements should be clear in the shopping area.
(vi) Operating procedures shall be efficient leaving time, patience and energy for shopping.

3.6 Public relations

(a) A corporate campaign is required to show EAL as an airport providing services and goods of high quality at comparable prices to the High Street.

(b) EAL needs to interact with local community, and be seen as a good corporate citizen.

(i) Sponsorship of local events.
(ii) Open days for shopping/visiting EAL.
(iii) Participation in local green projects.
(iv) Involve public in plans for new terminal from the start.

(c) Encourage business from airlines and travel agents.

(i) Press conferences
(ii) Open days
(iii) Press releases

(d) *Internal marketing*

(i) Educate operational staff about the revenue required from the commercial division to fund operations.

(ii) Quality circles will get people to work together.

(iii) Notice boards can be used to enhance employee awareness.

(iv) In house magazine will have a similar function.

(v) Publish results of in house market research:

(1) Attitudes to shopping;
(2) Behavioural studies;
(3) Airport facilities.

(e) Advertising. A number of advertising opportunities exist:

(i) Internally increase advertising sites where possible;
(ii) External advertising locations include the following:

(1) Women's magazines
(2) Travel agencies
(3) Joint advertising with tourist boards
(4) Local hotels
(5) Travel trade journals
(6) National press
(7) Local papers
(8) TV campaign to raise awareness and project corporate image (joint with concessionaries)

(iii) Travellers' club;
(iv) Literature within airport;
(v) Literature included in travel documents;
(vi) Direct marketing to UK/foreign travel agencies and all companies at local business centre.

4. SAMPLE OUTLINE PLAN (BY SYNDICATE C1)

Objective 1

4.1 Increase gross operating profit as follows:

1993	*1994*	*1995*	*1996*	*1997*
5%	5%	7%	9%	12%

An increase in revenue of 2% per annum for the next five years is an essential feature. Also £500 million must be invested over the next five years in airport expansion and development.

Strategy

4.2 (a) Reduce operating costs.

(b) Develop non duty free sales.

(c) Improve financial management.

(d) Ensure full utilisation of floor space relative to potential profitability.

(e) Investigate diversification and integration possibilities. These include 'hotel' business, joint ventures with other airports, integration with other transport providers (coach, taxis etc).

(f) Change the image of the airport.

Tactics (to achieve strategy)

4.3 *Reduce operating costs*

(a) Review salary structure.
(b) Job evaluation.
(c) Revise and develop reward schemes.
(d) Efficiency review studies can be set up.

(e) Methods and systems improvements.
(f) Sell display advertising vigorously.
(g) Special promotion offers and leaflet distribution.
(h) Increase return per square foot, particularly reviewing and improving the utilisation of catering space and other low return areas.

4.4 (a) *Develop non-duty free revenue.* A key tactic will be diversification into hotels, or hotel-related businesses.

(i) Delivery of luggage to airport without customer handling it.
(ii) Family room tariffs.
(iii) Flexible room arrangements.

(b) Ample car parking.

4.5 *Improve financial management*

(a) Debtor collection.
(b) Stabilise erratic dividend policy.
(c) Improve management reporting.
(d) Moderate increases in prices throughout.
(e) Increase charges for long and medium haul routes.
(f) More car parking facilities with special discounts for longer stays.

4.6 *Change image of airport*

(a) Media advertising.
(b) Special offers.
(c) Competitions.
(d) Publicity encouraging free exposure (biased environmentally).

4.7 *Joint ventures*

(a) Groups negotiating to strengthen position with concessionaires.
(b) Relationship marketing.
(c) Mixed mode transport.

Objective 2

4.8 *Risk reduction.* Reduce dependence on *duty free shops* as a percentage of revenue from 50.5% to 20% by the end of 1999. (*Note.* Sales to *increase* by 55% prior to 1999).

Strategy

4.9 The strategy to achieve this objective can be outlined as follows.

(a) Segment the market into business people, charter leisure customers, domestic flight customers and meet their needs.
(b) Improve accessibility to the airport and its shops.

(c) Create a friendly and relaxing atmosphere to shop in.
(d) Expand activities to include the business community.
(e) Improve its leisure emphasis (eg plane spotting).

Tactics

4.10 The tactics to support this strategy can include the following steps.

(a) Lobby local government to improve access routes.

(b) Shuttle service can be provided from the city centre.

(c) Percentage cut in all taxi fares.

(d) Improve promotion to business community.

(e) Conference and dining facilities can be provided.

(f) Shopping hours can be extended.

(g) Focus on the market segments.

(h) Market research should reflect segmented groups' buying behaviour.

(i) Attract the right kinds of concessionaires by improving traffic flow and demand for their goods via market research.

(j) Persuade tour operators to send people via the airport (tourist attraction and many destinations).

(k) Logical layouts.

(l) Clear signs.

(m) Clear flight calls and display boards particularly near shopping stores with clear intercom.

Objective 3

4.11 *Organisational structure*. Review within next 12 months, to ensure the most appropriate form is adopted to meet company aims and objectives.

Strategy

4.12 A strategy for organisation structure and culture can be outlined.

(a) Develop market orientation.

(b) Develop flatter more 'organic' structure to reduce bureaucracy and improve communications network.

(c) Review recruitment and selection criteria to meet new objectives.

Tactics

4.13 These tactics will help achieve the strategy.

(a) Develop internal marketing culture via training courses.
(b) TWM and quality circles.
(c) Commercial and operations divisions should have equal treatment.
(d) Team building.
(e) Re-negotiate terms with concessionaires.
(f) New terminal recruitment programme.
(g) Review the pay and rewards structure.
(h) Develop an appropriate personnel structure.
(i) Improve the negotiation skills of service staff.

4.14 This strategy can be illustrated by an Ansoff matrix.

	Existing products/services	*New products/services*
New markets	1 Visitors centre 2 Shopping centre	1 Exhibitions 2 Environment
Existing markets	1 Exploit duty free 2 Develop-car park 3 Catering	1 Leisure/hotels 2 New terminal 3 Catering 4 Enhanced car parking

4.15 A projected profit and loss account is provided below. Note that revenue is anticipated to increase by 12% per year.

	1993	*1994*	*1995*	*1996*	*1997*
	£m	£m	£m	£m	£m
Revenue	246.70	276.30	309.50	346.60	388.20
Operating costs	(98.70)	(124.34)	(139.28)	(155.97)	(174.69)
Operating profit	148.00	151.96	170.22	190.63	213.51
Interest received	7.50	8.30	7.90	8.10	8.50
Profit before tax	155.50	160.26	178.12	198.73	222.01
Tax charge	(33.40)	(46.65)	(48.08)	(63.44)	(59.62)
Profit for year	122.10	113.61	130.04	145.29	162.39
Dividend	-	(50.00)	(75.00)	(90.00)	(105.00)
Retained profit	122.10	63.61	55.04	44.29	60.39

5. DETAILED PLAN

5.1 A detailed plan, relating to the outline by Syndicate A2, is provided below.

5.2 Objectives

1. To increase use of EAL by airlines and passengers.
2. To reduce dependence on duty fee to 25% of total turnover by 1995 and to 15% by 1999.
3. To increase turnover to £335m by 1995, with a margin of 30%.
4. To establish market orientation within 12 months.

5.3 Strategy

1. Expand facilities by bringing a new terminal into use by 1999.
2. Develop new services and high value retail businesses, and investigate diversification into other areas such as hotels.
3. Optimise space utilisation to maximise profit potential.
4. Establish profit centres within the company.
5. Undertake a reorganisation to establish a dedicated marketing directorate, and establish an internal training and communications programme.

5.4 Quantified/timescaled objectives

	1992	*1993*	*1994*	*1995*	*1996*	*1997*	*1998*	*1999*
Turnover	£m	£m	£m	£m	£m	£m	£m	£m
Duty free revenue	66	70	73	83	85	86	87	88
Other retail	154	183	218	252	308	363	429	497
Total sales revenue	220	253	291	335	385	443	509	585
Gross profit	£m	£m	£m	£m	£m	£m	£m	£m
(average 30% margin)	66	76	87	100	115	133	153	176
Duty free as % of total sales revenue (%)	30	27.6	25.1	25	22.1	19.4	17.2	15

5.5 *Target markets*

(a) Travellers (AB, aged 25-54)

(i) International business, females *and* males
(ii) International leisure: family groups
(iii) Domestic business: females *and* males
(iv) Domestic leisure: family group

(b) Airlines

(i) Top 20
(ii) Local operators: the airport could position itself as a hub with local operators serving lesser airports as a spoke

(c) Major High Street retailers (as concessionaires)

5.6 *New terminal*

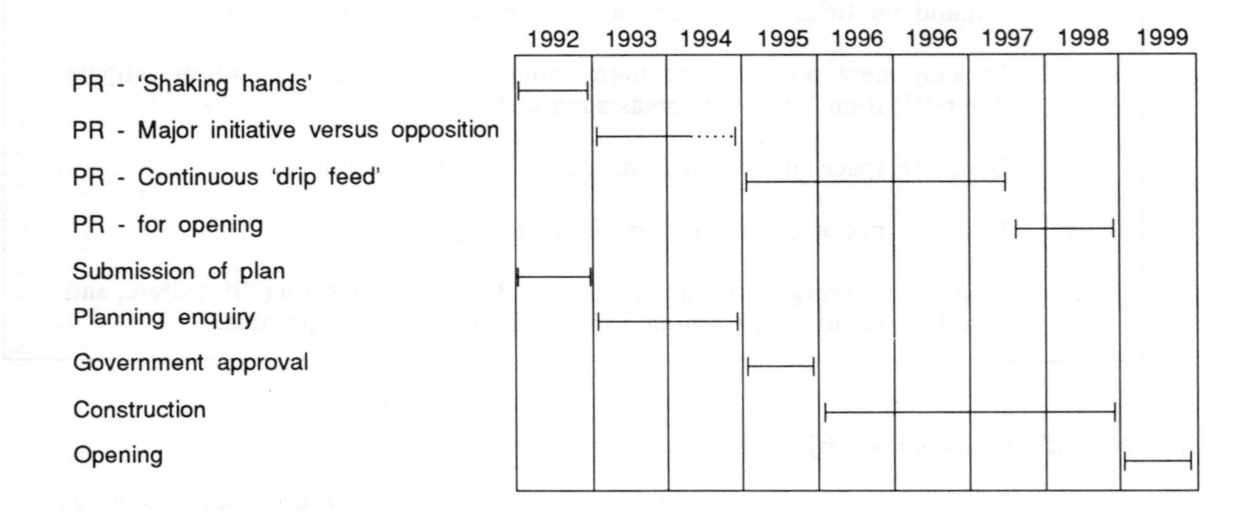

Terminal project progress and PR activities

Terminal project progress and PR activities.

5.7 Existing terminal.

During the next 12 months:

(a) review and reorganise existing and new facilities in existing terminals;
(b) use the extra 1,000ms as a 'test bed' for new ideas, including replacing duty free.

5.8 A detailed timescale is as follows.

(a) 1992 2nd quarter. Complete initial review and outline plan.

(b) 1992 3rd quarter. Present preliminary plan and approve detailed plan.

(c) 1992 4th quarter. Identify and negotiate with concessionaires and carry out any refurbishments in the terminal. Only 3 to 4 extra outlets are available because of 1,000m^2 space limit.

(d) 1993 1st quarter: the scheme is up and running.

(e) Review quarterly thereafter.

5.9 EAL is, ultimately, a service company, so the 4Ps are supplemented by People, Physical evidence, and Process.

Tactics

5.10 *People*

(a) Staff

(i) Training
(ii) Motivation
(iii) Remuneration
(iv) Fulfilment
(v) Job descriptions
(vi) Performance review
(vii) Organisation
(viii) Appearance

(b) *Customers*

(i) Not overcrowded
(ii) Stress-free surroundings

5.11 *Physical evidence*

(a) Airport design
(b) Retail shops and goods
(c) Signage, logos
(d) Luggage tags, maps

(e) Porterage
(f) Buses
(g) PA system, indicator boards
(h) Uniforms
(i) Trolleys
(j) Advertising space

5.12 *Process*

(a) Security
(b) Check-in
(c) Apron management
(d) Embark, disembark
(e) Arrive, park, pick-up, drop-off
(f) Flight information

5.13 *Product*

(a) Identify attractive market segments. Target facilities for smooth efficient flow and minimal queue time.

(b) Perhaps the new terminal should be for international segments.

(c) Services to airlines. A cost leadership approach should be adopted - lowest total *cost* to airline (compared with competition).

(d) Hotel with business facilities (joint venutre).

(e) Innovative advertising facilities.

5.14 *Price*

(a) Sensitivity research on whether low, medium or high.
(b) The price to concessionaires.

5.15 *Place*

(a) Work with local authority to improve transport.
(b) Lobby to get night flight ban limited.

5.16 *Promotion*

(a) PR to support planning application.
(b) Personal selling to major airlines and retail concessionaires.
(c) Corporate image advertising (press).
(d) Exhibit at 'World Travel Market'.
(e) Advertisements in trade journals - travel agents, airlines, retailers.
(f) Market research to understand buyer behaviour and wants.

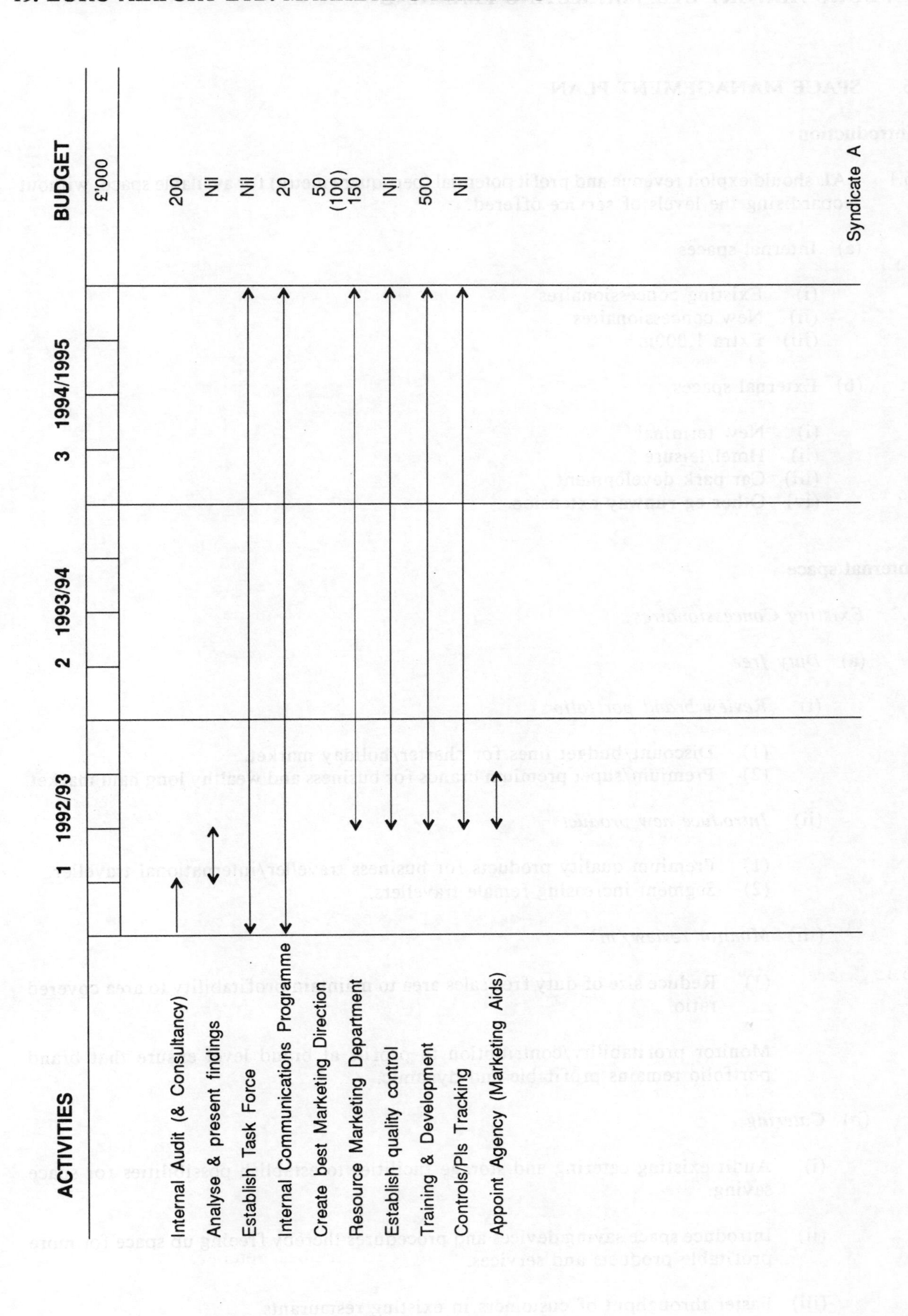
ACTIVITIES
Internal Audit (& Consultancy)
Analyse & present findings
Establish Task Force
Internal Communications Programme
Create best Marketing Directio
Resource Marketing Department
Establish quality control
Training & Development
Controls/PIs Tracking
Appoint Agency (Marketing Aids)
1 1992/93
2 1993/94
3 1994/1995
BUDGET
£'000
200
Nil
Nil
20
50
(100)
150
Nil
500
Nil
Syndicate A

6. SPACE MANAGEMENT PLAN

Introduction

6.1 EAL should exploit revenue and profit potential (per square metre) for available space, without jeopardising the levels of service offered.

(a) Internal spaces

(i) Existing concessionaires
(ii) New concessionaires
(iii) Extra 1,000m^2

(b) External spaces

(i) New terminal
(ii) Hotel/leisure
(iii) Car park development
(iv) Other eg runway extension

Internal space

6.2 *Existing Concessionaires*

(a) *Duty free*

(i) *Review brand portfolio*

(1) Discount/budget lines for charter/holiday market.
(2) Premium/super premium brands for business and wealthy long haul market.

(ii) *Introduce new products*

(1) Premium quality products for business traveller/international traveller.
(2) Segment increasing female travellers.

(iii) *Monitor review/*m^2

(1) Reduce size of duty free sales area to maintain profitability to area covered ratio.

Monitor profitability/contribution to profits at brand level ensure that brand portfolio remains profitable and dynamic.

(b) *Catering*

(i) Audit existing catering and storage facilities to establish possibilities for space saving.

(ii) Introduce space saving devices and procedures thereby freeing up space for more profitable products and services.

(iii) Faster throughput of customers in existing restaurants.

(iv) Possibly remove domestic waiter service restaurant to provide space for other activities.

(v) Food markets (concessionaires) can be established, eg sushi bars, all day breakfasts etc.

(c) *Services area*

(i) Banking, insurance, hotel reservations, car hire all located in one area, to minimise usage of space.

(ii) Raise percentage of turnover obtained from concessionaires to increase revenue.

6.3 *New concessionaires (pending market research)*

(a) Mini shopping malls:

(i) Jewellery eg Gucci, Rolex;
(ii) Clothing - Hermes;
(iii) Confectionery and Delicatessens:

(1) Thorntons, Lindt;
(2) Speciality teas;

(iv) Books (eg Dillons);
(v) Sports shop;
(vi) Gifts - adults and children;
(vii) Perfumeries/chemists.

(b) Extra 1,000 square metres should be used as a test bed for retail ideas (eg creche).

External space

6.4 *New terminal*

(a) The new terminal should be devoted to EC and short haul flights (helps market segmentation).

(b) Planning and design of the new terminal is awaiting the results of pending research competitors.

6.5 *Hotel/leisure.* A joint venture (eg Forte, Hilton) near to airport is possible.

6.6 *Car park development*

(a) Build the car park underground, so it is sympathetic with environment.
(b) Services to franchise include security, valet service, AA, RAC.
(c) There should be an emphasis on safety for women.

6.7 *Other*

The runway extension might be extended to $2\frac{1}{2}$ miles thus reducing noise levels and leading to an increased number of flights and night flights.

7. POSSIBLE OPPORTUNITIES FOR DEVELOPING BUSINESS

7.1 The flow chart below is a preliminary assessment of passengers' use of space at the airport, and might be a way of identifying new opportunities for earning revenue.

FLOW CHART - TYPICAL PASSENGER?

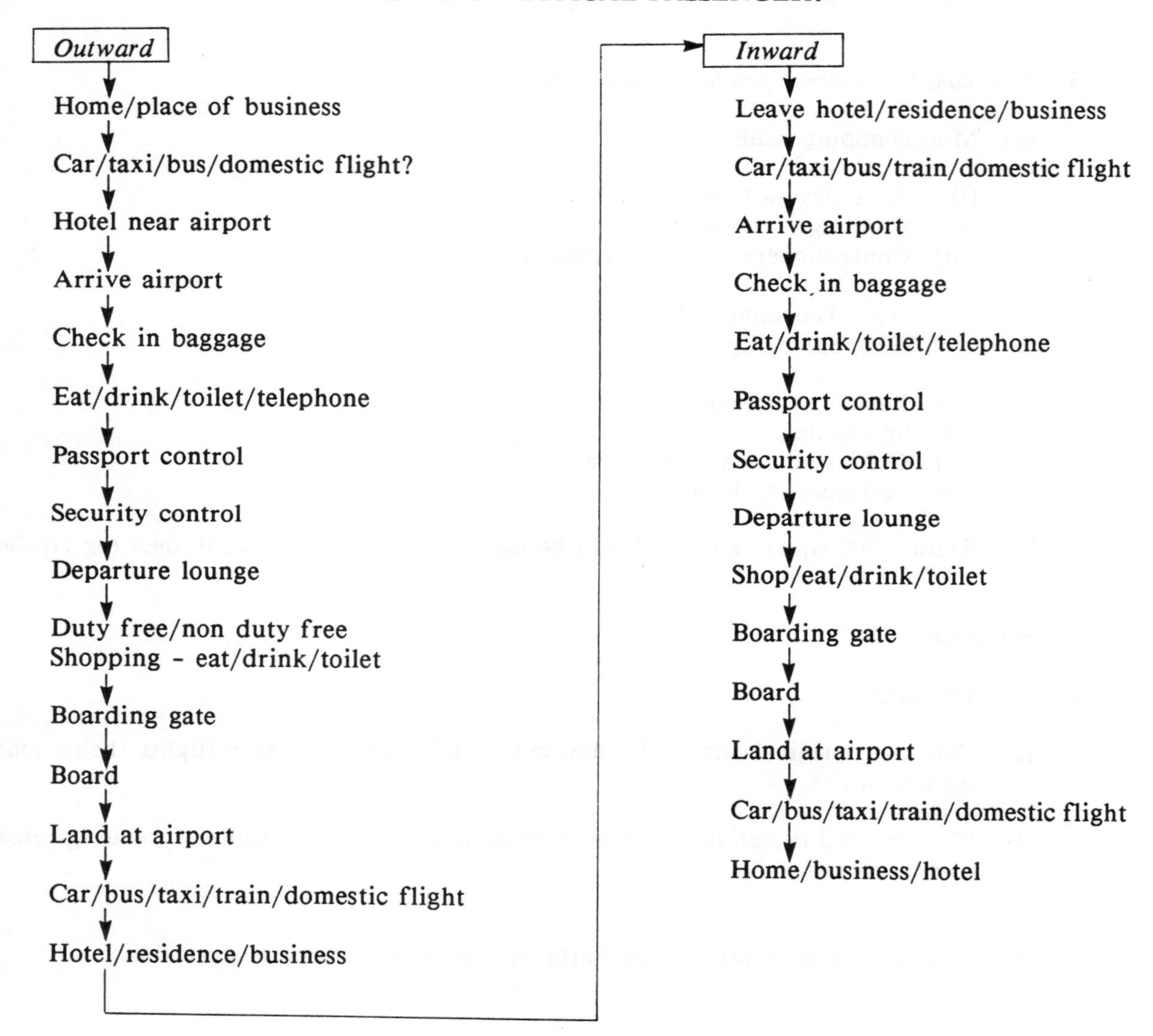

8. ENVIRONMENTAL ISSUES

Situational analysis

8.1 There has been a considerable build up of external pressures:

(a) Legislation;
(b) Protest groups (NIMBY);
(c) Congestion;
(d) Pollution (noise/smell);
(e) Safety.

8.2 This situation is charged and volatile. Certain aspects of it (eg fashion) are beyond EAL's direct control.

8.3 These pressures are, however, specifically linked to plans for the new terminal. Whilst the problems are immediate, strategies for solving them can be built into medium and long term planning.

8.4 **Objectives**

(a) Forge strong links between EAL's business activities and the local community: 0-4 years.

(b) Be increasingly proactive in handling these issues, and rigorously demonstrate EAL's principles in practice: 0 -10 years.

8.5 **Strategy**

(a) Devise an effective communications campaign.
(b) Segment and target specific problem groups.
(c) Deploy PR resources to EAL's best advantage.
(d) Establish links with the community and local business.

8.6 **Target audience**

(a) Governmental local and national levels
(b) The local community
(c) Protest groups and lobbyists
(d) Tourist boards
(e) Airlines
(f) Educational establishments

8.7 **Environmental issues market research**

A direct mail attitude survey to all target groups will refine current data and thinking, providing an important start point.

(a) Establish an environmental management programme and link this to other businesses in the area. Develop a corporate *environment statement*. Set 'green' performance targets.

(b) Appoint an *environment co-ordinator* with independent status (giving this person perceived independence and integrity) and form a project team with PR department members. Specific problem areas should have their own 'action executive'.

(c) Begin community forums as question and answer sessions. Include excerpts as part of local radio broadcasts and perhaps encourage phone-ins. Welcome criticism and respond to it. Public access to information should be easy.

(d) Introduce recycling targets as a key policy for both commercial and operations divisions. 'Be seen to be green' ie biodegradable cleaning materials, recycled non-bleached paper, bottle banks and waste collection areas, catalytically converted vehicles etc.

(e) Appoint full service advertising agency to develop a consistent, 'environment friendly' image, literature and advertising for EAL. Attention-grabbing poster campaign, national and regional press advertising, sales promotion activities are all possible.

(f) Produce a corporate brochure explaining the aims of the new terminal, and EAL's environmental policies. Scale document according to recipient - ie full, comprehensive publication for protesters and already interested parties, and a slimline version for the general public on the sidelines (who nevertheless have great influence).

(g) Offer improved community services as part of a new business development programme. These will include leisure services, direct rail links, extensive shopping facilities, free day trips, open days and so forth.

(h) Monitor the impact of aircraft and building plans on 'bio-diverse' life forms, with the help of local schools and colleges, paint eyes on planes to scare off birds and prevent them being killed by being sucked into the jet engines, or crashing into windscreens.

(i) Introduce an EAL environment advice line with trained staff to respond to questions.

(j) Sponsorship - local community activity.

8.8 Budget for environmental policy

	£'000	
Market research	60	
Recruitment	50	
Data analysis	15	
Agency/campaign	400	
Telephone service	20	
Sponsorship	15	
Joint ventures		
Access/rail links	2,000	
'Phased recycling'	1,000	
Community forums	20	
Total	3,580	(£3.58m)

Timescale

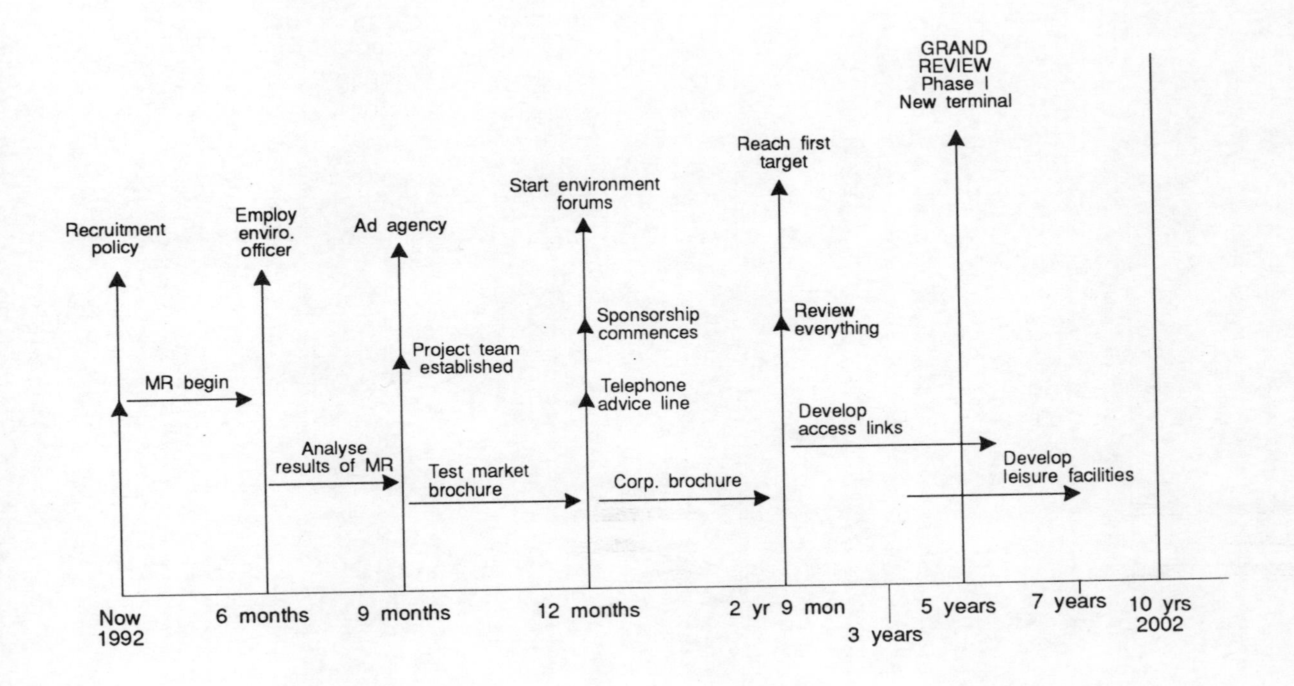

9. CONCLUSION

9.1 Just in case you have forgotten, you need to conduct two final steps in the recommended methodology.

9.2

CONSULT CHAPTER 6 FOR GUIDANCE NOTES
STEP 27 DRAW UP YOUR EXAMINATION PLAN **STEP 28 PRACTISE WRITING IN TRUE REPORT STYLE**
ALLOW AS LONG AS NECESSARY FOR THESE LAST TWO STEPS

9.3 Good luck in your second practice run exam!

Chapter 20

EURO AIRPORT LTD: THE EXAMINATION PAPER

This chapter covers the following topics.

EURO AIRPORT LTD

THE EXAM QUESTIONS ARE ON THE NEXT PAGE

DO NOT LOOK UNTIL YOU ARE READY TO SPEND

THREE HOURS ON DOING THESE AS A MOCK EXAM

1. THE EXAMINATION QUESTIONS

EURO AIRPORT LIMITED

Question 1

Detail your long-term proposals to counteract the potential loss of duty free revenue, by the strategy of increasing sales of non-duty free goods and services at the airport site. In making your proposals, you should pay due regard to the most important financial indicators by which the airport's commercial performance is currently measured, plus any non financial performance standards which you may additionally suggest. (40 marks)

Question 2

Suggest and justify changes in the current organisation structure and specify a set of internal marketing initiatives which might lead to a more unified approach (between operations and commercial divisions) to the marketing of the airport as a whole, to both passengers and airlines. (30 marks)

Question 3

Submit reasoned approaches which might create a more favourable and informed opinion within the local community, towards the airport's development plans for a new terminal and other possible future expansions. (30 marks)

2. EXAMINER'S REPORT

General comments

2.1 Overall, the pass rate was pleasingly higher than previous sittings. Students in all countries appear to have related well to the international airport setting and were able to make many creative suggestions within their answers.

2.2 A good case study should, given competent and thorough analysis, yield its key issues. These key issues should normally be the basis on which the examination questions are set, so as to preserve the integrity of the case. Most candidates (no doubt ably assisted by tutors) have not scrimped on their analysis and had therefore enjoyed their reward of some success in anticipating the likely question areas. Perhaps it should equally be pointed out that these questions were nevertheless highly demanding and will have occupied the minds of top marketing executives in the European airport market for some considerable time.

2.3 Unfortunately, however, standards varied *between* centres and *within* centres considerably, with some students clearly having conducted very little and analysis, evidently hoping to be able to waffle their way through the paper.

2.4 Regrettably, far too many candidates are still submitting answers in appropriate and unprofessional *essay style*, despite clear instructions calling for a more business-like report format and warnings that not to adopt this format is courting failure. Some candidates also did not adopt the role stipulated in the candidates brief, wrongly using statements such as 'What the new business development manager should do' or 'Irma needs to do'.

2.5 Papers from some centres failed to provide a single instance of costing or scheduling for any of the three answers given. This proliferates an impression of a lack of real management ability. Candidates wishing to be granted membership of the Chartered Institute of Marketing really must demonstrate their professionalism beyond the mere putting forward of ideas.

2.6 Candidates are again counselled to think clearly what the question is really about before writing out pre-prepared answers, the greater proportion of which are then irrelevant. A good method of ensuring the question is fully addressed is to identify its key words.

2.7 Distressingly many candidates spend inordinate amounts of time on presenting overly-detailed contents pages, followed by over-lengthy lists of pre-prepared objectives and assumptions. Marks are not normally awarded for assumptions in themselves, especially those which are deliberately and unrealistically contrived to alter the questions so as to bring them into line with pre-prepared answers. Examinees should avoid extremely long lists of objectives which confuse rather than clarify the direction the company should take. Equally, candidates should not produce extensive introductions and summaries which gain no marks in themselves. All this timewasting only serves to convey the impression that the candidate is avoiding answering the actual question set. Even if this is untrue, the candidate than has too little time left to devote to the real question and is obliged to produce a superficial answer of listing which are unacceptable for a pass standard in this paper.

2.8 A relatively new practice has emerged at least one centre whereby candidates attach appendices to their answers without referring the examiner to these in the text. The examiner therefore marks the question and has to re-mark upon finding the appendices. Worst still some candidates left blank pages in between their answers and the appendices, thereby running the risk of these being missed completely.

2.9 *Question 1*

(a) Many candidates confined their answers solely to providing unstructured lists of proposals which, however, good, were insufficient in themselves to secure a pass level.

(b) It has been hoped that examiners would preface their proposals with some *quantified* and *time-scaled* objectives so as to provide an appropriate perspective. Also it has been expected that the majority of answers would be structured into strategy and tactics, using Ansoff and marketing mix (for services) headings.

(c) Far too many candidates failed to proposed any marketing research whatsoever. Some of the few that did went overboard and covered research and screening exclusively, failing to come up with any other proposals - hardly the right stance for a new business development *manager* trying to make a name for herself in a new position.

(d) Whilst most candidates made some well substantiated proposals, quite a number strayed outside the limitations of the airport site as directed in the question.

(e) A surprising number of papers failed to allude to the most important financial indicators as asked, as well as to propose any non-financial performance indicators, as invited by the question. It was regrettable that some excellent creative thinking was spoiled by a general failure to answer the question fully.

2.10 *Question 2*

(a) A refreshingly high proportion of candidates had appreciated that Irma's ability to develop new business to replace lost duty free sales would be constrained by the current organisation and that she might feel obliged to make some constructive *suggestions* for changes.

(b) Quite a large number of students were also aware of the crucial role that *internal marketing* can play in service marketing, and were able to suggest practical initiatives behind the bland 'put in TQM' approach.

(c) Good candidates used simplified organisation charts to clarify their suggestions and indicated both timescales and costs. Poor candidates failed to justify changes and the worst seemed to think that creating a taskforce was the one miraculous solution to all problems. It needs to be emphasised that the mere appointment of a manager, or the formation of a committee, in itself achieves nothing.

(d) A number of students, mostly from overseas, suggested a matrix organisation or 'flattening' the current structure without any indication as to what they meant by this or indeed any real justification.

2.11 *Question 3*

(a) Regrettably, some candidates saw the words 'development plans for a new terminal' within the question and immediately pitched enthusiastically into their pre-prepared answers without reference to the rest of the question which was really about public relations.

(b) Other examinees submitted PR or communications plans without a thought as to different target audiences, and how they might have different motives requiring different approaches and messages.

(c) Scripts incorporating plans which included even marginal references to timing, sequencing or costs were extremely rate. All future candidates are urged to include these aspects *as a matter of course*, bearing in mind they have four weeks lead time to prepare for the examination.

(d) Having made these constructive criticisms it has to be said that there were many really excellent answers to this question and tutors at most centres are to be congratulated on instilling a keen sense of environmental responsibility and awareness in their students. The understanding of environmental issues and the good grasp of the complexity of PR demonstrated by most candidates, was very encouraging.

3. ILLUSTRATIVE MARKING SCHEMES

3.1 *Question 1*

Detail your long term proposals to counteract the potential loss of duty free revenue, by the strategy of increasing sales of non duty free goods and services at the airport site. In making your proposals, you should pay due regard to the most important financial indicators by which the airport's commercial performance is currently measured, plus any non financial performance standards which you may additional suggest. (40 marks)

(a) Most students will have prepared a marketing plan with at least one of the objectives hopefully being to profitably replace lost duty free sales by June 1999. There are effectively seven years in which to build up sales to a level at which this loss will not be crippling.

(b) *Reasonable* assumptions that not *all* the duty free sales will be lost, owing to the continued sale of duty free tobacco and alcohol to non-EC passengers and some retention of sale at a higher (non duty free) price to EC passengers are allowable, but not to the extent when the question is unanswered. Basically we are looking for a number of valid proposals to generate *new* business *from the airport site* (in other words the existing space plus any new space which becomes available eg the new terminal). Students are expected to realise that EAL is essentially a landlord. However, Irma can, and should, be able to take a partnership approach to the greater satisfaction of customer needs by concessionnaires, EAL commercial/operations divisions, and the airlines.

(c) Good answers will work through the format - objectives, strategies à la Ansoff and tactics at the marketing mix level including the 7 P's for services and market research. These answers should pay due regard to the *financial* indicators given in the case (turnover, sales/revenue per passenger and per square metre, profit, ROI, inflation, exchange rates, tax changes, growth in consumer expenditure etc).

(d) Really good answers will include non-financial standards of performance such as security, safety, environmental concerns, customer satisfactions, repeat patronage, reduction of tensions and the building of long-term relationships.

(e) *Marking scheme*

		Up to (marks)
1	Objectives - quantified and timescaled	3
2	Marketing research - information required, method	7
3	Proposals: strategy, tactics (7 P's)	15
4	Financial performance indicators - sales/revenue per passenger/ per square metre, profit, ROI etc	5
5	Non financial performance indicators - security, safety, customer satisfaction, environmental concern etc	5
6	Scheduling and costing	5
		40

3.2 *Question 2*

Suggest and justify changes in the current organisation structure and specify a set of internal marketing initiatives which might lead to a more unified approach (between operations and commercial divisions) to the marketing of the airport as a whole, to both passengers and airlines. (30 marks)

(a) It is expected that most candidates will submit revised organisation charts proposing some form of integration between commercial and operations divisions under Marketing.

(b) If this is suggested at *Director* level, then some discussion of the problems involved should occur.

(c) It might be possible to integrate commercial and operations under the marketing banner at terminal level or at least to giving marketing a functional authority (rather than an operational or line responsibility) as an interim or transitional stage.

(d) In any event, answers need to recognise that unification is not an overnight process and, if it is to work effectively, it requires the consensus of all the staff.

(e) Internal marketing and customer care training programmes for all staff should recognise the importance of safety and security procedures as well as the satisfaction of customers' needs for commercial goods and services. Other internal marketing initiatives might include suggestion schemes, open meetings, quality circles, special interest group discussions etc as well as formal training.

(f) Back to organisation, PR should ideally be a company-wide activity. Candidates need to recognise also that without active marketing to airlines, there would be no flights available and no passengers for retail sales.

(g) *Marking scheme*

		Up to (marks)
1	Valid suggestions for changes in the organisational structure	10
2	Justification of above changes	5
3	Specified internal marketing initiatives	10
4	Scheduling and costing	5
		30

(h) *Notes*

(i) In view of the organisational complexity (and the time it would take) it would perhaps be unrealistic to expect candidates to produce organisation charts in stages (eg current, interim, ultimate). However, some credit should be allowed for organisation charts submitted, within the above marking schemes.

(ii) The really good candidates will no doubt submit costings and schedules for their proposals and a modest amount of marks should be allowed for this.

3.3 *Question 3*

Submit reasoned approaches which might create a more favourable and informed opinion within the local community, towards the airport's development plans for a new terminal and other possible future expansions. (30 marks)

(a) Hopefully, candidates will submit an external PR plan based upon research aimed at identifying the target audiences and within these, the opinion leaders, deciders and influencers.

(b) Candidates should demonstrate an appreciation that adverse attitudes will need careful handling and some time to change these towards a more favourable orientation.

(c) The local community might be defined as follows.

(i) Local government.

(ii) Local branches of national institutions eg Chamber of Commerce, CBI, National Federation of Consumer Groups etc.

(iii) Special interest groups such as anti-noise, anti-pollution etc.

(iv) Local MPs and prospective parliamentary candidates.

(v) The general public.

(vi) Local needs.

(vii) Other.

Approaches could include visits in/out, providing speakers, conducting demonstrations aimed at convincing the 'antis' that airport activities are more beneficial to the local community than harmful etc.

(d) Candidates might also indicate that local communities can be influenced by national opinions. PR might therefore include national campaigns aimed at getting favourable media cover, approval of national government etc.

(e) *Marking scheme*

		Up to (marks)
1	Identification of local community audiences	5
2	Reasoned and valid approaches	20
3	Costing and schedule	5
		30

4. CONCLUSION

4.1 Well, how did you get on with your second mock exam? If you are still dissatisfied with your performance please do not despair. Further help is available at a price. Two other cases are examined in the Tutorial Text for this subject. An order form can be found at the end of this Workbook.

4.2 The chapter which follows tells you about some of this help and the appendices contain articles which you should find useful for your actual examination. BPP Study Texts are of course available for the other three CIM Diploma subjects which underpin this subject.

Chapter 21

CONSULTANTS' ANALYSIS OF EURO AIRPORT LTD

This chapter covers the following topics.

1. Introduction
2. Strategic considerations
3. The market
4. Marketing mix
5. Organisation
6. Finance

1. INTRODUCTION

1.1 The case study is published four weeks before the final examination. Whilst you are *not* supposed to research the industry, there are a number of *intensive revision courses* available to help you understand the wealth of data provided in the case. Also various consultancies provide analyses to help candidates marshall their thoughts.

1.2 Such analyses should be used in conjunction with a copy of the case study, sent from the Chartered Institute of Marketing.

1.3 This analysis is designed to help you to think through the problem areas confronting EAL, and to save you valuable study time. Such analyses do not point to a particular solution, and so they do not purport to be examination answers.

1.4 You are likely to have to make firm recommendations at the time of the examination. Make these, with appropriate justification, *without* regurgitating tracts of the case study or any analysis you might have consulted.

1.5 These analyses are lodged with the Chartered Institute of Marketing's examiners. Candidates will *not* gain marks by simply copying sections of them. Use them instead to help you arrive at, and justify, firm recommendations.

1.6 Such analyses are of necessity produced at great speed, but with every possible care. However, all material should be carefully scrutinised before basing recommendations on them, as errors are not impossible.

1.7 The analysis below is provided by *Northern Consultancy Associates* (65 Moorside North, Newcstle upon Tyne, NE4 9DU, UK), and is reproduced with their permission.

2. STRATEGIC CONSIDERATIONS

2.1 You are cast in the role of Irma Bergmann, the New Business Development *Manager*. As candidates do not assume the roles of director, it may be the case that there is less emphasis on *strategy* in this examination than in others. However, it is emphasised that you have been appointed with the threat of the loss of duty free sales in mind, but also with the aim of creating fresh thinking, and creating a unified approach to the marketing of the airport as a whole.

2.2 Nevertheless, as a middle manager, your decisions will be made within the context of corporate and marketing strategies. Moreover there *are* hints that opportunities exist for you to take a broader perspective within the firm. You are ambitious. You would certainly be ready to comment on strategic matters if invited.

2.3 One indication that you may be required to provide *less* in the way of strategic thinking in your answer is the amount of relevant information given in the case's text and appendices.

(a) A SWOT analysis is given by the case (Chapter 15, Paragraph 3.7) and also as part of the marketing audit. Some major constraints are also listed in the text (Chapter 15 Paragraphs 2.9 to 2.14). You should note these and think of them critically. Also, consider if there are any other issues which may have been omitted.

(b) Although you are instructed to do no further analysis for this examination, matters of general knowledge can be included. Thus the potential deregulation of airlines in Europe will open up competition and reduce prices. This should mean an increase in business, at least in the short term (before cartels re-establish themselves). European harmonisation, which is mentioned, will possibly mean an eventual common currency which would threaten a proportion of Bureau de Change activities. Are there any other issues to be considered?

(c) Indications for *objectives* are also listed (Chapter 15 Paragraphs 2.13 to 2.19). These are quantifiable, and provide a first opportunity to stress the difference between concessionaire's sales and the airport's revenue. Turnover for concessionaires depends on the margins and quantities sold. The airport's revenue depends on this but more directly on the terms negotiated with the concessionaires; and also of course on the number of flights and tariff per passenger to make up the non-commercial revenue, which has less importance to you.

(d) You should consider the broad *strategies* available to the airport; these will be outlined now, although more detail will be given elsewhere in the analysis.

(i) Ansoff would suggest that you might look to new market segments (or change emphasis). Segments such as Business vs Leisure must be considered. More widely, examine the different *markets* EAL appeals to: for example, the airline companies can be persuaded to fly from EAL, which in turn is an attraction for passengers. Adjustment can also be made to the products and services offered by the Commercial Division and this is certainly an important issue receiving treatment later.

(ii) You are encouraged to consider more adventurous, and perhaps risky ventures for the long term. You could have your own airport hotels specifically designed for the air traveller. For example, family room tariffs, ample parking, flexible meal arrangements and so on. You could move into your own retail operations, but this may prove too specialist a venture for you. Joint ventures with other airports to negotiate with concessionaires is a possibility. Running your own travel company to bus people to the nearest city centre (over ten miles away) is another.

(iii) It may be appropriate to consider another strategic model, from M E Porter. He proposes three options, namely *segmentation focus* and *cost leadership*. Segmentation we have dealt with.

(1) *Focus* suggests concentrating on the products which are suitable for particular markets. For example do domestic and international travellers both need the same products?

(2) In introducing cost leadership, Porter departs from Ansoff's model. This is a legitimate plan for a large company. For example, savings mainly from the operations sector would allow the airport to reduce its *passenger tariff*. More airlines might then fly from the airport, bringing more passengers who would use the terminals. This points to the benefits of a unified approach mentioned in the Candidates' Brief. All staff (both commercial and operational) must see themselves as a customer orientated whole to achieve greater successes. How do you sell this to them?

3. THE MARKET

Market segments

3.1 Market segmentation aims to subdivide the market into sections which will display different buying behaviour patterns, so that different offerings can be devised for each, assuming the segment is attractive enough. The very broad market components for EAL will be the *airlines* themselves, and the *passengers* they carry.

3.2 *Airlines* will be segmented by such criteria as size of company, type of plane, nationality and so on. We have little information on this in the case.

3.3 There is considerable information on the passenger market, notably in Chapter 15, para 3.3.

(a) The business market will probably buy and behave a little differently from the leisure passenger, and be approached accordingly. This is a legitimate form of segmentation.

(b) Domestic and international passengers will also behave differently. However, we find that 48% of those using the International terminal are actually Domestic passengers. Thus, it become difficult to target appropriate services specifically to International travellers at present. It is therefore not a particularly useful form of segmentation for Irma

Bergmann, but perhaps it should be. Can the different types of passenger be more clearly allocated to their own terminal? There may be operational reasons making this difficult, or it may be straightforward.

(c) There are other bases for segmentation mentioned: age, sex, social class. These would be of interest to the concessionaires, helping them to determine the type of merchandise to stock.

(d) Other types of segmentation are also mentioned in the case. These are important and suggest that passengers flying from, rather than to, the airport, and airside transfer passengers, are the ones most likely to buy commercial products. Promotional efforts are thus appropriate.

(e) Trends are also important in the market, and the fact that the leisure, long haul, and female passenger market segments are growing in numerical size must be noted.

3.4 *Buyer behaviour*

(a) It was stated above that segmentation is only useful if customers in different segments buy or behave differently. Behaviour patterns can be inferred from factual and demographic data. For example, there is likely to be a link between age and type of clothes worn. Behavioural criteria are likely to be of relevance for segmentation (eg benefit sought, heavy or frequent users as opposed to light or infrequent users, and psychographics (personality types).

(b) The problem is that it is difficult to access each segment. (Which newspapers do frequent users read, for example?) We have already stated that different categories of traveller may behave differently (eg outbound, inbound, transfers etc). The advantage here is that it should be possible to reach these appropriately in *different terminals*. It is always worthwhile studying buyer behaviour, but especially in this case.

(c) A general rule of buyer behaviour, is that customers will take greater care with a purchase (extensive problem solving) if they perceive a risk.

(i) *Organisational buying behaviour*

This applies to *airlines and their decision to use an airport*. Not only is this a major decision but the buyer will be accountable to senior management and shareholders. Risk will certainly be avoided and indeed this may be a decision of sufficient magnitude to warrant a group decision (Decision Making Unit). The seller can attempt to identify the key people and influence them.

Firms also make decisions on how their personnel fly. Whilst they will allow a business travel agent to make such decisions for them, They will take care will be taken in selecting such an agent. To the extent that individuals are involved, speed and comfort are likely to be more important than cost, depending on economic conditions.

(ii) *Individual buyer behaviour*

General points are made in Appendix 17 (Chapter 15 para 3.17) of the case.

(1) *Businessmen*. In the terminal businessmen and women may be regular travellers, therefore rather less interested in duty free products. If they have been away from home for some time they may wish to buy more expensive presents.

(2) *Charter/leisure*. These customers generally travel once or twice a year. As they cannot put spending on expense accounts, they will be looking for a bargain. This is guaranteed on the duty free and they will undoubtedly stock up. They may buy inexpensive toiletries such as toothpaste, but may be less certain of the relative value of clothes and electrical goods unless they have investigated beforehand, and therefore they may be cautious in buying these.

(3) Passengers on *domestic flights*, whether business or leisure are less likely to be major purchasers. They can check in late, often only half an hour before take-off, and will have little interest in browsing.

(4) The issue of *browsing* is an important one. Customers with more time available will shop more. When spending fairly large sums of money they will do so where they are sure of getting bargain, (ie the duty free). What if this facility disappeared? They would still have time to kill and perhaps switch spending to the next least risky item. Would this be where prices are generally known and therefore comparable, or where they are 'blurred' (eg fashion items?).

(5) The above logic can be used to consider appropriate offerings for travellers in general. In particular you may care to consider the appropriate type of catering facilities in terminals.

3.5 *Researching the market*

(a) Candidates are often asked to consider obtaining more data. It is impossible in an analysis such as this to cover all eventualities, and much information has been given to you. Some general principles may help.

(i) In research you must decide *who* you need to investigate and then decide on how to obtain a representative sample. This may be fairly large for consumer research, and together with the methods of obtaining data (eg structured questionnaire) will allow for quantified results (as in Chapter 15, paragraph 3.17 in the case).

(ii) Surveys on organisations may have to investigate more complicated issues and may require qualitative, less structured questioning with a relatively small number of respondents. A decision how to obtain the information must also be made (eg personal interviewing, telephone interviewing or observation). In preparing for questions in this area in the examination students should consider where more information is necessary, what type of information would be useful, and how to obtain it.

(iii) Certainly Irma Bergmann is used to obtaining research data in her previous job; some is already available to her now. This may merely whet her appetite however.

(iv) Irma will want as much in house data as possible. What data from concessionaires could be useful? Is there any more data about customers which would be valuable? Could it be broken down into helpful categories, eg market segments? Can new product ideas be researched or screened? A hint is dropped in the case (Chapter 3, paragraph

3.10 of this text) that a survey of competitor airports may be required to observe their retail mix. How would you go about this? (Possibly by observation on staggered days.) What would you be looking for? What difficulties would you anticipate and how would you overcome them?

3.6 *Competition*

(a) When reviewing the market it is necessary to consider competition. This is reviewed in two places in the case (Chapter 15, paras 2.23, 2.24, 3.8 and 3.9 of this text). This latter information we have already considered in noting that EAL is one of the less expensive airports for airlines. This may attract airlines. We find that there are over 100 destinations from EAL. Is this critical in attracting passengers? Or is it that it is near a major business centre, city centre of tourist attraction?

(b) Much is made of the superior design quality in EAL. Would this, or a superior duty free shop, attract passengers to an airport? Do customers merely regard stopovers at Schipol (Amsterdam) or Dubai (recognised as attractive airports) as a bonus or do they plan their routes to include them? You must look at the factors listed in the case (Chapter 15 Paragraphs 3.8) and draw your own conclusions as to their importance.

(c) Operating procedures use up time. If time is available to customers, they are 'captive' and this gives a clear advantage to the airport over shops in the high street. Nevertheless the customer is aware of prices in shops at say electrical goods shops such as Dixons. Airlines will make in flight brochures available, as competing suppliers.

How can the airport offset this? Not only must prices be competitive, but customers must perceive them to be so. Moreover whilst the high street might be only indirect competition with the airport customers have become used to shopping malls of quality.

4. MARKETING MIX

Products and services

4.1 As New Business Development Manager, you are charged with the responsibility of developing new projects to maintain the growth of the organisation, and to counter the threats posed by revenue earning activities which may decline or halt altogether.

4.2 The chief concern, and the biggest threat, is the likelihood that duty free sales will have to end by July 1st 1999. Political lobbying etc *might* remove this threat, but planning has to proceed on the basis that this is unlikely to succeed, and alternative sources of revenue have to be found. Analysis of the figures provided in the case study (Chapter 15 paragraph 3.2) proves just how big a problem this is.

4.3 Although duty/tax free shops account for by far the biggest share of the revenue (50.5%), they only account for 25.9% of space, so that they represent a very effective use of space. In contrast, catering accounts for 53.1% of space, but a meagre 5.3% of revenue. If using information from the table on p 14 of the case, we divide the percentage share of revenue by the share of space for each category of activity, we can show the relative effectiveness of the use of space.

Product/service	*Revenue % per space %*
Car rental	3.75
Hotel reservations	3.00
Duty/tax free shops	1.95
Banking/Bureau de Change	1.93
Bookshops	0.69
Insurance	0.67
Specialist shops	0.58
Payphones	0.46
Sundry	0.18
Catering	0.10
Advertising, car parks - terminal surface space not used	

The table is arranged in decreasing order of the effectiveness of the use of space, thus car rental provides the highest income per unit of space, and catering the lowest.

4.4 Both terminals have a waiter service restaurant, but 60% of those questioned in the survey of airport shoppers (Chapter 15, para 3.17) said they required self service facilities. Self service would be quicker, and might therefore process customers so that they would have more time to spend on other things, including shopping. Of other products and services, car parks represent the second biggest contribution to total revenue, and do not take up terminal space.

Given 1992 revenue of £220.3m, commercial activity accounts for 65% of this (£143.2m). By applying the share of commercial revenue in Chapter 15, para 3.2 to this, we can calculate actual revenue (eg duty free £143.2 × 0.505 = £72.31m). These figures can then be used to calculate the activity share of *total* EAL revenue. At 32.83%, duty free revenue accounts for almost as much as the whole of airline and passenger charges.

Activity	*% of EAL revenue*	*Turnover* £m
Duty/tax free shops	32.83	72.310
Car parks	12.61	27.780
Banking/Bureau de Change	3.77	8.310
Bookshops	3.71	8.162
Catering	3.45	7.580
Advertising	3.38	7.446
Specialist shops	2.28	5.020
Car rental	1.95	4.300
Hotel reservations	0.39	0.860
Pay-phones	0.39	0.860
Insurance	0.13	0.290
Sundry	0.13	0.286

4.5 Activities have been arranged in descending order of contribution. The table only shows commercial activities in terms of their contribution to *revenue*, not profit. Since most of the activities in the commercial area rely on concessions, these activities employ largely staff other than those of EAL (a shop for instance, would have to pay its own staff). On the other hand, most of the staff employed by EAL are on the operational side, concerned with income from the airlines. Thus although the commercial activities from retail concessions etc account for 65% of revenue, they almost certainly account for a higher share of the profit. This makes the potential loss of duty free income even more serious, since it means that not only does this business account for nearly 33% of EAL's turnover, but almost certainly a significantly larger share of profits.

New products/services

4.6 EAL should be constantly reviewing the *balance* of the retailing services on offer. Retailers constantly evaluate the share of space given to different products, and with a retailing background you will be very conscious of this. Concessionaries will themselves review the use of their own space. EAL needs to know that the right balance of space is given over to the different types of concessions, and that these are appropriate for each terminal (eg would the sports shop not be better situated in the international rather than the domestic terminal, since the clientele there has a higher proportion of leisure travellers?)

4.7 The 1,000 square metre facility mentioned in the case is a relatively small retail facility, but precisely because of this, it is capable of providing information as to the best use for sites with limited space. Basically, this requires either a very high turnover per square metre, or very high margins, or preferably both. For ideas you might examine the type of business that seems to do well in small spaces within large shopping centres. EAL could use this site as a test market for ideas, and encourage they appropriate type of concession to operate in it, or even try some ideas out as a directly run operation.

4.8 The new product development process requires idea generation, followed by screening, as mentioned in the memo from the commercial director in the case study (Chapter 15, para 3.12). This entails generating a range of ideas, and evaluating these ideas through various stages of development, to remove the ideas which are likely not to be able to meet the criteria that the company has for the performance of its new products. The most thorough, and sometimes costly research and evaluation is logically placed *before* a potentially expensive development stage. Projects that are most risky or require the highest development costs require the most careful screening. In contrast, those new product/service ventures which are not risky might be best tested by trying them out. A typical idea generation and screening process might take the following form.

Typical new product screening stages

1 Decide new product strategy
2 Idea generation
3 Initial screening
4 Detailed business analysis
5 Development
6 Testing
7 Commercialisation

4.9 For manufacturing organisations that require high capital investment before the development of a new product, screening might involve considerable collection of information. For retailers, where there is a decision to stock a new product, this can be done on a small scale, at little risk, to evaluate the prospects of the product. In the case of EAL, the unit might be a good 'test bed' for ideas.

4.10 In contrast, the design for the *new terminal* cannot be easily altered once it has been constructed, therefore ideas for it will require careful screening and analysis.

4.11 Some sources of ideas have been mentioned in the case (successful ventures in competitive airports) and some trends have been mentioned which might give rise to ideas (eg increased international, leisure and travel by women). Research could also be conducted to provide further ideas (eg focus groups, brainstorming sessions, and surveys). Focus is naturally on travellers themselves.

4.12 It might be possible to target people who come to the airport to meet or collect an arriving passenger. These people could sometimes have a considerable amount of time on their hands. People with even more time might be 'plane spotters' - those who come to observe. Could the new terminal have observation facilities to attract them?

4.13 The new terminal gives the opportunity for more radical long term ventures to be considered at the design stage, such as a *hotel*. This might take some of the place of the duty free revenue. Hotel booking does quite well, signifying that there would be a good chance of appropriate demand. The exact form that the hotel operation might take would need to be considered (eg whether it would be a luxury operation - higher costs, but higher prices, whether charging would be per person or per room for overnight accommodation, and whether it would have its own catering, or share restaurant facilities, saving space). It is significant that with this terminal, unlike the earlier ones, that commercial considerations rather than simply operational ones can be considered at the outset, thus making it a more effective revenue earner. Operational issues will still be important, and careful interaction and negotiation with those responsible for those will be necessary.

4.14 Joint ventures with other airports is also mentioned. It is hard to see what the forms could be for this.

(a) One possibility is for groups of airports to negotiate with large concessionaire groups for the rights to be sited in all the airports, thus increasing the airports bargaining power.

(b) Another possibility is to combine together with other airports in proposing services with travel and tourism operators on holiday packages/mixed mode transport which would bring increased business for all concerned. These types of ventures might benefit in particular from relationship marketing. This basically consists of building long term trusting relationships with other organisations. These relationships would result in arrangements that other firms would find hard to break into, even if temporarily they could offer a keener bargain. They would require a high standard of communication and good support. The highest possible profit might not be realised from a single transaction, but the business networks created would be stable and profitable in the long run.

Promotion

4.15 Although we are given scant detail of existing promotional activity in the case study it is made very clear to us that significant challenges lie ahead. We are shown in Chapter 15 paragraph 18 of the case study that EAL does not actively market the airport, and that only one competitor is identified as doing so. This represents an opportunity for the company which can be addressed by a combination of 'above the line' advertising, below the line promotion (special offers, competitions etc) and publicity (encouraging 'free' exposure in the media).

4.16 The various targets or 'publics' have to have their promotional needs addressed, is part of an overall promotional strategy. In physical design there is already a 'house style', but this is just a start.

External

4.17 External targets include at least the following.

(a) Local government
(b) Local residents and pressure groups
(c) Airlines
(d) Business travellers
(e) Actual and potential concessionaires
(f) Advertisers
(g) Leisure travellers

4.18 The airport does not have uncongested approach route. This inevitably reduces the attractiveness of the airport by increasing stress and travel time. Promotional efforts directed at local and regional government might help to get improvements in access by stressing the regional benefits that might ensue.

4.19 The airport is not within ten miles of a city centre, so that the number of people who might be affected by the new terminal will not be large, but may be disproportionately important. This does mean that a fairly intensive public relations campaign could be mounted in a cost-effective way to win over hearts and minds and overcome the 'not in my backyard' syndrome. You are expected to provide ideas for this. The diagram in Appendix 13 of the case (Chapter 15, para 3.13) shows that EAL has considerable public relations capability. Having considerable technical capability is not the same as having an effective *strategy*. The local community needs to be involved so that it feels the airport belongs to it.

4.20 Airlines have to be reminded of the benefits that using EAL brings to them, to reinforce the experience that they have. Personal relationships and good cooperation could be an important instrument here.

4.21 Promoting business travel not only means promotion to individual travellers, but also to their organisations and travel agents. For some business, travellers there will be no real competition because of geographical convenience, but there will be others for whom several airports might equally be feasible as departure points.

4.22 It is necessary to seek out and persuade concessionaires to take up concessions at the airport. These should be the organisations best able to be successful, since in so doing they would be able to afford to pay higher amounts to EAL. This can only be done by looking after their interests well, and creating increasing traffic to produce more income for them. If EAL can identify the products and services that would do best, they can carefully target the appropriate organisations.

4.23 Travellers have considerable spending power. This is evidenced by the bias towards ABC1 income groups. This is a powerful selling tool to use in promoting advertising space to firms and their advertising agents.

4.24 The leisure market is set to increase. This can be aided by persuading more tour operators to use EAL as one of their starting points. Since the airport is also near tourist attractions, it can also be promoted as a tourist destination.

Internal

4.25 There is promotion in the physical internal environment to consider (eg display advertising and special promotions with leaflets etc). Another kind of internal promotion may be crucial and far less obvious.

4.26 The tensions between operational and commercial aspects are potentially damaging, and probably have already caused some harm. part of the process of an organisation becoming truly market oriented is often internal marketing. The importance of commercial aspects needs to be communicated to those involved in operational aspects so that they are not simply seen as a nuisance. If passenger handling can be improved by those operational staff responsible, more time will be freed for shopping. Thus all sides could benefit by a campaign emphasising that different groups and departments in an organisation are all suppliers and customers internally. Techniques such as those used by *total quality management* programmes with such things as quality circles, interdisciplinary groups set to work together on problems, and quality circles, are all approaches that spring to mind. This issue is fairly urgent as the design for the new terminal will have to be finalised. This should be done by cooperation between commercial and operational interests rather than hostile negotiation. The organisation seems to be aware of this in that it is recognised at the highest level that commercial interests need to be considered at the outset rather than as something bolted on.

Price

4.27 Price may not seem to be an important variable, and certainly there is not much devoted to it in the case study. However, if even moderate increases can be sustained without reduction in business, profits might benefit considerably, since most of the organisation's costs are fixed or semi-fixed.

4.28 Appendix 9 (Chapter 15, para 3.9) of the case study shows us that although EAL's charges for typical aircraft types are second highest for short haul routes, they are second cheapest for long and medium haul routes. Airport C is cheaper for long haul routes, but unlike EAL is not near a business centre, and has fewer than 100 destinations. Airport D is cheaper for medium haul routes, but does not have good passenger facilities. Therefore it would seem that as long as EAL maintains a high standard of service to the airlines and provides good service to passengers, there is scope to increase charges to the airlines for long and medium haul routes.

4.29 Scope for obtaining the best possible prices from concessionaires will depend on negotiating skills and market knowledge (your background gives you those as Irma Bergmann).

4.30 Ultimately, only profitable concessionaires can pay highly, and so generating traffic, creating the right sort of retail environment and picking and persuading successful businesses to come to the airport will be crucial.

Place

4.31 We have seen that a unified design concept is a unique selling point. It is important that this be maintained in such a way as to create as relaxed and unstressed environment as possible, so that travellers are in the right mood to shop.

4.32 We have already seen that there are differences between the amount of space allocated to different services, and the revenue generated. The most extreme contrast being between the high revenue in relation to space for duty free sales, and the low revenue in relation to space characteristic of the catering services. It would be a mistake to assume that space occupied should be *directly* in proportion, but it would appear that scope for improvement is possible. The general principle is that space should be allocated so that marginal increases in space for each activity would bring in the same amount of revenue. Otherwise it would be more profitable to take space from one activity and give it to another. We must of course bear in mind that some essential services must be provided up at least to a minimum standard.

Another aspect of place is *location*. There is nothing you can do about that, but it is a variable to take into account. Being near a major tourist attraction and business centre are both major advantages, favouring both business and leisure use. The airport is more than 10 miles from a city centre. That may not be quite the disadvantage is seems. Firstly, although we know that there are objections to development on environmental grounds, these would be much more serious if the airport had been located so that noise and visual aspects affected a large city population. The site is affected by congestion on access routes and as much pressure should be brought to bear on authorities to improve this. If operations are slick, smooth and fast in the airport, this will save the passenger time, and help in some part to make up for congestion on the access routes themselves. Congestion *within* the airport would only compound the problem.

5. ORGANISATION

The role of new business development manager

5.1 You may be aware of a whole range of issues in the case study, but you must be especially careful to distinguish between the things you are responsible for, the things you can do, the things you can influence, and things you cannot affect.

5.2 Note that in the organisation chart, you (as Irma) report directly to the commercial director. You have responsibility for new business, and have the ear of someone responsible for all *commercial* activities, but not *operational* activities. No one reports to *you*, so that it appears that you have no line authority. Thus you cannot order anyone to do anything, but instead can exercise influence through persuasion, your knowledge and expertise, and in your ability to be an 'organisation person'.

Functional conflict

5.3 Various organisation researchers have noted that some conflict between different functions in an organisation is normal. This is so because in attempting to increase their own effectiveness and thereby improve their contribution to the organisation's achievement of its objectives, they must have their own sub-objectives which may impede the achievement of another function's sub-objectives.

5.4 EAL has a very elaborate, multi-layered organisation structure. This is understandable in such a large organisation with so many tasks to perform, but it means that formally at least, conflict between the operations and the commercial sections only can be resolved at chief executive level. There is no routine mechanism existing to reach compromises between operational efficiency and commercial interests. We are clearly told in the case in several places, that these conflicts are of some significance. Passengers taking longer than they should for shopping etc create problems for operational staff. One implication of this is the need to 'market' the worth and importance of commercial activities to operational staff. Less obviously, however, it also means that resources devoted to speeding up operational procedures will free time for shopping, and will help to create a relaxed unstressed atmosphere in which passengers are likely to spend.

5.5 Current fashion in organisational design is to create flatter structure with improved communication and clearly defined responsibility pushed down the organisation to the point where people can be aware of the detail required to produce solutions to problems. Applied to EAL, this would probably involve operational and commercial staff being under one manager at lower levels in the organisation, or creating task forces composed of staff from both functions. At this stage, it may be worth your while to make copies of the organisation charts in the case, and put them together to get a good understanding of the structure itself, and to see how any changes you might recommend could be incorporated. In your case study role, this is not your responsibility, but you are very much affected by the issue.

5.6 It is noticeable that *public relations* personnel does not report to the commercial director, but to the *chief executive*. From a marketing point of view, it is one more marketing activity and should be under the same head. Some public relations professionals would argue that PR needs to be both powerful and independent, and therefore should report to the chief executive.

5.7 It is certainly true that public relations is vital to the achievement of commercial activities for EAL, and coordination is required. Given the request from the public relations director that you get involved, cooperation seems to be forthcoming (Chapter 15, paragraph 3.16, Appendix 15 of the case). The size of the PR department shows that it is given considerable resources.

5.8 There may also be a suggestion of empire building, ie the establishment of an over large structure doing work in house that might be better handled outside. You are not, however, in a position to deal with that directly yourself, but it could be something you would need to take into account.

5.9 A final thought as far as the organisation is concerned, is that in service marketing we often think of a fifth 'P' - people. Human resources is a key element to providing quality service to customers and getting the best out of 25,000 employees.

6. FINANCE

6.1 Examiners consistently stress that they want candidates to demonstrate an awareness of *financial implications* of a case. Whilst the information provided does not suggest this will be a critical factor in the examination, opportunities should be taken to include appropriate financial aspects in your answers.

6.2 We now consider the data given in appendix 4 (Chapter 15, Paragraph 3.4). You are provided with normal final accounts (profit and loss and balance sheet) and a source and use of funds statement. Remember that revenue and costs in the profit and loss account refer to sales gained and services used up during the year. This does not mean that the cash has actually been received or paid.

6.3 These different statements therefore serve a different purpose and might apparently disagree. For example the dividends against the annual profit figures in the profit and loss account do not agree (by year) with figures shown in the source and application. This reflects that actual payment took place in the subsequent year. Looking at these accounts, the following points may be made.

(a) *Liquidity is rather low.* The current ratio is 1 or below. It is true that, for most service industries, a lower figures is acceptable since stocks will be negligible, but in this operation, debtors are large. There is little cash readily available.

(b) Profitability levels are generally good.

	1992	*1991*	*1990*
(i) Profit margin = profit/sales	41.1%	37.6%	21.8%
(ii) Asset turnover = sales/capital employed	0.33	0.31	0.31
(iii) Return on capital employed (ROCE) (profit margin × asset turnover)	13.7%	11.7%	6.8%

The company is making very high profits (on turnover) and this allows it to make acceptable return on capital despite its poor asset turnover, caused presumably by the very high assets required for this kind of operation. The profitability trend is very healthy.

(c) From the source and application of funds we can see the levels of funds generated. This is extremely healthy. Indeed it is rising faster than revenue demonstrating perhaps that costs and payments are under control

(d) One strange point is the erratic dividend policy. It is most unusual for a company to be able to pay no dividend (1992) from an operating profit of £90 million. One point worth noting is that, as already explained, any savings from this will not have reached the funds statement yet. The £32.6 million dividend for 1992 will be from the 1991 profit and loss. *Thus the funding benefit of the dividend decision in 1992 will come in 1993.*

(e) The company has low gearing. All funds are provided by shareholders or generated from revenues. It has virtually no loan capital and therefore it should be able to raise such funding fairly easily.

6.4 Apart from the above, it is perhaps worth making some general points. You are told you will have to justify any expenditure recommended. Remember commercial activities account for 65% of revenue and almost certainly an even greater proportion of profit.

6.5 Remember the criterion of revenue per square metre. You may not have specific figures, but use the argument. However, every item in a terminal cannot be for profit; customers do need food even if it does seem to be relatively unprofitable at present. Also do not forget you need to work in a unified way with operations. THey may not make as much profit s your department but their smooth operation is the main reason your customers arrive and their efficiency releases customers to spend time with concessionaires.

6.6 When discussing major long term ventures to do with the new terminal (or even diversification into hotels) you must first of all raise money (loans and dividend policy have already been discussed). Then having invested it, some mention or awareness of investment appraisal methods such as payback or (DCF) (discounted cash flow, which accountants and financiers regard as a for more accurate approach to investment decisions) to allow for the time lapse before receiving the money, and the inflation which will have occurred in the interim.

6.7 If discussing expansion of the *retail operations*, the importance of investment may not be so great. To the extent that you continue with concessionaires they can be made responsible for funding much of the investment in the commercial sector. However, the construction of the new terminal will be a major investment. This may be the reason that dividend payments have been suspended for the time being (ie to release liquid funds).

7. CONCLUSION: FOOD FOR THOUGHT

7.1 (a) Have you thought through development in a phased way, eg immediate plans, medium term for the new terminal, and long term strategic diversification?

(b) (i) Could you, if asked, comment on plans for the new terminal? You would need to do this in relation to the commercial requirements of which you are aware. Can operations assist you to hit target markets better by their terminal organisation?

(ii) What might be the best ideas to make up for the impending loss of duty free income, and how could the ideas be appraised?

(c) How can commercial values and requirements be 'sold' to operations staff? How can the two functions best integrate?

(d) Could you make suggestions for a PR campaign to minimise local resistance to the new terminal?

(e) What research would you commission to determine retail activities at competitor airports?

(f) What kinds of co-operative ventures might be possible with other airports?

(g) Could you make better use of the space available to commercial use?

(h) Have you any proposals for the reorganisation of EAL? Are any new posts required? What would the job description be in each case?

(i) Where would finance come from for large scale investment such as the new terminal? What would the implications of this be?

7.2 Remember, the examiner has seen a copy of this analysis and others like it.

Chapter 22

SIGNIFICANT CURRENT ISSUES

This chapter contains notes on issues which you should bear in mind in case study work.

1. Relationship marketing
2. Total marketing: total quality and the marketing concept
3. Improving marketing orientation
4. Internal marketing
5. Brand management: culture, values and change

1. RELATIONSHIP MARKETING

1.1 The essence of *relationship marketing* is stated by Martin Christoper, Adrian Payne and David Ballantyne in their book of this title (Butterworth-Heinemann 1991) as:

(a) focus on customer retention;
(b) orientation on customer benefits;
(c) long time scale;
(d) high customer commitment;
(e) high customer contact;
(f) quality is the concern of all.

1.2 It is claimed that gaining a new customer can cost four times as much as to keep one, so that a focus on customer retention makes a great deal of sense.

1.3 The longer term approach can also be said to be eminently suited to the 1990s in many ways. Studies of successful Japanese companies are likely to reveal an underlying long term strategy in that:

(a) they will accept losses in the short term in order to gain a dominant market share and lasting profitability in the longer term;

(b) they form long-term contractual relationships with all their staff rather than the 'hire and fire' approach taken by many British companies;

(c) they build long-term partnerships with their suppliers in the interests of the customers rather than the 'cheapest price on the day' approach adopted by many British managements;

(d) once a Japanese company wins a customer it works hard to build the relationship rather than easing up;

(e) a long term approach is also taken with regard to location and the development of good relationships with the community.

1.4 Relationship marketing's emphasis on high customer commitment is in keeping with the TQM approach being taken by many British companies in the 1990s. There is increasing recognition that internal customers and indirect customer contacts play crucial roles in the quality of external customer service. Put quite simply if someone in the despatch department drops a case rather too heavily on the pallet, a subsequent customer complaint of damaged goods is likely to result. Failure of the works office to respond quickly to a sales office telephone enquiry on progress of a job means a customer is let down and an expensively built-up relationship is tarnished.

2. TOTAL MARKETING: TOTAL QUALITY AND THE MARKETING CONCEPT

2.1 The following is a summary of an article by Barry J Witcher of Durham University Business School published in the Quarterly Review of Marketing (Winter 1990).

2.2 Witcher's main contention is that marketing, as currently understood by management and the marketing profession, is generally too narrow a concept. In fact, it can be argued that the marketing concept has a great deal in common with *total quality management* (TQM).

2.3 Going back to Kotler, marketing is about identifying customer needs and targeting organisation resources at them in the most appropriate way. Segmentation is an important technique for ascertaining customer needs, although only 47% of UK companies, according to a report published in 1987, can identify their main types of customer.

2.4 Witcher feels that companies still follow rival philosophies to the marketing concept.

(a) *Production orientation* involves a focus on costs, quality and reliability, 'a predeterministic rather than a flexible and responsive approach to customer needs'.

(b) *Product orientation* involves a concentration of *product features* rather than *customer benefits*, leading to a misunderstanding as to the significance of product changes on the competitive offer.

(c) A *selling orientation* results in an emphasis on promotion and 'a hit-and-run attitude towards the customer which gives a distinctly short-term emphasis to a company's operations.'

2.5 Witcher argues that the marketing concept goes much deeper than ideas about 'segmentation' and 'targeting'. He holds that three conditions must be met for a true marketing orientation.

(a) All aspects of a company's organisation and functioning must be directed to customers. This deals with issues of the marketing environment, keeping in touch with customers etc.

(b) The company must coordinate its efforts and activities with those of its customers. This deals with targeting, segmentation and competitive advantage.

(c) There should be a total marketing environment for the *whole company*. The marketing philosophy must be embraced by the *whole* company (eg including the accounts department).

Internal marketing

2.6 In most UK companies, marketing is a separate activity, devoted to outsiders. For the marketing philosophy to be adopted, it must overcome the pattern of communication within the company.

2.7 Some examples by which this can be achieved are:

(a) internal communication (eg mission statements);

(b) linking business functions (eg production and marketing personnel should be trained together;

(c) relationships between marketing and staff.

2.8 Witcher quotes the example of BT's TQM programme.

(a) A mission statement was drawn up for the company, expressing what was required from the company by its users, in terms of 'customer service, product quality, involvement of suppliers and attainment of a positive market position.'

(b) Cross-functional training and workshops tried to build bridges between different parts of the company.

(c) Full discussion of TQM was encouraged.

Total quality management (TQM)

2.9 'The purpose was to implement planning and management through the use of team working, and by so doing create an understanding which leads to a greater spread of responsibilities, and pro-activity... TQM tries to make the process continuous.'

Relationship marketing

2.10 TQM matches with the concept of relationship marketing. Relationship marketing is concerned with 'more than just a short term event in a market place'. Rather, 'relationships take time to establish, and all long term phenomena which involve complete series of exchanges (however defined). In short, relationship marketing is orientated towards 'strong, lasting relationship with individual accounts.'

2.11 A simple example can be provided in the service sector. A restaurant management will want satisfied customers to return, as repeat custom will be a more important factor in the restaurant's success.

Business to business marketing

2.12 Marketing to other businesses has a different set of problems than marketing to consumers. Arguably, if TQM is encouraging customers to have a more restricted number of suppliers, then business-to-business marketing, on a relationship basis, will become more important.

Marketing and TQM

2.13 Marketing is perhaps 'too basic to be noticed' and, as it is not considered in the abstract, the marketing department often has little connection with TQM programs.

(a) If 'quality' is fitness for use, then this should be part of internal marketing. Quality is not simply a matter of improving production processes.

(b) If 'total quality management' is to be introduced, so perhaps must 'total marketing' in order that the firm's productive capacity can be tailored to customer needs. This would mean *everybody* in the firm knowing, or at least considering, 'the demands of customers.'

2.14 Witcher suggests that UK companies are culturally ill-suited to this approach.

(a) The history of adversarial relations with suppliers does not encourage a 'partnership' approach, as noted in Paragraph 2.12.

(b) UK firms' activities are compartmentalised, so that there are significant divisions within the company.

2.15 'The insularity of UK-based companies has probably prevented the full application of marketing in its modern sense. This is a British marketing failure. For the future, British companies should look to their corporate cultures, and change them. The marketing concept, like the total quality concept, applies totally and to everything. Both these things must be brought together through training and company identity schemes as a common programme to influence culture. Management have to understand that the marketing idea is not a functional activity but a way of business life. In the Japanese way of stating things, it is an important part of 'continuous improvement. This is not generally understood at the moment, which is why companies do not seem to be implementing modern marketing ideas. The marketing profession must understand it first.'

3. IMPROVING MARKETING ORIENTATION

3.1 Richard Wilson and Noel Fook of Nottingham Business School argue, in *Marketing Business* (June 1990) that the adoption by organisations of the marketing orientation improves their effectiveness in marketing specifically, and then in the effectiveness of the organisation throughout its activities.

3.2 The authors feel that marketing is a process by which 'an enterprise seeks to maintain a continuous match between its products and services'. A more precise definition is that the 'marketing orientation is the process by which an enterprise's target customers' needs and wants are effectively and efficiently satisfied within the resource limitation and long-term survival requirements of that enterprise'.

3.3 However, how far does the marketing orientation actually exist in UK companies? If so, how can you recognise it? The authors suggest that the existence of an effective marketing orientation can be identified by the following characteristics.

(a) A 'good understanding of the needs, wants and behaviour patterns of targeted customers.'

(b) The organisation should be concerned with *profitable* sales rather than just turnover.

(c) The chief executive should be a marketing strategist, rather than fitting to implement it in the organisation.

(d) The mission should be market driven.

(e) Marketing should be 'seen as being more important than other functions and orientations'.

(f) The marketing orientation should be recognised as superior.

(g) All managers should use marketing inputs in decision making.

(h) The cost-efficiency of the marketing function should be analysed.

(i) The marketing function should be involved in new product development.

(j) Marketing professionals should be employed for marketing functions.

(k) Marketing is the responsibility of everyone in the organisation.

(l) Decisions with marketing implications are made in a well-coordinated way and executed in an integrated manner.

3.4 Wilson and Fook go on to connect these issues with the 7 S framework (shared values, style, structure, skills and staffing, systems, strategy) outlined by Kinsey.

3.5 Developing a marketing orientation 'is a long term process and needs to be thought of as a form of investment. To a large extent this investment is in changing the organisation's culture, so that common values relating to the need to highlight service to customers, a concern for quality in all activities and so forth, are shared throughout the organisation. This is not an appropriate target for a quick fix.'

3.6 Wilson and Fook suggest the following stages to increase the marketing orientation of an organisation.

(a) Secure the support of senior management with the prestige and authority to push it through and overcome skepticism.

(b) There should be a specified mission relating to the development of the marketing orientation.

(c) A task force should be set up:

(i) to identify the current orientation;

(ii) to carry out an analysis of deficiencies between the current orientation and the desired marketing orientation;

(iii) to advise on change and implementation.

3.7 Progress must be monitored to ensure that the firm does not snap back into its old ways.

4. INTERNAL MARKETING

4.1 Kevin Thomson writing in *Marketing Business* (September 1991) stated that 'looking at the employee as a valued customer is the focus of the new discipline of internal marketing'.

4.2 'If *total* customer satisfaction is the responsibility of marketing, then it is no longer good enough for marketing people to simply look at the external customer's requirements. Quality can only come from inside the organisation, so marketing must start to turn its attention this way.'

4.3 Internal marketing is not just the responsibility of training staff (employed by the personnel department) but of marketing personnel because only marketing personnel possess all of the following.

(a) Knowledge of the organisation's overall strategy.
(b) Understanding of the needs of external customers.
(c) Marketing techniques and tools.
(d) Ability to use techniques and tools on internal customers.
(e) Budgets.

4.4 Internal marketing is a means to 'reach and teach' the internal customer. Internal products and services include education, information, strategy and planning.

4.5 Internal marketing also can be integrated with a company's external marketing practice. Service businesses in particular, which depend on customers being made to feel welcomed, depend on those personnel dealing directly with the customers. Internal marketers can affect these employees, or indeed, any other aspect of the organisation/customer relationship (eg quality).

4.6 Internal marketing combines:

(a) marketing;
(b) human resources;
(c) training;
(d) behavioural science.

4.7 It operates at three levels.

(a) It can be integrated at overall policy-making level as one of the objectives of the company.

(b) It is a strategic tool in the *planning* of organisational change.

(c) It is part of a way of implementing organisational change, or supporting an external marketing effort.

4.8 Internal marketing sees internal communications, and so forth (eg company magazines, services to employees) as products to be 'sold' to customers.

4.9 Internal marketing it is hoped, will provide the right framework for quality management. Internal marketing - identifying and meeting customer needs - can be seen as giving focus to quality control.

5. BRAND MANAGEMENT: CULTURE, VALUES AND CHANGE

5.1 Neil Pickup and John Smith argue, in 'Marketing Business' (April 1990) that 'more organisations which have been successful in establishing a brand have directed their attention both inside and outside the organisation; not merely to the external environment within which the business operates, but also to the culture influencing and governing delivery of the package to the customer'.

5.2 Marketing has, traditionally had an 'external focus. However, communicating these external issues to other members of the organisation, has been relegated to standard internal communications 'as the sole means to initiate what may well be major cultural change'.

5.3 Especially in service businesses, creating a corporate brand by which the business is known, and delivering it successfully, often requires changes in corporate culture. The major issues involve:

(a) corporate culture;
(b) procedures and processes;
(c) organisational design.

5.4 If a business's culture is in conflict with customer expectations, than corporate branding is a liability, as it might make claims which cannot be satisfied.

5.5 The authors hold that internal research is necessary, before any attempt is made to set up a corporate brand. Furthermore:

(a) both management and staff need to understand why the organisation exists and the role of the brand;

(b) both management and staff should 'own' the culture;

(c) there should be an 'objective and pragmatic analysis of the culture(s) and values operating within the business';

(d) there should be a change management strategy.

5.6 The process of organisational change can be analysed in three phases.

(a) *Phase 1.* This is the 'pre-managerial' phase of a business. It thrives on entrepreneurial flare.

(b) *Phase 2.* However, this flair needs to be supported by good management if the business is to succeed. Management structures tend to become rigid in this phase.

(c) *Phase 3.* Businesses evolve from formal rigidities to Phase 3 and are held together, not so much by procedures, as by values.

5.7 In phase 1, the *corporate* brand image might be founded on the entrepreneur (eg 'Virgin' is Richard Branson). In phase 2, a corporate brand might be increased, as it were, from outside and imposed by formal procedures. However, as the brand is not connected with the underlying corporate culture, its claims, compared with the service actually provided, may founder.

In phase 3, the corporate brand will reflect the corporate culture, and will be shared by managers and staff.

5.8 Managing the introduction is a major task as it requires a thorough review of all the behaviour patterns. 'Shared values and agreed standards must become inherent in all management activity, whether routine dealings with external and internal customers or non-routine activities such as management development programs'.

5.9 Corporate branding though required changes in behaviour so that the brand's ideals can be matched.

6. CONCLUSION

6.1 These articles suggest some general principles.

(a) The marketing approach needs to be involved with all facets of an organisation's relationship with customers, including quality.

(b) For service businesses, or in service activities of non-service businesses, the success of external marketing may depend on the spread of marketing values *within* the organisations.

INDEX

FURTHER READING

BPP also publish a Tutorial Text for this subject. It contains background material from the other subjects relevant to the case study and also provides guidance, similar to that which you will find in this Workbook, on three different case studies: *Royal Mail* (June 1993). *GT Student Aids Ltd* (December 1993) and *Purbeck Financial Services* (June 1994).

To order your Tutorial Text, ring our credit card hotline on 0181-740 6808. Alternatively, send this page to our Freepost address or fax it to us on 0181-740 1184.

To: BPP Publishing Ltd, FREEPOST, London W12 8BR **Tel: 0181-740 6808**
Fax: 0181-740 1184

Forenames (Mr / Ms): ____________________

Surname: ____________________

Address: ____________________

____

Post code: ____________________

Please send me the following books:	*Quantity*	*Price*	*Total*
Strategic Marketing Management: Analysis and Decision Tutorial Text	......	£24.95	....

Please include postage:

UK: £2.50 for first plus £1.00 for each extra book ....
Europe (inc ROI): £5.00 for first plus £4.00 for each extra book
Rest of World: £7.50 for first plus £5.00 for each extra book ....

I enclose a cheque for £__________ or charge to Access/Visa

Card number | | | | | | | | | | | | | | | | |

Expiry date ______________ Signature ____________________

To order any further titles in the BPP CIM range, please use the form overleaf.

CIM - Diploma: Strategic Marketing Management: Analysis and Decision (2/95)

ORDER FORM

To order your CIM books ring our credit card hotline on 0181-740 6808. Alternatively, send this page to our Freepost address or fax it to us on 0181-740 1184.

To: BPP Publishing Ltd, FREEPOST, London, W12 8BR Tel: 0181-740 6808
Fax: 0181-740 1184

Forenames (Mr/Mrs): ______________________
Surname: ______________________
Address: ______________________
____
Post code: ____________ **Date of exam (month/year):** ____________

Please send me the following books:

	Price *Text*	*Price* *Kit Workbook*	*Quantity* *Text*	*Total* *Kit Workbook*	*Total*
Certificate					
Marketing Environment	15.95	7.95	....	....	....
Understanding Customers	15.95	7.95	....	....	....
Business Communications	15.95	7.95	....	....	....
Marketing Fundamentals	15.95	7.95	....	....	....
Advanced Certificate					
Promotional Practice	16.95	7.95	....	....	....
Management Information for Marketing and Sales	16.95	7.95	....	....	....
Effective Management for Marketing	16.95	7.95	....	....	....
Marketing Operations	16.95	7.95	....	....	....
Diploma					
Marketing Communications Strategy	17.95	8.95	....	....	....
International Marketing Strategy	17.95	8.95	....	....	....
Strategic Marketing Managemnet: Planning and Control	17.95	8.95	....	....	....
Strategic Marketing Management: Analsyis and Decision	24.95	16.95	....	....	....
Please include postage:					
UK: Texts £2.50 for first plus £1.00 for each extra			....	....	....
Kits £1.50 for first plus £0.50 for each extra			....	....	....
Europe (inc ROI): Texts £5.00 for first plus £4.00 for each extra			....	....	....
Kits £2.50 for first plus £1.00 for each extra			....	....	....
Rest of World: Texts £7.50 for first plus £5.00 for each extra			....	....	....
Kits £4.00 for first plus £2.00 for each extra			....	....	....
				Total	

I enclose a cheque for £__________ or charge to Access/Visa

Card number | | | | | | | | | | | | | | | | |

Expiry date __________ Signature ______________________

CIM - Diploma: Strategic Marketing Management: Analysis and Decision (2/95)

Name: ______________________________

How have you used this Workbook?

Home study (book only) ☐ With 'correspondence' package ☐

On a course: college____________ ☐ Other ____________

How did you obtain this Workbook?

From us by mail order ☐ From us by phone ☐

From a bookshop ☐ From your college ☐

Where did you hear about BPP Workbook?

At bookshop ☐ Recommended by lecturer ☐

Recommended by friend ☐ Mailshot from BPP ☐

Advertisement in ____________ ☐ Other ____________

Have you used the companion Tutorial Text for this subject? **Yes/No**

Your comments and suggestions would be appreciated on the following areas.

Topic coverage

Analytical breadth and depth

Errors (please specify, and refer to a page number)

Presentation

Other